MUTATION TESTING FOR THE NEW CENTURY

MUTATION 2000

A Symposium on Mutation Testing for the New Century

October 6-7, 2000

San Jose, California

Sponsored by

The IEEE Reliability Society

Telcordia Technologies

Software Engineering Research Center

The Kluwer International Series on
ADVANCES IN DATABASE SYSTEMS

Series Editor
Ahmed K. Elmagarmid

Purdue University
West Lafayette, IN 47907

Other books in the Series:

THE FRACTAL STRUCTURE OF DATA REFERENCE: *Applications to the Memory Hierarchy,* *Bruce McNutt;* ISBN: 0-7923-7945-4
SEMANTIC MODELS FOR MULTIMEDIA DATABASE SEARCHING AND BROWSING, *Shu-Ching Chen, R.L. Kashyap, and Arif Ghafoor*; ISBN: 0-7923-7888-1
INFORMATION BROKERING ACROSS HETEROGENEOUS DIGITAL DATA: A Metadata-based Approach, *Vipul Kashyap, Amit Sheth*; ISBN: 0-7923-7883-0
DATA DISSEMINATION IN WIRELESS COMPUTING ENVIRONMENTS, *Kian-Lee Tan and Beng Chin Ooi*; ISBN: 0-7923-7866-0
MIDDLEWARE NETWORKS: Concept, Design and Deployment of Internet Infrastructure, *Michah Lerner, George Vanecek, Nino Vidovic, Dad Vrsalovic;* ISBN: 0-7923-7840-7
ADVANCED DATABASE INDEXING, *Yannis Manolopoulos, Yannis Theodoridis, Vassilis J. Tsotras;* ISBN: 0-7923-7716-8
MULTILEVEL SECURE TRANSACTION PROCESSING, *Vijay Atluri, Sushil Jajodia, Binto George* ISBN: 0-7923-7702-8
FUZZY LOGIC IN DATA MODELING, *Guoqing Chen* ISBN: 0-7923-8253-6
INTERCONNECTING HETEROGENEOUS INFORMATION SYSTEMS, *Athman Bouguettaya, Boualem Benatallah, Ahmed Elmagarmid* ISBN: 0-7923-8216-1
FOUNDATIONS OF KNOWLEDGE SYSTEMS: With Applications to Databases and Agents, *Gerd Wagner* ISBN: 0-7923-8212-9
DATABASE RECOVERY, *Vijay Kumar, Sang H. Son* ISBN: 0-7923-8192-0
PARALLEL, OBJECT-ORIENTED, AND ACTIVE KNOWLEDGE BASE SYSTEMS, *Ioannis Vlahavas, Nick Bassiliades* ISBN: 0-7923-8117-3
DATA MANAGEMENT FOR MOBILE COMPUTING, *Evaggelia Pitoura, George Samaras* ISBN: 0-7923-8053-3
MINING VERY LARGE DATABASES WITH PARALLEL PROCESSING, *Alex A. Freitas, Simon H. Lavington* ISBN: 0-7923-8048-7
INDEXING TECHNIQUES FOR ADVANCED DATABASE SYSTEMS, *Elisa Bertino, Beng Chin Ooi, Ron Sacks-Davis, Kian-Lee Tan, Justin Zobel, Boris Shidlovsky, Barbara Catania* ISBN: 0-7923-9985-4
INDEX DATA STRUCTURES IN OBJECT-ORIENTED DATABASES, *Thomas A. Mueck, Martin L. Polaschek* ISBN: 0-7923-9971-4
DATABASE ISSUES IN GEOGRAPHIC INFORMATION SYSTEMS, *Nabil R. Adam, Aryya Gangopadhyay* ISBN: 0-7923-9924-2
VIDEO DATABASE SYSTEMS: Issues, Products, and Applications, *Ahmed K. Elmagarmid, Haitao Jiang, Abdelsalam A. Helal, Anupam Joshi, Magdy Ahmed* ISBN: 0-7923-9872-6
REPLICATION TECHNIQUES IN DISTRIBUTED SYSTEMS, *Abdelsalam A. Helal, Abdelsalam A. Heddaya, Bharat B. Bhargava* ISBN: 0-7923-9800-9
SEARCHING MULTIMEDIA DATABASES BY CONTENT, *Christos Faloutsos* ISBN: 0-7923-9777-0
TIME-CONSTRAINED TRANSACTION MANAGEMENT: Real-Time Constraints in Database Transaction Systems, *Nandit R. Soparkar, Henry F. Korth, Abraham Silberschatz* ISBN: 0-7923-9752-5
DATABASE CONCURRENCY CONTROL: Methods, Performance, and Analysis, *Alexander Thomasian, IBM T. J. Watson Research Center* ISBN: 0-7923-9741-X

MUTATION TESTING FOR THE NEW CENTURY

edited by

W. Eric Wong
Telcordia Technologies, U.S.A.

KLUWER ACADEMIC PUBLISHERS
Boston / Dordrecht / London

Distributors for North, Central and South America:
Kluwer Academic Publishers
101 Philip Drive
Assinippi Park
Norwell, Massachusetts 02061 USA
Telephone (781) 871-6600
Fax (781) 681-9045
E-Mail <kluwer@wkap.com>

Distributors for all other countries:
Kluwer Academic Publishers Group
Distribution Centre
Post Office Box 322
3300 AH Dordrecht, THE NETHERLANDS
Telephone 31 78 6392 392
Fax 31 78 6392 254
E-Mail <services@wkap.nl>

Electronic Services <http://www.wkap.nl>

Library of Congress Cataloging-in-Publication Data

Mutation testing for the new century / edited by W. Eric Wong.
p. cm. -- (Kluwer international series on advances in database systems ; 24)
Proceedings of Mutation 2000 : a symposium on mutation testing for the new century, October 6-7, 2000, San Jose, California.
Includes bibliographical references and index.
ISBN – 0-7923-7323-5 (alk. paper)
1. Mutation testing of computer programs--Congresses. 2. Computer programs--Testing--Congresses. I. Wong, W. Eric. II. Mutation 2000 (2000 : San Jose, Calif.) III. Series.

QA76.76.T48.M88 2001
005.1'4--dc21 2001029620

Printed on acid-free paper.

Table of Contents

Mutation Testing for the New Century

Keynote: Programs Determined by Mutation-adequate Tests

Panel: Future of Mutation Testing and Its Application

Interface Mutation

Tool Session

A Message From the Honorary Chair

In late autumn of 1975 I made one of my frequent trips from Atlanta to New Haven to collaborate with Richard Lipton. We were at that time working on some theoretical results in programming languages. We had also just begun discussing with Alan Perlis some ideas regarding proofs of software correctness. These discussions would eventually lead to our paper "Social Processes and Proofs of Theorems and Programs". Program correctness was therefore on my mind. I recall being a little late when I walked into a conference room where Lipton was meeting with Fred Sayward, Dave Hanson and a couple of graduate students, including Tim Budd. They were discussing a paper that Lipton had written several years before when he was a graduate student at Carnegie Mellon University. I was completely unprepared for the idea that I heard that day.

Edsgar Dijkstra is credited with observing (in defense of program proofs) that software testing can only prove the presence of errors, but not their absence. But what if, Lipton argued, there were only a finite number of possible errors. Then the Dijkstra axiom fails because a set of test cases on which the subject program succeeds but each of the finite number of possible erroneous programs gives an erroneous output demonstrates that the subject program does not contain any of the possible errors and is therefore correct. Cutting though the many obvious objections about the number of possible errors (even if there were only finitely many possible errors) and the difficulty of finding out what they were, Lipton and Sayward were in the process of beating David Hanson, an expert on programming languages and compilers, into submission on the question of whether or not such an exhaustive testing method could ever be efficiently automated.

Over the next three days, most of the central ideas of what was being called "perturbation testing" were worked out in rough form. Sayward and Budd had found some empirical basis for simple error models in Gannon's seminal paper. This led to an elegant scheme for creating and executing errors using perturbation operators that modified leaves of parse trees. There was still the troublesome issue of combinatorial growth in the number of possible simple errors that might conspire to cause a "real" software defect, but we decided to set this problem aside for awhile.

By the end of the academic year, Sayward and Budd had constructed a working interpreter for Fortran IV on Yale's PDP-10. I recruited Alan Acree to do the same for Cobol at Georgia Tech. Jerry Feldman at the University of Rochester had suggested that "mutation" testing was a more appealing (and more accurate) term than perturbation. Lipton and I spent the following summer at the famous Mathematic Research Center in Madison, Wisconsin. Many of the theoretical underpinnings of mutation were worked out that summer, including metainduction and the competent programmer hypothesis, equivalence checking, and the coupling effect.

The coupling effect was at that time and continues to be the most controversial aspect of the theory, but to us it was not so startling. We spent some time trying to invent counterexamples but except for the academic examples that are now well known was always led back to the coupling of simple errors. I found a collection of science fiction short stories by Robert Silverberg in which he explains: "Mutations are seldom spectacular. Those mutants that are startlingly different from their parents tend not to survive long, either because the mutation renders them unable to function normally or because they are rejected by those who sired them."* I have always been struck by the elegant simplicity of this passage and thought that it was really the only sensible way to justify the coupling effect. I have planned for many years to use it in our growing but still unfinished monograph on Mutation Analysis. Since that project may never be complete, it is probably best to insure that it gets used at least once in the way I planned.

It is especially gratifying that, after 25 years, this workshop has convened to consider the state of research in Mutation Analysis. My colleague Aditya Mathur's article in the Encyclopedia of Software Engineering provides the most complete roadmap and technical attribution for mutation testing. The workshop organizers comprise the core of the active research community and the technical program carries forward the important empirical and theoretical themes that have long been associated with mutation analysis.

That autumn morning in 1975, I thought that "perturbing" programs in just the right way for the explicit purpose of falsifying Dijkstra's assumption about software testing was one of the most powerful ideas I had ever encountered. The many students and colleagues who over the years have added depth to the ideas and validated the basic concepts have helped create what is in my biased view the most scientific, rational approach to assuring that computer programs work as they are intended.

*Mutants, edited by Robert Silverberg, Thomas Nelson Publishers, 1974, page 1.

Richard A. DeMillo
Vice President and General Manager
Computer Sciences Research
Telcordia Technologies

Message from the Symposium Chairs

Welcome to Mutation 2000--the first symposium in an area that grew from an idea by Richard Lipton in 1971 and spearheaded by Richard DeMillo since then.

This symposium is intended to bring together, for the first time, a wide range of researchers who will present outcomes of their most recent and cutting edge research in mutation testing. Through keynotes, presentations, and discussions, they will provide answers to key questions related to mutation and raise questions yet to be answered. Proceedings of the symposium will serve as reference and educational material for researchers, practitioners, and students of software engineering.

Extensive research and development over more than two decades has produced mutation tools for languages such as Fortran, Ada, C, and IDL; empirical evaluations comparing mutation with other test adequacy criteria; empirical evidence and theoretical justification for the coupling effect; and techniques for speeding up mutation testing using various types of high performance architectures. Mutation has received the attention of software developers and testers in such diverse areas as network protocols and nuclear simulation.

The program committee of Mutation 2000 invited original unpublished papers in the area of mutation testing. Each paper was reviewed by at least four members of the program committee. After a rigorous reviewing process, thirteen high quality papers were selected: eight as regular papers and five as short papers. In addition, three selected papers will also be published in a special issue of the Journal of Software Testing, Verification, and Reliability.

Many individuals have contributed to this symposium and it would not have been possible without their help and support. We would like to thank the authors for sharing their ideas with us and the reviewers for providing valuable feedback on the papers they reviewed. Our thanks go as well to all the PC members for taking time from their busy schedules to help us organize this symposium. Thank you also to Rosemary Hoehler, Sue McDonald, Vannessa Vouse, and Frank Warren (all from Telcordia Technologies) for their invaluable help in creating the conference web page, assisting on-line registration, negotiating a hotel contract, and many similar activities without which it would be difficult, if not impossible, to proceed. Finally, we are grateful to Telcordia Technologies for its strong support of this symposium.

Thank you for attending Mutation 2000. We hope that you enjoy the program and have a pleasant stay in San Jose.

Aditya Mathur, Perdue University
Eric Wong, Telcordia Technologies

Organizing Committee

Honorary Chairs

Richard A. DeMillo
Applied Research
Telcordia Technologies
rad@research.telcordia.com

Richard J. Lipton
Department of Computer Science
Princeton University
rjl@cs.princeton.edu

General Chair

Aditya P. Mathur
Department of Computer Science
Purdue University
apm@cs.purdue.edu

Program Chair

W. Eric Wong
Applied Research
Telcordia Technologies
ewong@research.telcordia.com

ISSRE 2000 Liaison

Allen P. Nikora
Jet Propulsion Laboratory
Allen.P.Nikora@jpl.nasa.gov

Program Committee

John A. Clark, University of York, UK
Bob Horgan, Telcordia Technologies, USA
William E. Howden, University of California at San Diego, USA
Kim N. King, Georgia State University, USA
Jose C. Maldonado, University of Sao Paulo at Sao Carlos, Brazil
W. Michael McCracken, Georgia Tech, USA
Jeff Offutt, George Mason University, USA
Martin Woodward, University of Liverpool, UK

Additional Reviewers

Sudipto Ghosh, Colorado State University, USA
Plinio Vilela, Telcordia Technologies, USA
Mladen Vouk, North Carolina State University, USA

Keynote

Why Software Falls Down

Rich DeMillo
Applied Research
Telcordia Technologies*

Abstract

This talk advocates the analysis of system level software failures. The title and content are inspired by the famous book by Mario Salvadori and Matthys Levi, "Why Buildings Fall Down". As software engineering makes the transformation to a mature engineering discipline, the community must develop way to learn from engineering failure if serious engineering attempts to prevent failure are to succeed. Engineering principles that lead inevitably to more reliable, stable software are rare. Concepts like form resistance in civil engineering and architecture would be useful for software developers because such concepts lead to construction styles and methods that are inherently stable. Unfortunately, even simple applications of simple principles like redundancy have been only sporadic and have met with mixed results.

Part of the reason is that there has been little groundwork on a system level understanding of what can go wrong with software. This talk analyzes four common sources of engineering failure from the point of view of software engineering:

1) structures undermined by shifting sands
2) underdesign
3) lack of redundancy
4) combinations of rare events

In each case a thorough analysis of software failures can lead to definite design methods and architectural models that tend to avoid the root cause of the failure.

What can be learned from watching programs fall down?

- Ways to abstract the combinations of rare events
- Engineering rules of thumb that avoid disasters
- Architectural principles
- What to measure

*Since Mutation 2000, Dr. DeMillo has left Telcordia for a position at Hewlett-Packard.

Keynote

Mutation: The Early Days

Dick Lipton
College of Computing
Georgia Institute of Technology
&
Applied Research
Telcordia Technologies

Abstract

The start of the testing method that we now call *mutation* was back when I was a graduate student at CMU. My initial idea was to use the same method that was used in hardware. Hardware testing then (and now) was based on the idea of "stuck-at-faults". A test set was considered adequate provided it could distinguish between all stuck-at-faults. My idea was then to replace stuck-at-faults by simple changes to the program. One basis of this was the thesis of Young. He showed that many errors in programs were quite simple.

I actually did a thesis on a totally different topic. After arriving at Yale I began to work on mutation once Rich DeMillo joined in. Without Rich mutation would have remained an "idea". Once Rich was involved we began to move quickly. First, we did some toy experiments. Fred Sayward and others were critical. Then, Rich and his team took over and began to build a series of mutation systems.

Mutation: Application, Effectiveness, and Test Generation (I)

Investigating the Effectiveness of Object-Oriented Strategies with the Mutation Method

Sunwoo Kim
John A. Clark
John A. McDermid

High Integrity Systems Engineering Group
Department of Computer Science
University of York, Heslington, York
YO10 5DD, United Kingdom
{sunwoo,jac,jam}@cs.york.ac.uk

Abstract

The mutation method assesses test quality by examining the ability of a test set to distinguish syntactic deviations representing specific types of faults from the program under test. This paper describes an empirical study performed to evaluate the effectiveness of object-oriented (OO) test strategies using the mutation method. The test sets for the experimental system are generated according to three selected OO test methods and their effectiveness is compared by determining how well the developed test sets kill injected mutants derived from an established mutation system Mothra, and our own OO-specific mutation technique which is termed Class Mutation.

The Relationship Between Program Dependence and Mutation Analysis

Mark Harman,
Rob Hierons,
Brunel University,
Uxbridge, Middlesex,
UB8 3PH, UK.
Tel: +44 (0)1895 274 000
Fax: +44 (0)1895 251 686
Mark.Harman@brunel.ac.uk
Rob.Hierons@brunel.ac.uk

Sebastian Danicic,
Goldsmiths College,
University of London,
New Cross,
London SE14 6NW, UK.
Tel: +44 (0)20 7919 7856
Fax: +44 (0)20 7919 7853
Sebastian@mcs.gold.ac.uk

Keywords: Slicing, Dependence Analysis, Test Data Generation, Equivalent Mutant Detection

Abstract

This paper presents some connections between dependence analysis and mutation testing. Specifically, dependence analysis can be applied to two problems in mutation testing, captured by the questions:

1. How do we avoid the creation of equivalent mutants?
2. How do we generate test data that kills non-equivalent mutants?

The theoretical connections described here suggest ways in which a dependence analysis tool might be used, in combination with existing tools for mutation testing, for test-data generation and equivalent-mutant detection.

In this paper the variable orientated, fine grained dependence framework of Jackson and Rollins is used to achieve these two goals. This framework of dependence analysis appears to be better suited to mutation testing than the more traditional, Program Dependence Graph (PDG) approach, used in slicing and other forms of program analysis.

The relationship between dependence analysis and mutation testing is used to defined an augmented mutation testing process, with starts and ends with dependence analysis phases. The pre-analysis removes a class of equivalent mutants from further analysis, while the post-analysis phase is used to simplify the human effort required to study the few mutants that evade the automated phases of the process.

Introduction

In mutation testing, a program is mutated to create a mutant by a small syntactic change. These changes are likely to make the mutant behave differently when compared to the original. Such behavioural differences can be found by running the program with an input which reveals the differing behaviour. An execution which does this 'kills' the mutant in the nomenclature of mutation testing[1]. Running a mutant is 'testing' the original program in the sense that bugs in the original program are simulated by the mutations. Broadly speaking, a test set which kills many mutants is considered to be better at finding bugs than one which does not. In this way mutation testing can be used to assess the effectiveness of a test set or to help in the construction of an effective test set.

Mutation testing has been shown to be highly effective in empirical studies [6, 22]. It is also theoretically appealing because it is tailored to the program under test and because it can be used to emulate the effect of other coverage based test adequacy criteria. However, there is a downside. Typically, many mutants can be created from even the simplest original program under test and some of these may be equivalent to the original program semantically (though they differ syntactically). The problem of finding a set of test data which kills all non-equivalent mutants is also far from trivial.

Two currently important problems for mutation testing are thus summed up as two questions. The first question is 'How do we avoid the creation of equivalent mutants?' The second question is 'How do we (automatically) generate test data that kills all non-equivalent mutants?'.

Clearly, in considering adequacy criteria, only non-equivalent mutants should be used. However, the problem of detecting equivalent mutants is undecidable, and so removing equivalent mutants is non-trivial. The automatic generation of test data which satisfies some test data adequacy criterion is known to be a hard problem and the mutation-inspired adequacy criteria

[1] Mutants are always executed on test cases for which this original program behaves correctly. If a test case reveals an error, the original program must be corrected and the mutation analysis restarted *ab initio*.

are no exception.

This paper shows how dependency analysis can be used to attack these two problems. The rest of the paper is organised as follows. Sections 2 and 3 introduces the forms of mutation testing and dependence considered in this paper. Section 4 establishes the theoretical connection between these forms of mutation testing and program dependence analysis, showing how it can be used to support test data generation and equivalent mutant detection. Section 5 provides examples which illustrate the claims in the preceding section. Section 6 presents related work on compiler-optimisation and constraint-based approaches to test data generation and equivalent mutation detection. This suggests a combined mutation testing process presented in Section 7. The process combines dependence analysis and constraint based approaches to mutation testing. Section 8 concludes with directions for future work.

2 Forms of Mutation Testing

2.1 Strong, Weak and Firm Mutation

Mutants are always created in the same way: a single simple syntactic alternation is made to a node, n, of the original program. Mutants are 'killed' when a test case reveals mutant behaviour which differs from that of the original program. In order to kill a mutant, its behaviour must therefore be inspected in some way. There are three approaches to the way in which a mutant is inspected, known as 'strong', 'firm' and 'weak' mutation.

In the original form of mutation testing, now called *strong mutation testing*, input σ kills a mutant p' of a program p if p and p' produce different output when executed on σ.

Woodward and Halewood [32] suggested using the final state of the program in place of the output. This is a helpful generalisation because the output sequence can be considered to be denoted by a variable. Their definition of this 'state-based' approach to mutation subsumes the traditional 'output based' approach. It also simplifies the formal exposition presented later. Hereinafter, we shall, without loss of generality, assume that testing a mutant consists of inspecting some set of variables, which we call the *inspection set*.

Strong mutants are theoretically hard to kill because the effect of the mutation can be lost before the program reaches the final state.

Under *weak mutation testing* [15], p' is killed by input σ on inspection set I if the execution of p and p' on σ leads to different values of some $\mathbf{x} \in I$ immediately after *some* execution of the mutation point at node n.

Woodward and Halewood [32] introduce *firm mutation testing* as a compromise between strong and weak mutation. In firm mutation, p is mutated at some point n to form p'. The original program, p and the mutant, p' are compared on some inspection set I at some node i. Both weak mutation and strong mutation are special cases of firm mutation: in weak mutation $i = n$ and in strong mutation i is the exit node of the program. Firm mutation testing therefore subsumes strong and weak mutation. Hereinafter it will be assumed, without loss of generality, that firm mutation is being used. The point i will be termed the *probe point*.

The view of mutation testing adopted in this paper is summarised in Definition 2.1 below.

Definition 2.1 (Mutant)
In this paper, a *mutant* will be considered to be a program p' constructed from a program p by a single syntactic change affecting node n of p. The mutant p' will be tested by executing p and p' on input σ and checking the values of the variables in some inspection set I at some probe point i. If the value of any variable in I at i is different for the execution of p and p' then the mutant p' is killed.

Definition 2.2 (Equivalence)
Equivalence of a mutant p' is dependent upon the choice of probe set and probe point, as well as the particular mutation applied to the original program. If p' is not killed by any possible input for a inspection set I at a point i, we shall say that p' is *equivalent* to p with respect to I and i. If, for all inspection sets, p' is not killed by any possible input we shall say that p' is equivalent at i. If for all inspection sets I and for all mutation points i, a mutant p' is equivalent with respect to I and i, then we shall simply say that p' is *equivalent*.

2.2 Reference–Preserving Mutation Operators

In considering the connections between dependence analysis and mutation testing, the set of reference-preserving mutation operators are an important class. A mutation operator is reference-preserving if it does not change the set of referenced variables of any node of any program it mutates. Referenced variables are those mentioned in expressions, either on the RHS of an assignment node or as variables mentioned in the boolean expression of a predicate node.

The concept of reference preserving can be illustrated by considering the Mothra system [18]. Mothra contains 22 meta mutation operators. We call the Mothra operators 'meta operators' because each defines a family of individual primitive mutation operators. The Mothra operators are well known and will not be described in detail here. However, we shall consider a few operators to illustrate reference preservation.

ABS composes an expression with the absolute value function, while CRP replaces a source constant with a different constant. Neither of these can add or remove a variable reference and they are thus reference preserving. SVR replaces a scalar variable with an alternative and so is clearly not reference preserving when applied to the right-hand side of an assignment or to the boolean expression of a predicate. SDL deletes a statement and so will only be reference preserving in the few rare cases where the deleted statement references no variables.

AOR and ROR stand for Arithmetic and Relational Operator Replacement respectively. Each includes primitive mutation of erators LEFTOP and RIGHTOP, which delete the left and right operand of the binary expression they are applied to. While the bona fide operator replacement primitive mutation operators in AOR and ROR meta mutation sets are reference preserving, LEFTOP and RIGHTOP will not generally be reference preserving.

In dependence analysis, programs which are identical up to referenced variable sets contain identical dependencies under the approximation used in most dependence analysis algorithms [4]. This means that when reference-preserving mutations are considered, it will not be necessary to re-compute dependence information from the original program. As many mutation operators are reference preserving, this makes the combination of dependence analysis and mutation testing more efficient than it might otherwise be. Where dependence information needs to be re-computed, an incremental approach [28, 29, 33, 34] will be highly applicable since, by definition, mutation involves only very minor changes.

3 Dependence Analysis

Jackson and Rollins [16] introduce a form of program dependence, which we shall call 'JR–Dependence'. As we will show, JR–dependence is a useful aid in tackling various problems in mutation testing, including reducing the input set in the search for mutant killing states.

JR–dependence is 'finer grained' than the Program Dependence Graph (PDG) [5, 13, 14] often used in program analysis, and particularly in slicing [7, 10, 31]. It allows us to relate (variable, node) pairs rather than simply to relate nodes. This allows us to say that the definition of a variable x at node n_1 can influence the value of a variable y at node n_2, rather than merely saying that node n_1 can influence node n_2.

JR–dependence is better suited to the analysis of mutants, because we shall want to know which sets of variables are important at certain points in the program, not merely which nodes are important. Specifically, we shall want to know the set of variables which can be used to kill a mutant and which set of variables store values which cannot be used to kill a mutant.

In the JR–approach, dependence relations are constructed from two basic dependence relations, *du* and *ucd*, which we now explain.

Every atomic program statement (node of the CFG) is represented as a relation, *du*, between pairs. For example, an assignment statement at node 5:-

```
5:    x:=y+z;
```

has

$$du = \{((x,5),(y,5)),((x,5),(z,5))\}$$

Node 5 defines {x} and uses {y, z}. The relation *du* is thus *internal* in the sense that it relates variables of the *same* node. In the above example, the value of x defined at node 5 depends upon the value of y referenced at node 5. Hence there is a relationship from $(x,5)$ to $(y,5)$ in *du*. Similarly, the value of x at node 5 depends upon the value of z at node 5, so there is also a relationship from $(x,5)$ to $(z,5)$ in *du*.

A *du* relation will always mention the same node in all relationships. That is

$$((v_1,n_1),(v_2,n_2)) \in du \quad \Rightarrow n_1 = n_2$$

Thus relationships in *du* are 'intranode' but 'intervariable'. It is because the relationship is intranode that we call it an 'internal relation'.

The external relationship between nodes is expressed by a relation, *ucd*, which captures the control and data dependence relations of the PDG (augmented to allow variables to be identified in addition to nodes). For data dependence, *ucd* expresses the connection between the use of a variable at node n_i with the definition of the same variable at a different node n_j. The *ucd* relation is also used to express control dependence between (variable, node) pairs. A control dependence[2] exists from a node x to a node y if y chooses whether or not node x gets executed. In such a control dependence, the node y will always be a predicate.

Control dependence is achieved in *ucd* using a coding, in which an assigned variable depends (in *du*) upon a special variable ε, the 'execution variable'. The ε variable of node n is dependent (in *ucd*) upon a variable τ, which is defined in all nodes which control n. In this way control dependence is captured in *ucd* as if it were a data dependence upon special variables τ and ε.

By composing *du* and *ucd* in various ways, and restricting the resulting domains and ranges, we can use JR–notation to express, and hence to compute[3] the dependencies which will be of interest in program analysis and, in particular, in mutation analysis.

Jackson and Rollins define several compositions. Here only one will be required: the UD relation.

$$UD = ucd \circ (du \circ ucd)^*$$

Here, R^* is the reflexive transitive closure of R and relational composition is from left to right i.e.

$$r_1 \circ r_2 = \{(x,y) | \exists z \text{ such that } (x,z) \in r_1 \text{ and } (z,y) \in r_2\}$$

By closing the relation $du \circ ucd$, the propagation of dependence information is achieved. The composition of the closure

[2]More precisely, a control dependence exists from node x to node y if x is always executed when one branch of node y is executed, but there is also a path from y to the exit which does not contain x[5].

[3]The JR–notation is written in a functional style. This provides both a relatively high level 'specification orientated' style of notation, and a relatively simple way of prototyping implementations in a functional language such as ML.

with *ucd* is merely required to ensure that the resulting relation, UD is of an appropriate type. That is, one from uses of variables to the definitions upon which they depend.

4 The Relationship Between JR–Dependence and Mutation Testing

This section establishes the relationship between JR–Dependence and Mutation Testing. It is used as the theoretical basis for the augmented mutation testing process proposed in section 7.

Let p be the original program under test and let p' be a mutant of p created by mutating node n of p. Let the probe point be i and the inspection set be I and let Var be the set of all variables. Let *start* be the entry node of the CFG.

To kill p' we are looking for a state σ which *distinguishes* between p and p' with respect to (i, I). Some initial program variables will be interesting and some will not. Those which are uninteresting can be varied arbitrarily without killing the mutant p'. That is, the value of these variables cannot be used to produce different behaviour in the mutant and the original program. Those which are interesting may potentially affect the outcome of execution of the mutant in a way that will allow us to determine that it is different from the original.

Clearly, such a set of variables will depend both upon the mutant and the program from which it is created. It will also depend upon the probe point and inspection set, as these are the lens through which the mutant and original are inspected. If a mutant is hard to kill it may be because it is equivalent. This may occur either because the mutant is so similar to the original that no inspection can detect it, or simply because the (inspection-set, probe-point) pair are inappropriate (the lens is too weak).

Using JR–notation, we shall define the set T of 'interesting variables' which is such that any variable outside this set need not vary in our test set. To generate test data to kill a mutant, we should be sure to consider only variables in the set T. If T is empty then the mutant is equivalent, and should not be analysed further (or the probe point and/or inspection set should be varied).

Let $\mathbf{ran}(\mathrm{R})$ be the range of a relation R. With a slight abuse of notation we shall refer to variables in this range. Strictly these are the variables in the first element of each pair in the range.

Using the JR–dependence notation [16], consider the relation

$$R = (I \times \{i\}) \lhd UD_p \rhd (Var \times \{\text{start}\})$$

Any variable outside $X = \mathbf{ran}(\mathrm{R})$ cannot possibly affect I at i. i.e. Any two initial states differing only on variables outside $\mathbf{ran}(\mathrm{R})$ will always behave the same at (i, I).

Similarly,

$$R' = (I \times \{i\}) \lhd UD_{p'} \rhd (Var \times \{\text{start}\})$$

is such that any variable outside $X' = \mathbf{ran}(\mathrm{R})'$ cannot possibly affect I at i.

Therefore if we are looking for states which can kill the mutant, we only need consider states which differ on variables in $X \cup X'$.

$$\text{i.e. } T = X \cup X'$$

We can improve on this, however. A 'killing state' must also affect the mutant at node n, otherwise it cannot possibly distinguish between p and p'.

Now consider the relation

$$S = (Var \times \{n\}) \lhd UD_p \rhd (Var \times \{\text{start}\})$$

For program p, any two initial states differing only on variables outside $\mathbf{ran}(\mathrm{S})$ will always behave the same at n.

Similarly, let

$$S' = (Var \times \{n\}) \lhd UD_{p'} \rhd (Var \times \{\text{start}\})$$

For program p', any two initial states differing only on variables outside $\mathbf{ran}(\mathrm{S})'$ will always behave the same at n.

Let $Z = \mathbf{ran}(\mathrm{S})$ and $Z' = \mathbf{ran}(\mathrm{S})'$. Any two states which only differ outside $Z \cup Z'$ must behave the same *everywhere* with respect to p and p'.

So the space where we look for killing states can be limited further to states differing only on $(X \cup X') \cap (Z \cup Z')$.

$$\text{i.e. } T = (X \cup X') \cap (Z \cup Z')$$

Observe that choosing a variable z, which *is* in T does not guarantee that the mutant will be killed. This is not merely because the right value has to be chosen for the 'influencing' variable in order to kill the mutant. This lack of a guarantee also arises because it is sadly possible for dependence analysis to produce 'false positives'. All dependence analysis must be safe: it will always include a dependency if one exists. However, for the usual, well-known, decidability reasons, such analyses will not always fail to include a dependency where none exists.

Therefore, T is sufficient in the sense that any variable outside T cannot have a bearing on whether the mutant is killed. Therefore, although there is some imprecision inherent in dependence analysis, it is nonetheless possible to make the following two definite statements about T:

- In selecting test data, only the initial values of variables in T should be varied.
  All other variable values are definitely irrelevant.

- If no variable in T can be varied in the initial state, then the mutant is definitely equivalent.
  The most obvious way in which this can happen is for T to be empty. However, in certain domain-specific problems there may be non-empty sets, T, for which no variable in T can be varied. For instance, the only variables in T may have values which depend upon the input to some physical environment sensor, which cannot be easily set to an arbitrary value by the tester.

```
x = y+z;      /* mutation point */
:
x = 0;    /* re-initialise */
:
printf("%d",x);      /* probe point */
```

Figure 1: A set of Equivalent Mutants

```
x = 42;     /* mutation point */
:     /* does not define or reference x */
if (z==2)
   y = x+1;
else z = x*x;
:
x = 0;       /* re-initialise */
:    /* does not define y or z */
printf("%d",x);      /* probe point */
```

Figure 2: Poor Choice of Inspection Set

5 Examples

In this section we present a few simple motivating examples which illustrate the way in which the foregoing formal analysis can be used to help focus attention upon interesting variables when generating test data and how we can avoid the creation of certain classes of equivalent mutants.

5.1 Avoiding the Creation of Equivalent Mutants

Mutants which fail to propagate 'corrupted data' to the inspection set at the probe point will be equivalent and should be avoided.

For example, consider the program in Figure 1. In this program, the value of x at the mutation point fails to propagate to the probe point because it is killed on all paths from the mutation point to the probe point (in this simple example, there is only one such path).

In this case, equivalence arises because of the control flow structure of the original program. The re-initialisation of the variable x effectively destroys the previous value, and so any mutation analysis which places the mutation point on one side of the assignment and the probe point on the other, without affecting the control flow, will fail to detect any mutation which retains x as the defined variable. This situation (in which variables are re-initialised) is common in embedded systems, where the number of variables is not large. Paucity promotes re-use, leading to just this sort of re-initialisation.

In general, it is not easy to determine which variable values can reach a particular program point, and so it will not be easy to spot these equivalent mutants manually. Fortunately, dependence analysis is designed to automate the production of answers to just these sort of questions.

In the previous example, the mutant was equivalent because the value of a variable was set during computation. This form of program is likely to cause the creation of equivalent mutants in strong mutation testing, but less so in weak mutation testing where the value of the mutated variable does not have to propagate to the probe point. Mutants may also be equivalent, because the inspection set is poorly chosen. In such situations, either the mutation needs to be reconsidered or the (inspection set, probe point) pair should be altered.

For example, consider the program fragment in Figure 2. In this program fragment, the value of x defined at the first line, will not reach the `printf` statement at the last line because of the intervening initialisation. In this respect the example is similar to the previous one. However, in this example there is a difference. The value of x can reach the probe point through the variables y and z, which store a value dependent upon x and which are not re-initialised on the way to the probe point. Therefore, a better choice of inspection set would be $\{y, z\}$ rather than $\{x\}$.

5.2 Generating Test Data to Kill Non-Equivalent Mutants

Consider the CFG in Figure 3. In this figure, code blocks indicated by question marks contain arbitrary code, but do not reference or define the variables $\{a, b, c, d, x, y, z\}$.

Suppose the predicate p4 is mutated using a reference-preserving mutation. Clearly, this mutation can only be killed if a suitable set of values is chosen for the input variables to the program. The inputs in this case, are, a, b, c, d, x, y and z. If each variable is a 16-bit integer then the input is therefore $16 \times 7 = 112$ bits long. There are thus $2^{112} \approx 10^{33}$ potential values in the space to be searched. However, it turns out that *only* the variables a and b can affect the values of b and c at the predicate node p4 and therefore, only these two variables need be considered when attempting to find an input to kill the mutant. This observation reduces the search space to $2^{32} \approx 10^9$, a reduction of order 22 in the number of possible test cases to consider.

Determining that the values of b and c at node p4 are affected by only the variables a and b in the initial state is precisely the role of dependence analysis. This analysis does not determine the input values needed to kill the mutant. That (harder) problem is the preserve of constraint solving approaches [21, 23, 24]. However, dependence analysis can dramatically reduce the space that needs to be considered in order to determine the crucial killing values and can be applied when constraint-based techniques fail to give an answer.

Reducing search space size in this way may also find application in the area of search-based test data generation systems, such as those based on genetic algorithms [17, 25, 26, 30].

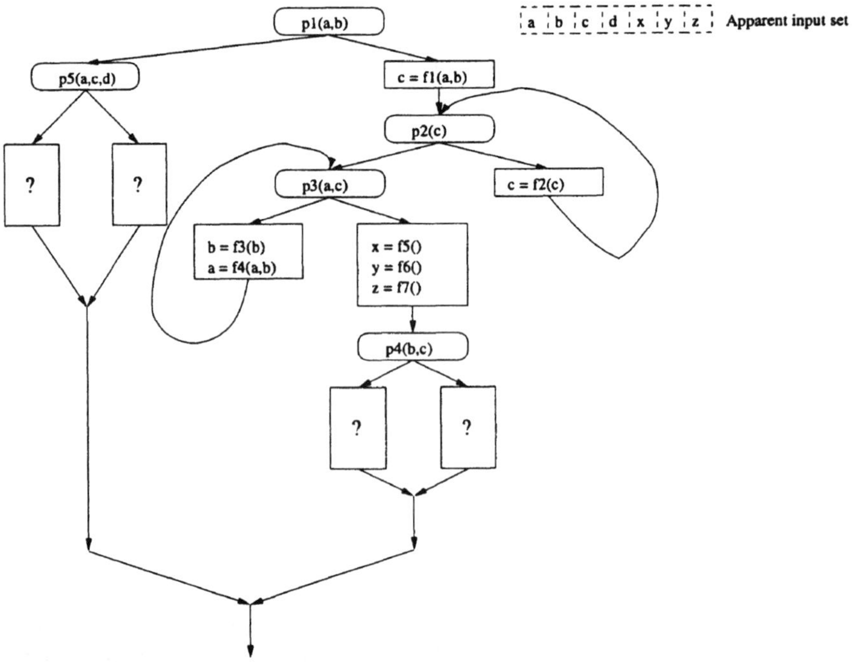

Figure 3: Generating Test Data to Kill a Mutant

6 Related Work

Voas and McGraw [27] were the first to suggest that dependence analysis (specifically program slicing) might be useful in mutation analysis. They observed that syntax-preserving slicing can identify points unaffected by some statement and that these make poor candidates for fault injection, because the mutants so-created are 'guaranteed' to be equivalent. This is slightly inaccurate [12]. The observation becomes true when only reference preserving mutations are considered.

The present authors [12] developed the initial proposal of Voas and McGraw, showing how amorphous slicing [3, 8, 9, 11] can be used to assist human analysis of particularly stubborn mutants. This work considered slicing as a means of assisting the human analysis, rather than as a way of determining equivalence.

Offut et al. [19, 20, 21, 22, 23] have considered the problems of test data generation and equivalent mutant detection extensively, using both constraint-based techniques and compiler optimisations.

Initial work focussed on compiler optimisations [19]. The idea was originally proposed by Baldwin and Sayward [2] as early as 1979, but remained unexplored until 1994, when Offutt and Craft implemented a set of compiler-optimisation heuristics and evaluated them. The approach consists of looking at mutants which appear to implement traditional peep-hole compiler optimisations [1]. Such compiler optimisations were designed to create faster, but equivalent programs and so a mutant which implements a compiler optimisation will, by definition, be an equivalent mutant regardless of the probe point and inspectio set. Offutt and Craft's empirical study of this idea, indicated tha while helpful, there was some way to go if the equivalent mu tant problem was to be overcome. They found that the set c heuristics they implemented was able to detect about 10% of th equivalent mutants.

This work on compiler optimisation was improved upon i work by Offutt et al. [20, 21, 22, 23], which focussed o constraint-based approaches which seek to determine muta equivalence by formulating a set of constraints. These co straints were originally used to generate test data (by solving th constraints). The more recent work also indicated that heuri tics designed to determine when such a set of constraints fails be satisfiable is also rather effective as a means of determini equivalence. Empirical studies showed that the approach cou achieve a detection rate of about 50%.

Initially [21, 22, 23], the approach considered constraints ov logical formulæ whose free variables were input variables to t program. Later work [20] used set-based constraints, where se of intervals of possible input values were propagated through t program under test. Both these techniques are more fine grain than the work presented here. They are capable of providing v ues of test data, rather than simply identifying which variab are significant. This observation motivates the augmented mu tion testing process which we propose in the next section.

7 A Dependence and Constraint Based Mutation Analysis Process

We do not propose dependence analysis as a replacement for constraint-based approaches. Rather we suggest that it should form an additional tool in the armory of the mutation analyst. In particular, where constraint based approaches have failed to produce test data, dependence analysis will help to focus the manual search for test data by constraining the input domain to the interesting variables. Furthermore, an initial dependence analysis may help to avoid the creation of certain classes of equivalent mutants, which would save later effort using a constraint-based system.

This symbiotic relationship is now developed into a process for mutation testing which combines dependence analysis, amorphous slicing and constraint-based test data generation and constraint based detection of equivalent mutants.

The process is depicted in Figure 4. The first phase is the creation of mutants. The process proposed here is independent of the approach taken to mutant creation. The next phase consists of detecting equivalent mutants using dependence analysis. This is a natural next phase as dependence analysis is less computationally expensive than constraint based approaches. This means that those mutants which dependence analysis can detect as equivalent are quickly disposed of. The next phase is the constraint-based approach developed by Offutt et al. This generates test data which kills some mutants and determines others to be equivalent.

The mutants which remain are those which are not determined to be equivalent by either dependence analysis or by constraint based analysis. These we call 'stubborn mutants'. These may be equivalent, but our two technologies of dependence analysis and constraint-based analysis simply proved too weak to detect them.

Stubborn mutants will ultimately have to be considered by a human. However, before the human is forced to look at the program code of a mutant, two more phases of automatic processing take place. The first of these is amorphous slicing (as described in more detail in [12]). This produces a simplified program tailored to the question of whether or not the mutant is equivalent. The second is domain reduction which can be achieved using the JR–dependence approach as described in this paper.

Thus the human mutation tester is finally presented with a set of stubborn mutants to analyse. Each is simplified using amorphous slicing and the human is guided in their choice of test data to consider by JR–dependence analysis.

8 Conclusions and Future Work

This paper has shown how dependence-based analysis can be used to assist in the detection of equivalent mutants and in the narrowing of the search space which needs to be considered in the generation of test data to kill a mutant.

It has been argued that the Jackson and Rollins style of dependence analysis (JR–Dependence) is more suited to mutation testing than the more widely used, Program Dependence Graph driven approaches. This is because the JR–style of analysis is more fine grained, relating not only nodes, but also the variables which are important at given nodes. This allows us to ask, for example, which variables are important at the entry node to the program and which variables need to be inspected at chosen probe points in order to avoid the equivalent mutant problem.

These dependence based techniques do not subsume constraint-based techniques, which may also detect equivalent mutants and which additionally generate test data. However, dependence analysis provides the tester with a complementary technology, to be used in tandem with constraint-based approaches to reduce the number of equivalent mutants which enter the constraint-based phase and to help to narrow the search space for data where constraint based approaches are unable to create data.

The paper culminates in a process for mutation testing which augments the existing constraint-based process with three additional dependence-based steps. One of these was previously proposed by the present authors, and is based upon amorphous slicing as a 'last resort' assistant to human analysis of stubborn mutants. The other two are new, and form a pre- and post- analysis phase, augmenting the existing mutation testing process. They avoid generation of mutants which JR–dependence can determine to be equivalent and help restrict attention to the effective set of input variables, where constraint based techniques are unable to generate killing test data.

Acknowledgements

We would like to thank Jeff Offutt and Martin Woodward for helpful discussions concerning mutation testing which helped to shape our ideas on the integration of dependence analysis techniques into the classic mutation testing process. The four anonymous referees also provided helpful comments which have improved the presentation of the paper.

This work is supported in part by EPSRC grants GR/M58719 and GR/M78083.

References

[1] AHO, A. V., SETHI, R., AND ULLMAN, J. D. *Compilers: Principles, techniques and tools.* Addison Wesley, 1986.

[2] BALDWIN, D., AND SAYWARD, F. Heuristics for determining equivalence of program mutations. *Research Report 276, Department of Computer Science, Yale University* (1979).

[3] BINKLEY, D. W. Computing amorphous program slices using dependence graphs and a data-flow model. In *ACM Symposium on Applied Computing* (The Menger, San Antonio, Texas, U.S.A., 1999), ACM Press, New York, NY, USA, pp. 519–525.

[4] DANICIC, S. *Dataflow Minimal Slicing.* PhD thesis, University of North London, UK, School of Informatics, Apr. 1999.

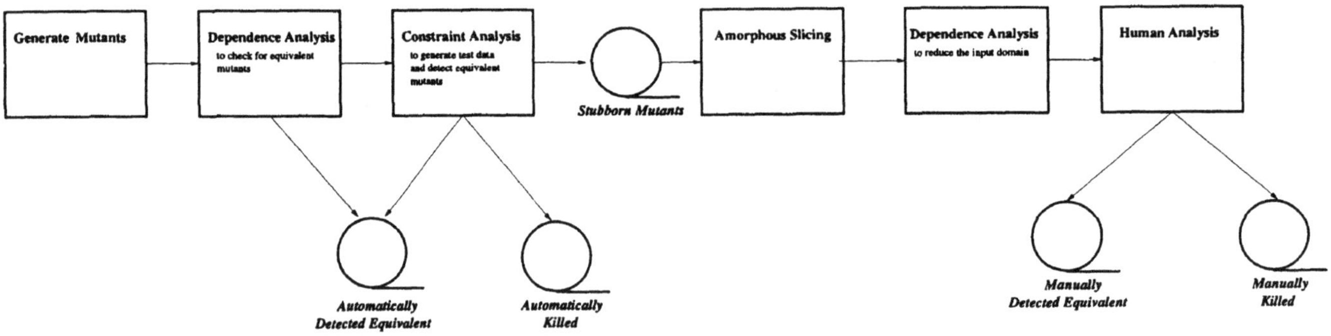

Figure 4: A Mutation Testing Process which Combines Dependence and Constraint Analysis

[5] FERRANTE, J., OTTENSTEIN, K. J., AND WARREN, J. D. The program dependence graph and its use in optimization. *ACM Transactions on Programming Languages and Systems 9*, 3 (July 1987), 319–349.

[6] FRANKL, P. G., WEISS, S. N., AND HU, C. All-uses vs mutation testing: An experimental comparison of effectiveness. *Journal of Systems Software 38* (1997), 235–253.

[7] GALLAGHER, K. B., AND LYLE, J. R. Using program slicing in software maintenance. *IEEE Transactions on Software Engineering 17*, 8 (Aug. 1991), 751–761.

[8] HARMAN, M., AND DANICIC, S. Amorphous program slicing. In 5th *IEEE International Workshop on Program Comprehesion (IWPC'97)* (Dearborn, Michigan, USA, May 1997), IEEE Computer Society Press, Los Alamitos, California, USA, pp. 70–79.

[9] HARMAN, M., FOX, C., HIERONS, R. M., BINKLEY, D., AND DANICIC, S. Program simplification as a means of approximating undecidable propositions. In 7th *IEEE International Workshop on Program Comprehesion (IWPC'99)* (Pittsburgh, Pennsylvania, USA, May 1999), IEEE Computer Society Press, Los Alamitos, California, USA, pp. 208–217.

[10] HARMAN, M., AND GALLAGHER, K. B. Information and Software Technology, Special issue on program slicing, volume 40, numbers 11 and 12.

[11] HARMAN, M., SIVAGURUNATHAN, Y., AND DANICIC, S. Analysis of dynamic memory access using amorphous slicing. In *IEEE International Conference on Software Maintenance (ICSM'98)* (Bethesda, Maryland, USA, Nov. 1998), IEEE Computer Society Press, Los Alamitos, California, USA, pp. 336–345.

[12] HIERONS, R. M., HARMAN, M., AND DANICIC, S. Using program slicing to assist in the detection of equivalent mutants. *Software Testing, Verification and Reliability 9*, 4 (1999), 233–262.

[13] HORWITZ, S., AND REPS, T. The use of program dependence graphs in software engineering. In 14th *International Conference on Software Engineering* (Melbourne, Australia, 1992), pp. 392–411.

[14] HORWITZ, S., REPS, T., AND BINKLEY, D. Interprocedural slicing using dependence graphs. *ACM Transactions on Programming Languages and Systems 12*, 1 (1990), 26–61.

[15] HOWDEN, W. E. Weak mutation testing and completeness of test sets. *IEEE Transactions on Software Engineering 8* (1982), 371–379.

[16] JACKSON, D., AND ROLLINS, E. J. Chopping: A generalisation of slicing. Tech. Rep. CMU-CS-94-169, School of Computer Science, Carnegie Mellon University, Pittsburgh, PA, July 1994.

[17] JONES, B., STHAMER, H.-H., AND EYRES, D. Automatic structural testing using genetic algorithms. *The Software Engineering Journal 11* (1996), 299–306.

[18] KING, K. N., AND OFFUTT, A. J. A FORTRAN language system for mutation-based software testing. *Software Practice and Experience 21* (1991), 686–718.

[19] OFFUTT, A. J., AND CRAFT, W. M. Using compiler optimization techniques to detect equivalent mutants. *Software Testing, Verification and Reliability 4* (1994), 131–154.

[20] OFFUTT, A. J., JIN, Z., AND PAN, J. The dynamic domain reduction approach to test data generation. *Software Practice and Experience 29*, 2 (January 1999), 167–193.

[21] OFFUTT, A. J., AND PAN, J. Detecting equivalent mutants and the feasible path problem. In *Annual Conference on Computer Assurance (COMPASS 96), IEEE Computer Society Press* (Gaithersburg, MD, June 1996), pp. 224–236.

[22] OFFUTT, A. J., PAN, J., TEWARY, K., AND ZHANG, T. An experimental evalutation of data flow and mutation testing. *Software Practice and Experience 26* (1996), 165–176.

[23] OFFUTT, J., AND PAN, J. Automatically detecting equivalent mutants and infeasible paths. *Software Testing, Verification, and Reliability 7*, 3 (Sept. 1997), 165–192.

[24] PAN, J. Using constraints to detect equivalant mutants. Master's thesis, George Mason University, 1994.

[25] PARGAS, R. P., HARROLD, M. J., AND PECK, R. R. Test-data generation using genetic algorithms. *The Journal of Software Testing, Verification and Reliability 9*, 4 (1999), 263–282.

[26] TRACEY, N., CLARK, J., AND MANDER, K. Automated program flaw finding using simulated annealing. In *International Symposium on Software Testing and Analysis* (March 1998), ACM/SIGSOFT, pp. 73–81.

[27] VOAS, J., AND MCGRAW, G. *Software Fault Injection.* Wiley, 1998.

[28] WAGNER, T. A., AND GRAHAM, S. L. Integrating incremental analysis with version management. In *Proceedings of the* 5th *European Software Engineering Conference (ESEC'95)* (Sept. 1995), W. Schäfer and P. Botella, Eds., Lecture Notes in Computer Science Nr. 989, Springer-Verlag, pp. 205–218.

9] WAGNER, T. A., AND GRAHAM, S. L. Incremental analysis of real programming languages. In *Proceedings of the ACM SIGPLAN Conference on Programming Language Design and Implementation (PLDI-97)* (New York, June 15–18 1997), vol. 32, 5 of *ACM SIGPLAN Notices*, ACM Press, pp. 31–43.

0] WEGENER, J., STHAMER, H., JONES, B. F., AND EYRES, D. E. Testing real-time systems using genetic algorithms. *Software Quality 6* (1997), 127–135.

1] WEISER, M. Program slicing. *IEEE Transactions on Software Engineering 10*, 4 (1984), 352–357.

2] WOODWARD, M. R., AND HALEWOOD, K. From weak to strong, dead or alive? an analysis of some mutation testing issues. In *Proceedings of the Second Workshop on Software Testing, Verification, and Analysis* (Banff, Canada, July 1988).

3] YUR, J., RYDER, B. G., AND LANDI, W. A. An incremental flow-and context-sensitive pointer aliasing analysis. In *Proceedings of the 21st International Conference on Software Engineering* (May 1999), IEEE Computer Society Press, Los Alamitos, California, USA, pp. 442–452.

4] YUR, J.-S., RYDER, B. G., LANDI, W. A., AND STOCKS, P. Incremental analysis of side effects for C software systems. In *Proceedings of the 19th International Conference on Software Engineering (ICSE '97)* (May 1997), IEEE Computer Society Press, Los Alamitos, California, USA, pp. 422–432.

Mutation of Model Checker Specifications for Test Generation and Evaluation

Paul E. Black
National Institute of
Standards and Technology
Gaithersburg, MD 20899
paul.black@nist.gov

Vadim Okun   Yaacov Yesha
University of Maryland
Baltimore County
Baltimore, MD 21250
{vokun1,yayesha}@cs.umbc.edu

Abstract

Mutation analysis on model checking specifications is a recent development. This approach mutates a specification, then applies a model checker to compare the mutants with the original specification to automatically generate tests or evaluate coverage. The properties of specification mutation operators have not been explored in depth. We report our work on theoretical and empirical comparison of these operators. Our future plans include studying how the form of a specification influences the results, finding relations between different operators, and validating the method against independent metrics.

Keywords: specification mutation, mutation operators, test generation, model checking.

1 Introduction

Mutation analysis is typically performed on program code. However, a specification provides additional valuable information. For instance, specification-based testing may detect a missing path error [15], that is, a situation when an implementation neglects an aspect of a problem and a section of code is altogether absent. Further, code-based analysis is not possible for some systems because testers do not have access to the source code. Analysis on a specification can also proceed independently of program development, and any results should apply to all implementations of the specification, e.g. ports to other systems. Model checking and specification-based mutation analysis are combined in a novel method to automatically produce tests from formal specifications [3] and measure test coverage [2]. We briefly introduce model checking here.

1.1 Model Checking

Model checking is a formal technique based on state exploration. Input to a model checker has two parts. One part is a state machine defined in terms of variables, initial values for the variables, environmental assumptions, and a description of the conditions under which variables may change value. The other part is a set of temporal logic expressions over states and execution paths.

Temporal logic is an extension of classical logic for dealing with systems that evolve with time. The properties such as "It will be the case that p", "It will always be the case that p" can be compactly specified in temporal logic.

Conceptually, a model checker visits all reachable states and verifies that each temporal logic expression is consistent with the state machine, i.e., satisfied over all paths. If an expression is not satisfied, the model checker generates a counterexample in the form of a trace or sequence of states, if possible.

The SMV Model Checker

We use the SMV [19] model checker. Its temporal logic is Computation Tree Logic (CTL) [11]. Typical formulas in CTL include:

- `AG safe`

  All reachable states are safe.

- `AG (request → AF response)`

  A request is always followed by a response sometime in the future.

Figure 1 is a short SMV example. "Request" is an input variable, and "state" is a variable with possible values "ready" and "busy." The initial value of state is "ready." The next state is "busy" if the state is "ready" and there is a request. Otherwise the next state is "ready" or "busy" nondeterministically. The SPEC clause is a CTL formula which states that whenever there is a request, state will eventually become "busy."

Some might object that SMV's description language is at too low a level for wide-spread use, and we agree. A

```
MODULE main
VAR
    request : boolean;
    state : {ready, busy};
ASSIGN
    init(state) := ready;
    next(state) := case
        state = ready & request : busy;
        1 : {ready, busy};
    esac;
SPEC AG (request -> AF state = busy)
```

Figure 1. A Short SMV Example

practical system must extract state machines and temporal logic expressions from higher level descriptions such as SCR specifications [4], MATLAB stateflows [5], or UML state diagrams.

Notice that choosing a different model checker naturally leads to a different specification language and therefore potentially different mutation operators and effects. We comment on the interaction between the form of a specification and the results of mutation analysis in Section 4.

In Section 2, we describe how we use a model checker and mutation analysis on specifications to generate tests. In Section 3, we report some of our findings, such as, which mutation operators are better than others in terms of coverage and the number of mutants. Finally in Section 4 we present some open questions and the research directions we have planned to take to address them.

2 Mutations for Test Generation

Ammann and Black used mutation analysis, along with model checking, to automatically produce tests from formal specifications [3] and measure test coverage [2]. Since our work has been in the framework of this approach, we briefly explain it here.

One begins with a finite state machine representation, or specification, of the system to be tested. Each transition of the state machine is reflected as a CTL clause. For instance, the first case of the state variable in Figure 1 may be expressed as the following clause.

SPEC AG (state = ready & request → AX state = busy)

Methods of turning order-dependent guards into order-independent CTL, expressing constructs which have no parallel in CTL, making the default case explicit, and minimizing expressions are given in [2]. The set of clauses derived from all state machine transitions, which are consistent with the state machine, are combined with any pre-existing clauses to serve as the specification.

Although other test criteria[1] could be applied [8, 14], we confine ourselves here to a specification mutation adequacy criterion. Simply stated, the criterion is that a test set must kill all mutations of a specification produced with some set of mutation operators. A mutant is killed if the mutant CTL clause is shown to be inconsistent with the trace, or history of execution states, of a test case. An equivalent, or consistent, mutant is true for all traces.

For program-based mutation analysis, detecting equivalent mutants is, in general, an undecidable problem. However, to use model checkers we restrict ourselves to a finite domain in which equivalent mutant identification is decidable. In fact, model checkers are designed to perform this equivalence check efficiently. The model checker finds equivalent mutants to be consistent with the state machine, so they may be automatically discarded.

To generate tests, one mutation operator is applied to all the CTL clauses. Applying each mutation operator in turn yields a set of mutant clauses. The model checker then compares the original state machine specification with the mutants. When the model checker finds a clause to be inconsistent, it produces a counterexample if possible. The counterexamples contain both stimulus and expected values, so they may be automatically converted to complete test cases. To reduce the number of tests, duplicate counterexamples are combined, and counterexamples which are prefixes of others are discarded.

Note that the number and type of mutation operators, as well as the form of the CTL clauses, influences the number and breadth of tests produced.

A variant of this approach may be used to evaluate coverage of a test set. Each test is turned into a finite state machine constrained to express only the execution sequence of that test. The model checker compares each constrained finite state machine with the set of mutants produced previously. A mutation adequacy coverage metric is the number of mutants killed divided by the total number of mutants. This simple metric may be made more precise and accurate by removing consistent mutants and all but one of semantically duplicate mutants, as explained in [2]. Let N be the number of unique, inconsistent mutants generated by all operators, and k be the number of mutants killed. The coverage is k/N. We use this metric to compare operators in Section 3.4.

2.1 Applicability

Model checking, a vital part of the method, can be applied to specifications for large software systems, such as TCAS II [9].

[1]After [15], a test criterion is a decision about what properties of a specification must be exercised to constitute a thorough test.

To avoid the model checker's state space explosion problem, several approaches are used, such as abstraction, partial order reduction, and symmetry [10]. A reduction called finite focus was proposed to increase feasibility of model checking for test set generation [1]. In that reduction, some finite number of states is mapped one-to-one to states in the reduced specification, while all other states are mapped to a single state.

2.2 Related Work on Specification Mutation

Gopal and Budd [16] applied a set of mutation operators to specifications given in predicate calculus form. The method relies on having a working implementation, as the program under test must be executed in order to generate test output. Woodward [24] investigated mutation operators for algebraic specifications. Weyuker et. al [23] proposed strategies for generating test data from the specifications represented by Boolean formulas and assessed their effectiveness using mutation analysis.

Fabbri et. al [12] devised a mutation model for finite state machines and used the mutation analysis criterion to evaluate the adequacy of the tests produced by standard finite state machine test sequence generation methods. Fabbri et. al [13] categorized mutation operators for different components of Statecharts specifications and provided strategies to abstract and incrementally test the components. Mutation analysis in the context of protocol specifications written in Estelle, an extended finite state machine formalism, was studied in [21].

3 Specification Mutation Operators

Ammann and Black defined some mutation operators, but did not consider the relative merits of the operators. We describe a set of mutation operators we developed for formal specifications together with their respective fault classes. We investigate the relationships between detection conditions for several fault classes analytically and compare the effectiveness of the mutation operators experimentally. A detailed description of the results presented in this Section can be found in [7].

3.1 Categories of Mutation Operators

Mutation categories should model potential faults [24]; therefore, it is important to recognize different types of faults. We design each mutation operator to uncover faults belonging to the corresponding fault class.

Some of these fault classes are related to the classes forming Kuhn's hierarchy. We use a term "simple expression" that closely corresponds to the Boolean variable in [18]. A simple expression is a Boolean expression that has no Boolean operators. For example, relational expressions and Boolean variables are simple expressions. (Other commonly used terms are "clause" and "condition").

Each fault class has a corresponding mutation operator. Applying a mutation operator gives rise to a fault in that class. For example, instances of the missing condition fault (MCF) class can be generated by a missing condition operator (MCO). Note that the abbreviation of the mutation operator ends in O, and the abbreviation of the corresponding fault class ends in F.

Although mutation operators are independent of any particular specification notation, here we present them for CTL specifications. Table 1 contains mutation operators for common fault classes and selected illustrative mutants generated from three formulas: the "`SPEC`" clause in Figure 1, the formula `AG (x & y → z)` (for ASO), and the formula `AG (WaterPres < 100)` (for RRO).

Operators and Example Mutants	
ORO	Operand Replacement
	AG (request → AF state = ready)
SNO	Simple Expression Negation
	AG (!request → AF state = busy)
ENO	Expression Negation
	AG (!(request → AF state = busy))
LRO	Logical Operator Replacement
	AG (request & AF state = busy)
RRO	Relational Operator Replacement
	AG (WaterPres <= 100)
MCO	Missing Condition
	AG AF state = busy
STO	Stuck-At
	AG (request → AF 1)
ASO	Associative Shift
	AG (x & (y → z))

Table 1. Mutation Operators and their Illustrative Mutants.

The function of some operators can be easily guessed from the name; we briefly explain what other, less obvious operators do. ORO replaces an operand by another syntactically legal operand. It does not replace a number with another number, since this may result in too many mutants. The current implementation of the operator handles two kinds of operands: state variables and symbolic constants. State variables may be of Boolean, scalar or integer type. The value of a scalar variable is drawn from a finite set of constants. An integer variable takes values from a finite range. An SMV specification may also contain symbolic constants defined by the user to represent integers.

MCO deletes simple expressions from conjunctions, disjunctions, and implications. STO replaces a simple expression with 0 and 1. ASO changes the association between variables, e.g., $x \rightarrow y_1 y_2 y_3$ is replaced with $(x \rightarrow y_1) y_2 y_3$.

If the number of atoms (variables and constants) in a specification is V and the number of value references is R, ORO results in $O(V * R)$ mutants, whereas SNO, LRO, MCO, STO, ASO and RRO result in $O(R)$ mutants.

ORO$^+$ operator, a combination of ORO and RRO, generates a class of faults closely matching VRF in [18].

Additionally, we defined Simple Expression Replacement Operator (SRO) which replaces a simple expression by every other syntactically valid simple expression of atoms in the model. This operator generates a class of faults identical to VRF. SRO sometimes generates higher order mutants, so by Woodward's principle [24], it should not be used for test generation.

We analyzed the relationships between several fault classes and studied the mutation operators experimentally.

3.2 Analysis of Fault Classes

Our operators model fault classes similar to those analyzed in Kuhn [18]. By comparing the conditions under which different types of faults are detected, Kuhn derived a hierarchy of fault classes. We extended Kuhn's analysis and tied it to mutation operators.

The detection conditions for a predicate P are the conditions under which a change to P affects the value of P. A test detects an error if and only if a faulty predicate P' evaluates to a different value than the correct predicate P. To simplify analysis, we only considered specifications S with formulas in disjunctive normal form (DNF).

Let S_{FAULT} be the detection conditions for fault class $FAULT$. We discovered the following relationships:

$$\begin{array}{ccccc} S_{SRF} & \rightarrow & S_{SNF} & \rightarrow & S_{ENF} \\ & \nearrow & & & \\ S_{STF} & \rightarrow & S_{MCF} & & \end{array}$$

Formal analysis is presented in [7]. Informally, to determine the detection conditions for an arbitrary fault in a particular fault class, an exclusive-or of an original specification and its faulty version is computed.

It follows from the relationships, for instance, that a test that detects a Simple Expression Replacement Fault (SRF) for a simple expression in a predicate, also detects a Simple Expression Negation Fault (SNF) for the same simple expression. Hence, SRO detects SNF. Also since ORO$^+$ can be considered as a practical approximation to SRO, ORO$^+$ is very likely to detect SNF.

3.3 Mutation Generator

To study the mutation operators and empirically confirm the theoretical results above, we developed an extensible tool for systematically making small syntactic changes to SMV specifications.

The tool uses portions of SMV code: the parser, abstract syntax tree (AST) manipulation routines and low level functionalities, such as dynamic memory allocation and manipulation of data structures (e.g., hash tables).

Mutation generator performs the following steps:

1. Parse a given SMV file and build a tree data structure in memory.

2. Process the tree to extract information necessary for performing mutations, e.g., collect information about types and domains of variables.

3. For each selected mutation operator, traverse the tree invoking the corresponding mutation routine. When the routine recognizes an opportunity for a mutation, it creates a mutant. The mutant is then written to a file.

Resulting individual mutations may be left in individual SMV files or written to a single file. The former yields a large number of files. The overhead of starting a new SMV process for each mutant is intolerable even for specifications of moderate size. Since SMV builds a state machine transition relation for a given input file only once and checks CTL formulas independently, using an option that writes mutations into a single file results in very efficient processing.

The tool allows us to selectively apply mutation operators. It can be extended to add new operators. In addition, the mutation generator optionally mutates state machines to generate tests which a correct implementation should fail.

The source code and documentation are available from the authors.

3.4 Empirical Comparison of Operators

We compared the mutation operators in terms of the number of test cases produced and the specification coverage. We ran experiments on several sample SMV specifications. Below we present the results for Safety Injection specification [6]. The results for other samples were similar. After reflection, this specification contains 22 CTL formulas and 5 variables, including a Boolean, 3 scalars, and an integer which takes values between 0 and 200, but is only compared with 2 different symbolic constants.

Out of a total of 730 mutants generated by applying all mutation operators to the specification (since SNO mutants

Operator	Mutants	Counter-examples	Unique Traces	Coverage
ORO$^+$	202	99	21	100%
ORO	130	63	17	94.2%
SNO	83	51	15	90.7%
ENO	144	104	15	90.7%
LRO	122	82	10	83.7%
RRO	72	36	10	50.0%
MCO	79	50	13	87.2%
STO	166	51	15	90.7%
ASO	17	17	5	47.7%

Table 2. Safety injection example results.

are a subset of ENO mutants, we did not include SNO mutants in the total), 86 were semantically unique, inconsistent. The method produced 21 unique test cases or traces.

We present details in Table 2. "Mutants" is the total number of mutants generated by each operator, including consistent and duplicate mutants. Next we give the number of counterexamples found in the SMV runs. "Unique traces" is the number of traces after duplicate traces and prefixes are removed. "Coverage" is the metric described in Section 2.

ORO$^+$ generates the largest number of mutants, but provides the same set of test cases as all the operators combined. Consequently, it has 100% coverage.

SNO provides second best coverage while generating significantly fewer mutants.

We define UT_{OPER} to be the set of unique traces generated by mutation operator $OPER$. For the Safety Injection specification, as well as several other examples, we found the following relationships between the sets of unique traces:

$$\begin{array}{l} UT_{ORO} \supseteq UT_{SNO} \supseteq UT_{ENO} \\ \quad \rotatebox{-90}{$\supseteq$} \\ UT_{STO} \supseteq UT_{MCO} \end{array}$$

These results agree with the analysis in Section 3.2. In particular, they support the idea that ORO is sufficient to detect faults in ORF, SNF, and ENF. Therefore, the Simple Expression Negation Operator (SNO) and Expression Negation Operator (ENO) are not needed if the Operand Replacement Operator (ORO) is used.

The above hierarchy is not guaranteed to hold for specifications with formulas not in disjunctive normal form. We discuss this in the following Section.

4 Open Questions

Based on our current understanding of the method and its challenges, we define the following research topics and questions.

4.1 How Does Form Influence Results?

Semantically equivalent specifications may be written in different ways. Since mutation analysis makes syntactic changes, the results may depend on what form the specification is in.

Form of Specifications

Kuhn's analytical technique applies to specifications in restricted form, i.e., with formulas in disjunctive normal form (DNF). Realistic specifications are generally not in DNF, and the mutants of a DNF representation are significantly different from the mutants of the original.

Consequently, if we apply mutation operators to the unaltered specification, the theoretical results do not strictly apply. We will empirically study the degree to which the test set generated from a specification with formulas in DNF differs from the test set produced from an original specification. To study this, we will mechanically convert specification formulas to DNF, then compare the test sets generated from original with those from the converted specifications.

Specification Languages

Although we use SMV, the method is not limited to any particular type of model checker. Most of the interest has centered around two types of model checkers [22]: branching time model checkers for Computation Tree Logic (CTL) and linear time model checkers for the propositional Linear Temporal Logic (LTL). SPIN [17] is a popular LTL model checker. We plan to study whether our research is applicable to both CTL and LTL model checkers.

4.2 What is the Relation Between Operators?

This has different facets, in particular, what is the trade off between choosing some operators which produce more mutants, but give better coverage, and performing selective mutation without the most expensive operators, that is, choosing operators which produce far fewer mutants, but give slightly worse coverage. Using Kuhn's analytical technique, we found the subsumption relationship between several operators. Subsumed operator does not need to be used if the subsuming operator is applied. We will look for such relationships for other operators. We are also interested in discovering other analytical techniques for comparing mutation operators. Finally, are some operators better for different applications, sizes or forms of specifications? The latter was discussed above.

New Operators and Sets of Operators

Efficiency of the test generation and evaluation method is determined, in part, by the cost of mutation. We plan to extend our work on comparing mutation operators based on their coverage and the number of mutants generated. We found that ORO^+ gives maximum coverage, and SNO gives very good coverage using far fewer mutants. We will look for other operators or sets of operators which provide high fault detection capabilities at reduced cost. We will extend the mutation generator program to apply a richer set of mutation operators to SMV specifications.

Experimental Base

The Safety Injection specification used in this paper has only five variables and a single module. However, many realistic specifications are composed of a number of modules and contain dozens of variables. To verify scalability of the method and applicability of the experimental results to realistic specifications, we plan to use larger specifications, such as the Flight Guidance System [20] and other specifications from industry. By improving the mutation generator to handle the general SMV syntax, we will extend the pool of specifications available for our experiments.

4.3 How Does the Method Compare with Others?

We want to compare the coverage of specification mutation analysis with existing methods to get some idea of the quality of this method.

An objective comparison of the specification-based mutation analysis with commonly accepted criteria is necessary. Our goal is to reduce the number of faults in the actual programs written from the formal specifications. Therefore, it is necessary to study usefulness of the tests generated from formal specifications for detecting bugs in the corresponding implementations.

Many coverage measures exist [25]. Branch coverage of generated tests for Cruise Control example was examined in [3]. Branch coverage (decision coverage) checks whether boolean expressions tested in control structures evaluated to both true and false.

We plan to investigate the program-based coverage of the tests using several coverage metrics, in particular, a practical variation of path coverage, such as length-n subpath coverage which checks whether all subpaths of length less than or equal to n in a program have been followed. Path coverage metric is powerful yet unrelated to mutation analysis, hence it is an important standard measure. Another possible measure is a fault-based coverage metric.

5 Conclusions

Standard mutation analysis is based on program source code. In contrast, a recent mutation analysis scheme uses model checkers to automatically generate complete test sets from formal specifications and to evaluate coverage of existing test sets. Using a model checker avoids the problem of equivalent mutants, since model checking is decidable, and takes advantage of 20 years of industrial model checking experience.

We described the specification-based mutation analysis method and reported our recent work: defining a set of specification mutation operators in the context of this method and comparing them based on their effectiveness and cost.

We posed three questions to confirm the practicality of this method: how does form influence results, what is the relation between mutation operators, and how does this method compare with others? We also outlined some of our research planned to address these questions.

References

[1] P. Ammann and P. E. Black. Abstracting formal specifications to generate software tests via model checking. In *Proceedings of the 18th Digital Avionics Systems Conference (DASC99)*, volume 2, page 10.A.6. IEEE, October 1999. Also NIST IR 6405.

[2] P. E. Ammann and P. E. Black. A specification-based coverage metric to evaluate test sets. In *Proceedings of Fourth IEEE International High-Assurance Systems Engineering Symposium (HASE 99)*, pages 239–248. IEEE Computer Society, November 1999. Also NIST IR 6403.

[3] P. E. Ammann, P. E. Black, and W. Majurski. Using model checking to generate tests from specifications. In *Proceedings of the Second IEEE International Conference on Formal Engineering Methods (ICFEM'98)*, pages 46–54. IEEE Computer Society, Dec. 1998.

[4] J. M. Atlee and M. A. Buckley. A logic-model semantics for SCR software requirements. In *Proceedings of the 1996 International Symposium on Software Testing and Analysis*, pages 280–292, Jan. 1996.

[5] C. Banphawatthanarak, B. H. Krogh, and K. Butts. Symbolic verification of executable control specifications. In *Proceedings of the Tenth IEEE International Symposium on Computer Aided Control System Design (jointly with the 1999 Conference on Control Applications)*, pages CACSD–581–586, Kohala Coast - Island of Hawai'i, Hawai'i, Aug 1999.

[6] R. Bharadwaj and C. L. Heitmeyer. Model checking complete requirements specifications using abstraction. Memorandum Report NRL/MR/5540-97-7999, U.S. Naval Research Laboratory, Washington, DC 20375, November 1997.

[7] P. E. Black, V. Okun, and Y. Yesha. Mutation operators for specifications. In *Proceedings of* 15th *IEEE International Conference on Automated Software Engineering (ASE2000)*, September 2000. To be published.

[8] J. Callahan, F. Schneider, and S. Easterbrook. Automated software testing using model-checking. In *Proceedings 1996 SPIN Workshop*, Rutgers, NJ, August 1996. Also WVU Technical Report #NASA-IVV-96-022.

[9] W. Chan, R. J. Anderson, P. Beame, S. Burns, F. Modugno, D. Notkin, and J. D. Reese. Model checking large software specifications. *IEEE Transactions on Software Engineering*, 24(7):498 – 520, July 1998.

[10] E. M. Clarke, O. Grumberg, and D. Peled. *Model Checking*. MIT Press, 1999.

[11] E. M. Clarke, Jr., E. A. Emerson, and A. P. Sistla. Automatic verification of finite-state concurrent systems using temporal logic specifications. *ACM Transactions on Programming Languages and Systems*, 8(2):244–263, April 1986.

[12] S. C. P. F. Fabbri, J. C. Maldonado, M. E. Delamaro, and P. C. Masiero. Mutation analysis testing for finite state machines. In *Proceedings of the Fifth International Symposium on Software Reliability Engineering*, pages 220–229, Monterey, CA, November 1994. IEEE.

[13] S. C. P. F. Fabbri, J. C. Maldonado, T. Sugeta, and P. C. Masiero. Mutation testing applied to validate specifications based on statecharts. In *Proceedings of the Tenth International Symposium on Software Reliability Engineering*, pages 210–219, Boca Raton, Florida, November 1999. IEEE.

[14] A. Gargantini and C. Heitmeyer. Using model checking to generate tests from requirements specifications. In *Proceedings of the Joint 7th European Software Engineering Conference and 7th ACM SIGSOFT International Symposium on Foundations of Software Engineering*, Toulouse, France, September 1999.

[15] J. B. Goodenough and S. L. Gerhart. Toward a theory of test data selection. *IEEE Transactions on Software Engineering*, 1(2):156–173, June 1975.

[16] A. Gopal and T. Budd. Program testing by specification mutation. Technical Report TR 83-17, University of Arizona, Nov. 1983.

[17] G. J. Holzmann. The model checker SPIN. *IEEE Transactions on Software Engineering*, 23(5):279–295, May 1997.

[18] D. R. Kuhn. Fault classes and error detection in specification based testing. *ACM Transactions on Software Engineering Methodology*, 8(4), October 1999.

[19] K. L. McMillan. *Symbolic Model Checking*. Kluwer Academic Publishers, 1993.

[20] S. P. Miller. Specifying the mode logic of a flight guidance system in CoRE and SCR. In *Second Workshop on Formal Methods in Software Practice*, Clearwater Beach, FL, March 1998.

[21] R. L. Probert and F. Guo. Mutation testing of protocols: Principles and preliminary experimental results. In *Protocol Test Systems, III*, pages 57–76. Elsevier Science Publishers B.V. (North-Holland), 1991.

[22] W. C. Visser. *Efficient CTL* Model Checking Using Games and Automata*. Dissertation, The University of Manchester, June 1998.

[23] E. Weyuker, T. Goradia, and A. Singh. Automatically generating test data from a boolean specification. *IEEE Transactions on Software Engineering*, 20(5):353–363, May 1994.

[24] M. Woodward. Errors in algebraic specifications and an experimental mutation testing tool. *Software Engineering Journal*, pages 211–224, July 1993.

[25] H. Zhu, P. A. V. Hall, and J. H. R. May. Software unit test coverage and adequacy. *ACM Computing Surveys*, 29(4):366–427, Dec. 1997.

Mutation: Cost Reduction

Evaluating N-Selective Mutation for C Programs: Unit and Integration Testing

José Carlos Maldonado
Ellen Francine Barbosa
Auri Marcelo Rizzo Vincenzi
Instituto de Ciências Matemáticas e de Computação
Universidade de São Paulo
{francine, jcmaldon, auri}@icmc.sc.usp.br

Márcio Eduardo Delamaro
Departamento de Informática
Universidade Estadual de Maringá
delamaro@din.uem.br

Abstract

Mutation Testing has been found to be an effective fault-revealing criterion. However, its high cost of application, mainly due to the high number of mutants created and the effort to determine the equivalent mutants, has motivated the proposition of alternative approaches for its application. One of them, named N-*Selective Mutation, aims at reducing the number of generated mutants through a reduction on the number of the most prevalent mutant operators expecting that would not occur a significant reduction on the effectiveness. Previously, other researchers investigated the* N-*Selective Mutation in the context of FORTRAN language, for the unit testing. The results showed that it is possible to have a large cost reduction preserving a high mutation score. Recently, the underlying mutation concept has been explored at the integration testing phase by the proposition of the Interface Mutation criterion. In the same research line, this work investigates the* N-*Selective Mutation for C programs, considering the unit and the integration testing phases, in the perspective of contributing to the establishment of low-cost, effective mutation-based testing strategies.* N-*Selective Mutation is also compared with other Selective Mutation criteria as well as with Randomly Selected Mutation.*

Keywords: N-Selective Mutation, Mutation Analysis, Interface Mutation, Unit and Integration Testing.

1 Introduction

Software testing, which has as objective the identification of not-yet-discovered errors, is one of the most important activities to guarantee the quality and the reliability of the software under development. Since the exhaustive test is, in general, impracticable, criteria that allow the selection of an input domain subset preserving the probability of revealing the existent errors in the program are necessary.

There is a large number of criteria available to evaluate a test set for a given program against a given specification [25]. A tester may use one or more of these criteria to assess the quality of a test set for a program and enhance the test set, if it is the case, by constructing additional test cases needed to fulfil the testing requirements.

Considering the diversity of testing criteria as well their complementary aspects, some theoretical and empirical studies have been conducted, aiming at the establishment of an effective, low-cost testing strategy [3, 5, 15, 17–19, 22–24]. Effectiveness, cost and strength are the three most meaningful bases for the comparison and evaluation of testing criteria. Effectiveness is related to the fault detection ability of a criterion; cost indicates the effort to satisfy a criterion; and strength refers to the difficulty of a test set T to satisfy a criterion C_2 given that T already satisfies another criterion C_1.

Mutation Testing (Mutation Analysis), proposed by DeMillo *et al.* [11], although powerful, is computationally expensive [17, 23, 24]. Its high cost of application, mainly due to the high number of mutants created and the effort to determine the equivalent mutants, has motivated the proposition of alternative criteria for its application [1, 14, 17, 18]. One of these alternatives, the N-Selective Mutation, tries to reduce the cost of Mutation Testing by discarding the most prevalent mutant operators – the ones that generate more mutants –, expecting that it would not occur a significant reduction on its effectiveness [18].

This work investigates the application of N-Selective Mutation in the context of C language, considering both the unit and the integration testing phases. We carried out two experiments. In Experiment I, at the unit testing phase, we used two program suites and the testing tool *Proteum* (*PROgram TEsting Using Mutants*) [8] – a tool that supports the testing of C programs at the unit level. In Experiment II, at the integration testing phase, we used one program suite from the Experiment I – a set of 5-Unix programs. Experiment II was conducted using Proteum/IM [6] – *IM* stands for Interface Mutation. Interface Mutation is a criterion that extends Mutation Testing to the integration testing phase [7, 9]. We compare the results obtained by applying N-Selective Mutation with other alternative approaches for the Mutation Testing application: Sufficient Mutation [3, 4] and Randomly Selected Mutation [1]. Using the same suite of programs in Experiments I and II enabled us to make some observations and conjectures to the establishment of an incremental strategy for applying N-Selective Mutation throughout the software development process: implementation and integration phases.

The remainder of this paper is organized as follows. In Section 2, an overview of Mutation Testing is provided as well as related works are described. Section 3 contains the description and analysis of both experiments we carried out. The results are also compared with some other alternative mutation approaches. In Section 4, our conclusions and future work are presented.

2 Mutation Testing: an Overview

Mutation Testing is based on the assumption that a program is well tested if all so-called "simple faults" are detected and removed. Simple faults are introduced into the program by creating different versions of the program, known as mutants, each of which containing a simple syntactic change. The simple faults are modeled by a set of mutant operators applied to a program P under test. The definition of the mutant operators set is a key point to the criterion. It should be observed that complex faults are assumed to be coupled to simple faults, in such a way that a test set that detects all simple faults in a program should also detect most complex faults. This is the so-called coupling effect assumption [11].

The quality of a test set T is measured by its ability to distinguish the behavior of the mutants from the behavior of the original program, in the sense of different outputs in the scope of this work. So, the goal is to find a test case that causes a mutant to behave differently from the original program. A mutant is equivalent if no such test case exists. If P behaves as per the specification when T is applied, then the quality of T is demonstrated, otherwise, a fault has been detected and the debugging activity should take place.

A test set that kills all the non-equivalent mutants is said to be adequate with respect to Mutation Testing, denoted by MT-adequate. The mutation score is the ratio of the number of dead mutants to the number of non-equivalent mutants. It measures the adequacy of a given test set T to test a program P.

Mutation Testing has been mostly used at the unit testing, mainly because the errors the mutant operators aim at are restricted to unit errors. Interface Mutation criterion [7, 9] extends Mutation Testing to the integration level. When applying Interface Mutation the tester is concerned with those errors related to a connection (the interface) between two units and the interactions along that connection. We refer to Mutation Testing when no distinction is relevant. When necessary, we refer to the application of Mutation Testing to the unit testing as Mutation Analysis and Interface Mutation as its application to the integration testing.

2.1 Alternative Mutation Testing Criteria

Empirical studies have provided evidences that Mutation Testing is among the most promising criteria in terms of fault detection [6, 9, 17, 22–24]. However, as previously highlighted, Mutation Testing often imposes unacceptable demands on computing and human resources because the large number of mutants that need to be executed on one or more test cases and that need to be examined for possible equivalence with the program under test.

The test community, to deal with the cost aspects, has investigated some approaches derived from Mutation Testing: Randomly Selected Mutation [1], Constrained Mutation [14] and Selective Mutation [17, 18]. The goal is to determine a set of mutations in such a way that if we obtain a test set T, able to distinguish those mutations, T will also be MT-adequate. In other words, the idea is that a subset of mutations can lead to the same test case selection, so that we can use subsets of operators or mutants that lead to the selection of test sets as effective as the total set of operators and mutants would.

Randomly Selected Mutation, proposed by Acree *et al.* [1], considers a percentage of the mutants generated by each operator. Empirical studies conducted for FORTRAN and C programs [5, 23] indicate that it is possible to obtain high mutation scores even with a reduced number of mutants. However, the randomly selection of mutants ignores the fault detection capability of individual mutant types [22]. Budd *et al.*'s fault detection experiments [5] found that mutants generated with respect to one mutant operator may be more effective in detecting certain types of faults than mutants generated with respect to other operators. This suggests that while mutants are selected for examination, they should be differently weighted depending on their respective fault detection capability.

Mathur proposed a variant of Acree *et al.*'s idea: Constrained Mutation [14], afterwards called Selective Mutation [18]. In Constrained Mutation we select a subset of mutant operators to be used for mutant generation. Motivating results have been obtained [23, 24]. It is important to observe, however, that Constrained Mutation does not establish a method for selecting the operators to be used; in general, these operators are intuitively selected based on the testers' experience. The definition of systematic ways for selecting the operators, as proposed by Barbosa *et al.* [3,4], may lead to better results.

Offutt *et al.* introduced N-Selective Mutation [17]. In this approach, the method for selecting the operators is related to the amount of mutants that each operator generates. The operators that create more mutants are not applied. So, N-Selective Mutation omits the N most prevalent operators. In that study, Offutt *et al.* explored 2, 4 and 6-Selective Mutation. On the average, the 2-Selective Mutation adequate test sets achieved a mutation score of 0.999 and a cost reduction of 24%, in terms of generated mutants, over ten subject programs. The 6-Selective Mutation adequate test sets achieved a mutation score of 0.997,with a cost reduction of 60%.

Motivated by the results from 6-Selective Mutation, Offutt *et al.* [17] investigated whether further reductions in the number of operators could yield effective mutation testing. In fact, Offutt *et al.* introduced the concept of sufficient mutant operators set. The idea is to determine a set of sufficient mutant operators S in a such way that if a test set T S-adequate is obtained, T would also lead to a very high mutation score. The experiment for the determination of sufficient mutant operators for FORTRAN language [17] was conducted using the Mothra tool [10]. The 22 mutant operators implemented in this tool were divided into three mutation classes: Replacement of Operands, Expression Modification and Statement Modification. Offutt *et al.* compared the mutation classes pairwise and noticed that with the five operators of Expression Modification class it was possible to obtain a significant reduction in the number of generated mutants (77.6%), preserving a high mutation score with respect to Mutation Analysis (above 0.98). One important point to be observed is that all the sufficient mutant operators determined were not among the six most prevalent FORTRAN operators, meaning that this approach would improve the 6-Selective Mutation.

Mresa and Bottaci [16] have also investigated sufficient FORTRAN operators using Mothra, taking into account the mutation scores provided by the individual operators and their associated costs (including test set generation and equivalent mutant detection) in order to determine the most efficient operators. According to the authors, the results show that the use of the most efficient operators can provide significant gains for Selective Mutation if the acceptable mutation score is not very close to 1.0, otherwise, Randomly Selected Mutation provides a more efficient strategy than a sufficient set of operators. Mresa and Bottaci have also raised the point that it can not be assumed that a test set that kills 99% of all the mutants is able to detect 99% of the real faults that would be detected by an adequate test set.

In another experiment, conducted by Wong *et al.* [22], Selective Mutation was investigated in the context of C and FORTRAN. For C language, *Proteum* [8] was used. It allows measuring the adequacy of the test sets with respect to (w.r.t.) 71 mutant operators, categorized into four mutation classes [2]: Statement (15), Operator (46), Variable (7) and Constant (3). Six selective mutation categories were constructed, based on 11 of the 71 mutant operators. These mutant operators were selected based on the authors' judgment of their relative usefulness. According to the authors, 6 of the 11 operators may constitute a very good starting point for establishing a sufficient set of mutant operators to use in an alternate cost-effective mutation.

Barbosa *et al.* [3, 4] reproduced the experiments conducted by Offutt *et al.* and Wong *et al.* for two other sets of C programs: a 27-program suite taken from Kernighan and Plauger [13], and a 5-Unix-program suite previously used by Wong *et al.* [21]. Applying the strategy of Offutt *et al.* on the 27-program suite it was obtained the Constant Mutation class as the sufficient set, with a mutation score of 0.97 and a cost reduction around 78%, in terms of the number of generated mutants. For the 5-program suite it was obtained the Operator Mutation class as the sufficient set, with a mutation score of 0.99 and a cost reduction about 66%. Applying the operators investigated by Wong *et al.* [22] it was obtained a mutation score close to 0.98 and a cost reduction around 80% for the 27-program suite, and a mutation score of 0.99 with a cost reduction over 83% for the 5-program suite.

The results obtained with the "intuitive" set of operators proposed by Wong *et al.* were a little better than the results obtained with the sufficient set obtained with the application of Offutt *et al.*'s strategy in the context of C language for the two suites of programs. It should be highlighted that some of the sufficient operators determined by Offutt *et al.*'s approach were among the most prevalent ones for C language, conflicting with N-Selective Mutation. Moreover, the sufficient operators were completely different for each program suite.

Barbosa *et al.* have also defined the *Sufficient Procedure* [3, 4], a systematic way to select a set of sufficient mutant operators. The *Sufficient Procedure* has six steps, based on the following guidelines:

i. **Consider mutant operators that determine a high mutation score**: To guarantee that the sufficient mutant operators set determines a high mutation score w.r.t. Mutation Testing, we should select the operators that determine the greatest mutation scores w.r.t. the total set of mutant operators. In some aspect, this capture the mutant operator effectiveness in the sense used by Offutt *et al.* [17], i.e., its mutation score against the full set of operators.

ii. **Consider one operator of each mutation class**: Each mutation class models specific errors in certain elements of a program (e.g. statements, operators, variables and constants). Thus, it is desirable that the sufficient set has, at least, the most representative operator of each class.

iii. **Evaluate the empirical inclusion among the mutant operators**: The mutant operators that are empirically included by other mutant operators of the sufficient set should be removed since these operators increase the application cost of the sufficient set, in terms of the number of mutants and equivalence determination. Thus, they do not effectively contribute to the testing activity improvement.

iv. **Establish an incremental strategy**: Given the application cost and the test requirements that each mutation class determines, it is interesting to establish an incremental strategy of application among the mutant operators of the sufficient set. The idea is to apply, at first, the mutant operators that are relevant to certain minimal testing requirements (e.g., all-nodes and all-edges coverage). Next, depending on the criticality of the application and the budget and time constraints, the mutant operators related to other concepts and test requirements may be applied.

v. **Consider mutant operators that provide an increment in the mutation score**: In general, independently of the quality of the test set, 80% of the mutants are killed at the first execution [5]. Considering that just around 20% of the mutants effectively contribute to the quality improvement of the test set, an increment of 1% in the mutation score represents 5% of the mutants that are really significant. Thus, the non-selected operators that if included in the sufficient set would increase the mutation score should be analyzed.

vi. **Consider mutant operators with high strength**: Other operators that should be considered to determine the sufficient set are those that have a high average strength w.r.t. each operator of the total set of operators.

The *Sufficient Procedure* was applied in the 27-program and 5-program suites. For the 27-program suite a mutation score of 0.997 and a cost reduction about 65% were obtained, and for the 5-program suite a mutation score of 0.998 and a cost reduction around 82%. However, the operators selected applying the *Sufficient Procedure* were among the most prevalent ones for C, again.

Vincenzi *et al.* [19] reproduced the Barbosa *et al.*'s study at the integration testing level, considering the Interface Mutation criterion and using the Proteum/IM testing tool. The sufficient set for the 5-Unix-program suite provided a mutation score of 0.998 and a cost reduction over 73%. At the integration level, similarly to the unit level, some of the interface sufficient operators were among the most prevalent ones. A complete description of the mutant operators can be found in [2, 6]. These operators were designed for C language, and are implemented in *Proteum* and Proteum/IM, for the unit and the integration testing, respectively.

Two main points motivated us to carry out the study reported herein. The first is that the authors are not aware of previous systematic studies of N-Selective Mutation for C language. Second, the conflicting results between Sufficient and N-Selective Mutation approaches, at the unit and the integration testing phases.

3 Experiments

We tried out the N-Selective Mutation approach in the context of unit and integration testing. At the unit testing phase, we considered two program suites: a 27-program suite and a 5-Unix-program suite. At the integration testing phase, we used the 5-Unix-program suite. The methodology used in the experiments comprises five phases: Program Selection, Tool Selection, Test Set Generation, N-Selective Mutation Application and Data Analysis.

3.1 Experiment I: Unit Testing

3.1.1 Program Selection

The first program suite is composed by 27 small programs, part of a simplified text editor [13]. These programs, previously used by Weyuker [20], were originally written in Pascal [13] and subsequently converted to C. As illustrated in Table 1, these programs range in size from 11 up to 71 executable statements and have from 119 up to 1631 mutants. The second suite comprises 5 Unix-utility programs, previously used by Wong *et al.* [21]. These programs range in size from 76 up to 119 executable statements and have from 1619 up to 4332 mutants (Table 1(b)). We have on the average 32 and 24 mutants/LOC for the 27-program and the 5-program suites, respectively.

Table 1 also provides, for each program, information on the total number of mutants and on the number of equivalent mutants (manually determined) per mutation class. Observe that the Operator Mutation class is the one that on the average generates the greatest number of mutants and the greatest number of equivalent ones for both program sets. For the 27-program suite, the exceptions are: change, command, getcmd, makepat and subst, although for three of them – change, command and getcmd – the number of equivalent mutants is still the greatest. For the 5-program suite, the Operator Mutation class does not generate the greatest number of equivalent mutants only for three programs: cal, checkeq and look. In fact, for the 27-program and the 5-program suites, the Operator and Variable Mutation classes are responsible for about 80% and 90% of all the equivalent mutants, respectively.

3.1.2 Tool Selection

We used ***Proteum*** testing tool [8], developed at University of São Paulo, which supports the application of Mutation Analysis to C programs, at the unit testing phase.

3.1.3 Test Set Generation

For the 27-program suite, one *ad hoc* test set was generated for each program based on its specification, i.e., none functional criterion was used. Next, the test sets were improved based on their adequacy w.r.t. Mutation Analysis: new test cases were added to obtain a *MA*-adequate test set for each one of the 27 programs. We kept in these sets only the effective test cases, i.e., test cases that when executed killed at least one mutant.

Table 1. Number of LOC and Mutants: 27-Program Suite.

(a)

Program	*LOC*	*Mutants Tot/Eq*	*Statement Tot/Eq*	*Operator Tot/Eq*	*Variable Tot/Eq*	*Constant Tot/Eq*
append	13	387 / 64	54 / 5	183 / 34	80 / 19	70 / 6
archive	14	514 / 75	57 / 0	222 / 19	61 / 28	174 / 28
change	13	119 / 19	59 / 5	15 / 8	33 / 3	12 / 3
ckglob	23	730 / 234	76 / 15	340 / 99	172 / 78	142 / 42
cmp	13	430 / 41	78 / 1	129 / 6	119 / 34	104 / 0
command	71	1207 / 243	230 / 26	248 / 89	345 / 86	384 / 42
compare	18	482 / 43	74 / 2	157 / 21	153 / 16	98 / 4
compress	14	454 / 87	69 / 0	215 / 53	110 / 34	60 / 0
dodash	15	1071 / 202	62 / 1	423 / 71	341 / 91	245 / 39
edit	23	524 / 139	105 / 13	211 / 63	126 / 45	82 / 18
entab	18	370 / 39	89 / 2	144 / 20	79 / 17	58 / 0
expand	15	389 / 37	67 / 0	210 / 20	60 / 17	52 / 0
getcmd	32	860 / 19	574 / 1	44 / 14	10 / 4	232 / 0
getdef	31	840 / 134	136 / 7	308 / 54	208 / 47	188 / 26
getfn	11	494 / 88	50 / 0	245 / 48	90 / 26	109 / 14
getfns	23	627 / 135	64 / 5	233 / 54	162 / 44	168 / 32
getlist	21	678 / 93	86 / 4	310 / 56	150 / 30	132 / 3
getnum	17	564 / 73	71 / 2	252 / 19	107 / 31	134 / 21
getone	23	834 / 122	98 / 4	397 / 67	205 / 38	134 / 13
gtext	16	804 / 82	55 / 3	331 / 37	224 / 39	194 / 3
makepat	29	1683 / 266	151 / 4	516 / 98	594 / 108	422 / 56
omatch	36	840 / 220	146 / 18	313 / 100	196 / 57	185 / 45
optpat	13	444 / 138	68 / 7	218 / 75	70 / 23	88 / 33
spread	19	1061 / 79	86 / 0	418 / 40	355 / 35	202 / 4
subst	36	1631 / 300	154 / 9	497 / 105	739 / 149	241 / 37
translit	33	1125 / 121	140 / 5	447 / 73	301 / 37	237 / 6
unrotate	28	984 / 43	92 / 0	441 / 20	189 / 19	262 / 4
Total	618	20146 / 3136	2991 / 139	7467 / 1363	5279 / 1155	4409 / 479

(b)

Program	*LOC*	*Mutants Tot/Eq*	*Statement Tot/Eq*	*Operator Tot/Eq*	*Variable Tot/Ea*	*Constant Tot/Eq*
cal	119	4332 / 221	352 / 3	1409 / 86	791 / 117	1780 / 15
checkeq	76	3099 / 206	268 / 1	937 / 99	783 / 106	1111 / 0
comm	119	1728 / 166	405 / 5	642 / 111	367 / 35	314 / 15
look	107	2056 / 143	319 / 23	720 / 36	646 / 55	371 / 29
uniq	103	1619 / 93	348 / 0	621 / 64	406 / 28	244 / 1
Total	524	12834 / 829	1692 / 32	4329 / 396	2993 / 341	3820 / 60

For the 5-program suite, 11 *MA*-adequate test sets were used for each one of the 5 programs. Initially, we generated a pool of test cases composed by: 1) ad hoc functional test cases, based on the program specification; and 2) randomly generated test cases. From that pool, 11 *MA*-adequate test sets were generated for each program: we run each test set against the mutants and, when necessary, added test cases to these sets to obtain a *MA*-adequate test set.

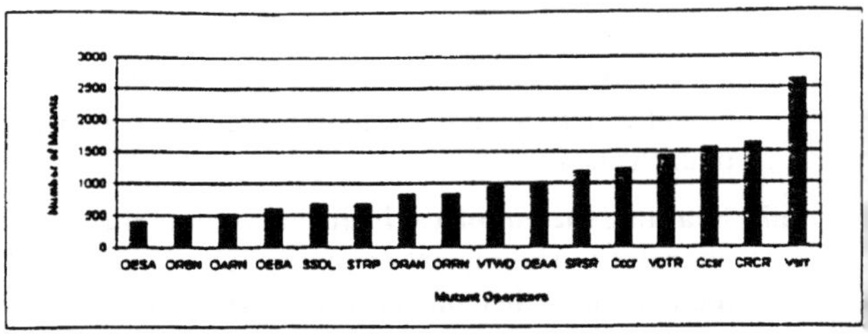

(a)

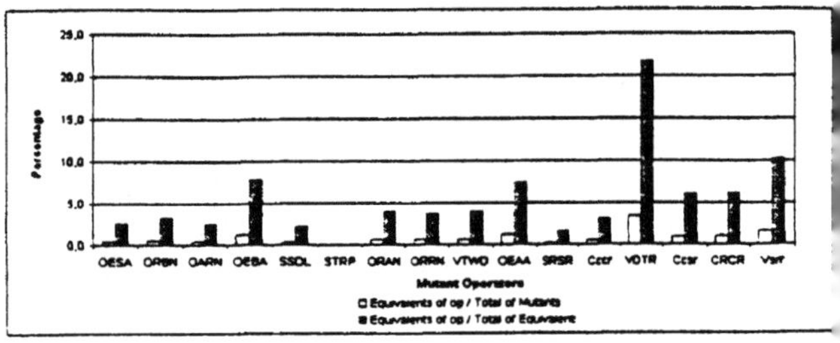

(b)

Figure 1. 27-Program Suite: Mutant Operators Cost per Number of: (a) Generated Mutants and (b) Equivalent Mutants.

3.1.4 *N*-Selective Mutation Application

For each program, the cost of the mutant operators was determined. For the 27-program suite, we provide in Figure 1 information on the mutant operators cost in terms of a) number of generated mutants and b) number of equivalent mutants compared with the total of mutants and with the total of equivalent ones. We consider the 16 most prevalent operators. The same information is provided in Figure 2 for the 5-program suite.

To the 27-program suite, out of 71 operators, only 39 were applicable (i.e., generate at least one mutant): 10 of Statement Mutation class, 21 of Operator Mutation class, 5 of Variable Mutation class and 3 of Constant Mutation class. To the 5-program suite, 56 operators were applicable: 14 of Statement, 33 of Operator, 6 of Variable and 3 of Constant. All the 39 operators that were applicable to the 27-program suite were also applicable to the 5-program suite. From Figure 1 and Figure 2 we can observe that 8 operators are in the intersection of the 10 most prevalent operators in both sets. It can also be observed that VDTR is the operator that generates, in both experiments, the greatest percentage of equivalent mutants compared either with the total number of its mutants or with the total number of all the mutants. Moreover, 6 operators are in the intersection of the 10 most prevalent operators in terms of equivalent mutants, in both experiments.

For the 27-program and the 5-program suites we tried out the *N*-Selective Mutation approach, from 1-Selective to 38-Selective and to 55-Selective, respectively; i.e., discard-

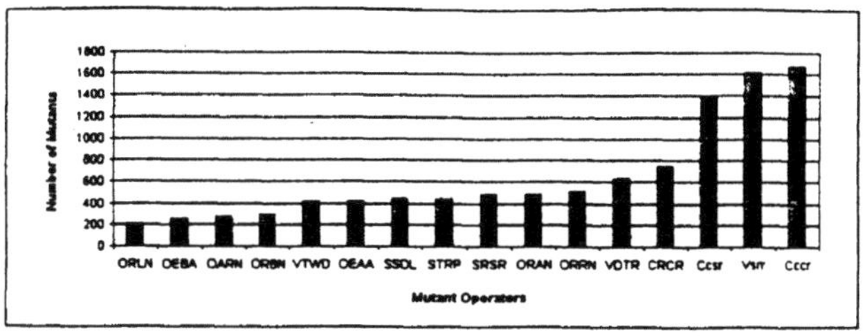

(a)

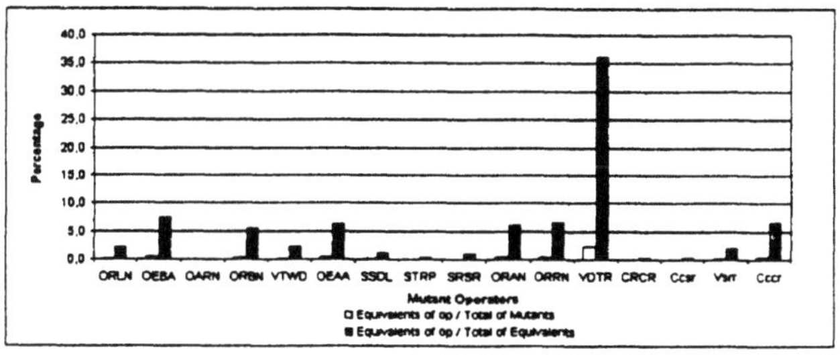

(b)

Figure 2. 5-Program Suite: Mutant Operators Cost per Number of: (a) Generated Mutants and (b) Equivalent Mutants.

ing at a time each one of the applicable operators, from the most to the least prevalent ones. Table 2 presents the average mutation score w.r.t. Mutation Analysis, the number of generated mutants by applying each N-Selective criterion and the cumulative cost reduction w.r.t. the total of mutants. The number of equivalent mutants and the associated cumulative cost reduction w.r.t. the total of equivalent mutants discharged are also provided. For the 5-program suite, the same information is synthesized in Table 3.

It is important to note that we could have stopped applying the N-Selective criteria at a certain coverage level, since from some point on there is no sense to further exclude some operators. However, we have decided to keep all the N-Selective criteria in order to provide a complete overview.

3.1.5 Data Analysis

In this section we analyze the cost/benefit of the N-Selective criteria and also carry out a comparison among N-Selective Mutation, some other selective criteria obtained considering previous work [4] and the Randomly Selected approach, in the context of C language. We use:

- *SS*: the sufficient set, composed of the operators obtained by applying the *Sufficient Procedure*.
- *CSS*: the constrained sufficient set from *SS*, composed of the most representative operator of each mutation class, i.e., the operator that determines the greatest mutation score for that class.
- *S-Offutt*: the operators obtained by applying the Offutt *et al.*'s strategy.
- *S-Wong*: the operators proposed by Wong *et al.*
- Some Randomly Selected Mutation criteria (10%, 20%, 30% and 40%).

Table 2. 27-Program Suite: N-Selective Mutation Application.

Criterion	MA Score	Generated Mutants Total	Generated Mutants Red(%)	Equivalent Mutants Total	Equivalent Mutants Red(%)
1-Sel	0.9989	17526	13.0	2811	10.4
2-Sel	0.9987	15895	21.1	2619	16.5
3-Sel	0.9967	14336	28.8	2430	22.5
4-Sel	0.9953	12899	36.0	1745	44.4
5-Sel	0.9924	11680	42.0	1647	47.5
6-Sel	0.9924	10487	47.9	1598	49.0
7-Sel	0.9923	9477	53.0	1364	56.5
8-Sel	0.9846	8519	57.7	1241	60.4
9-Sel	0.9831	7689	61.8	1125	64.1
10-Sel	0.9805	6859	66.0	1002	68.0
11-Sel	0.9805	6182	69.3	1001	68.1
12-Sel	0.9788	5506	72.7	933	70.2
13-Sel	0.9785	4900	75.7	687	78.1
14-Sel	0.9784	4366	78.3	610	80.5
15-Sel	0.9747	3868	80.8	506	83.9
16-Sel	0.9665	3464	82.8	426	86.4
17-Sel	0.9665	3108	84.6	392	87.5
18-Sel	0.9652	2776	86.2	344	89.0
19-Sel	0.9591	2444	87.9	301	90.4
20-Sel	0.9283	2158	89.3	299	90.5
21-Sel	0.9283	1888	90.6	272	91.3
22-Sel	0.9249	1621	92.0	211	93.3
23-Sel	0.9238	1396	93.1	155	95.1
24-Sel	0.8786	1215	94.0	154	95.1
25-Sel	0.8740	1037	94.9	137	95.6
26-Sel	0.8381	859	95.7	111	96.5
27-Sel	0.8267	724	96.4	99	96.8
28-Sel	0.8179	589	97.1	99	96.8
29-Sel	0.8162	454	97.7	44	98.6
30-Sel	0.7772	325	98.4	34	98.9
31-Sel	0.7100	235	98.8	21	99.3
32-Sel	0.6264	190	99.1	19	99.4
33-Sel	0.6174	152	99.2	19	99.4
34-Sel	0.5325	114	99.4	15	99.5
35-Sel	0.4610	77	99.6	12	99.6
36-Sel	0.1686	46	99.8	12	99.6
37-Sel	0.1221	24	99.9	12	99.6
38-Sel	0.0000	6	100.0	6	99.8

Concerning N-Selective Mutation, from Table 2 and Table 3 we can observe for both program suites:

- To achieve a mutation score over 0.99 for the 27-program suite we can use up to the 7-Selective criterion with associated cost reduction around 53% on the number of generated mutants and around 56% on the number of equivalent mutants. For the 5-program suite we can use up to the 18-Selective criterion to achieve the same test objective with a cost reduction around 83% and around 89% on the number of generated mutants and equivalent ones, respectively.
- To achieve a cost reduction over 90%, in terms of generated mutants, we would have to accept a smaller mutation score provided by the 21-Selective and the 24-Selective for the 27-program suite and for the 5-program suite, respectively.

For the comparison of N-Selective with other Selective and Randomly approaches we have to consider Table 2 and Table 4 for the 27-program suite, and Table 3 and Table 5 for the 5-program suite. Table 4 and Table 5 provide the Mutation Analysis score determined by the selective and randomly criteria and the respective cost reduction w.r.t. the total number of generated and equivalent mutants.

Table 3. 5-Program Suite: *N*-Selective Mutation Application.

Criterion	MA Score	Generated Mutants Total	Generated Mutants Red(%)	Equivalent Mutants Total	Equivalent Mutants Red(%)
1-Sel	1.0000	11158	13.1	774	6.6
2-Sel	0.9998	9537	25.7	757	8.7
3-Sel	0.9998	8144	36.5	754	9.0
4-Sel	0.9998	7393	42.4	752	9.3
5-Sel	0.9987	6760	47.3	452	45.5
6-Sel	0.9986	6245	51.3	397	52.1
7-Sel	0.9979	5755	55.2	346	58.3
8-Sel	0.9978	5271	58.9	337	59.3
9-Sel	0.9978	4823	62.4	334	59.7
10-Sel	0.9973	4377	65.9	324	60.9
11-Sel	0.9970	3952	69.2	271	67.3
12-Sel	0.9953	3530	72.5	252	69.6
13-Sel	0.9951	3236	74.8	206	75.2
14-Sel	0.9951	2966	76.9	206	75.2
15-Sel	0.9946	2711	78.9	145	82.5
16-Sel	0.9937	2505	80.5	127	84.7
17-Sel	0.9932	2309	82.0	92	88.9
18-Sel	0.9925	2127	83.4	91	89.0
19-Sel	0.9870	1957	84.8	91	89.0
20-Sel	0.9859	1788	86.1	88	89.4
21-Sel	0.9828	1626	87.3	80	90.3
22-Sel	0.9737	1466	88.6	79	90.5
23-Sel	0.9737	1331	89.6	51	93.8
24-Sel	0.9728	1208	90.6	45	94.6
25-Sel	0.9721	1096	91.5	45	94.6
26-Sel	0.9680	991	92.3	44	94.7
27-Sel	0.9580	900	93.0	43	94.8
28-Sel	0.9576	810	93.7	43	94.8
29-Sel	0.9534	728	94.3	43	94.8
30-Sel	0.9530	647	95.0	43	94.8
31-Sel	0.9508	566	95.6	16	98.1
32-Sel	0.9508	510	96.0	16	98.1
33-Sel	0.9346	456	96.4	15	98.2
34-Sel	0.9339	406	96.8	15	98.2
35-Sel	0.9247	363	97.2	14	98.3
36-Sel	0.9247	327	97.5	13	98.4
37-Sel	0.9211	294	97.7	13	98.4
38-Sel	0.9034	261	98.0	12	98.6
39-Sel	0.9034	231	98.2	12	98.6
40-Sel	0.8793	202	98.4	11	98.7
41-Sel	0.8523	175	98.6	11	98.7
42-Sel	0.8516	150	98.8	11	98.7
43-Sel	0.8508	126	99.0	11	98.7
44-Sel	0.8282	103	99.2	10	98.8
45-Sel	0.7111	85	99.3	8	99.0
46-Sel	0.7102	70	99.5	7	99.2
47-Sel	0.5799	58	99.5	7	99.2
48-Sel	0.5799	48	99.6	4	99.5
49-Sel	0.5789	38	99.7	4	99.5
50-Sel	0.5789	28	99.8	4	99.5
51-Sel	0.5424	18	99.9	4	99.5
52-Sel	0.3103	10	99.9	3	99.6
53-Sel	0.3009	4	100.0	0	100.0
54-Sel	0.0899	2	100.0	0	100.0
55-Sel	0.0899	1	100.0	0	100.0

For the 27-program suite, from Table 2 and Table 4 we can observe that, on the average, the *SS*-27 and *CSS*-27 sets perform better than *N*-Selective Mutation. *S-Wong* performs slightly better and *S-Offutt*-27 performs slightly worst. Randomly Selected Mutation is better than *N*-Selective Mutation in all the cases:

- The *SS*-27 criterion determines a mutation score over 0.99. Considering the *N*-Selective criteria, the closest value is provided by the 3-Selective criterion. However, the cost reduction obtained with *SS*-27, in terms of generated mutants, is around 65% (and around 56% on the equivalent ones), while the cost reduction obtained with 3-Selective is less than 29% (and less than 23%). To obtain a cost reduction close to the one provided by *SS*-27, we have to consider the 10-Selective criterion, however the mutation score would be around 0.98. Observe that the cost reduction, in terms of equivalent mutants, is greater for the 10-Selective criterion than for the *SS*-27.
- The *CSS*-27 criterion determines a mutation score over 0.98. Considering the *N*-Selective criteria, the closest value is provided by the 8-Selective criterion. However, the cost reduction obtained with *CSS*-27 is around 80% (and around 84% on the equivalent ones), while the cost reduction obtained with 8-Selective is less than 58% (and less than 61%). To obtain a cost reduction close to the one provided by *CSS*-27, we have to consider the 15-Selective criterion, however the mutation score would be less than 0.98, again, below 0.99.
- The *S-Offutt*-27 criterion determines a mutation score over 0.97. Considering the *N*-Selective criteria, the closest value is provided by the 15-Selective criterion. The cost reduction obtained with *S-Offutt*-27 is over 78% (and over 84% on the equivalent ones), while the cost reduction obtained with 15-Selective is over 80% (and over 83%). To obtain a cost reduction closer to the one provided by *S-Offutt*-27, we have to consider the 14-Selective criterion, with a cost reduction over 78% (and over 80%), and a mutation score greater than the one provided by *S-Offutt*-27. Notice in this case that *N*-Selective Mutation would perform better.
- The *S-Wong* criterion determines a mutation score close to 0.98. Considering the *N*-Selective criteria, the closest value is provided by the 11-Selective criterion. The cost reduction obtained with *S-Wong* is over 79% (and over 70% on the equivalent ones), and the cost reduction obtained with the 11-Selective criterion is close to 69% (and close to 68%). To obtain a cost reduction close to the one provided by *S-Wong* we have to consider the 15-Selective criterion, but the mutation score would be smaller than the one provided by *S-Wong*. Notice that *S-Wong* set performs slightly better than *N*-Selective Mutation.
- The 30%-Randomly determines a mutation score over 0.99. Considering the *N*-Selective criteria, the closest value is provided by the 7-Selective criterion. The cost reduction obtained with the 30%-Randomly and 7-Selective criteria is around 69% and around 53%, respectively. To obtain a cost reduction close to the one provided by 30%-Randomly, we have to consider the 11-Selective criterion, with a cost reduction over 69% and a mutation score about 0.98.

For the 5-program suite, considering Table 3 and Table 5, we can observe that, on the average, the *SS*-5 criterion performs better than the *N*-Selective criteria. *CSS*-5,

S-Wong and *N*-Selective Mutation are almost equivalent and *S-Offut-5* performs slightly worst than *N*-Selective. Randomly Selected Mutation and *N*-Selective Mutation performs almost equal in all the cases:

- The *SS*-5 criterion determines a mutation score over 0.99. Considering the *N*-Selective criteria, the closest value is provided by the 9-Selective criterion. However, the cost reduction obtained with *SS*-5 is about 82% (and about 46% on the equivalent ones), while the cost reduction obtained with 9-Selective is less than 63% (and close to 60%). To obtain a cost reduction close to the one provided by *SS*-5, we have to consider the 17-Selective criterion. Notice that the reduction on the number of equivalent mutants is greater for the 9-Selective and 17-Selective criteria than for the *SS*-5.
- The *CSS*-5 criterion determines a mutation score over 0.99. Considering the *N*-Selective criteria, the closest value is provided by the 18-Selective criterion. However, the cost reduction obtained with *CSS*-5 is over 89% (and over 89% on the equivalent ones), while the cost reduction obtained with 18-Selective is less than 84% (and close to 90%). To obtain a cost reduction close to the one provided by *CSS*-5, we have to consider the 23-Selective criterion, however the mutation score would be around 0.97.
- The *S-Offutt*-5 criterion determines a mutation score close to 0.99. Considering the *N*-Selective criteria, the closest value is provided by the 18-Selective criterion. The cost reduction obtained with *S-Offutt*-5 is around 77% (and around 59% on the equivalent ones), while the cost reduction obtained with 18-Selective is over 83% (and around 89%). To obtain a cost reduction close to the one provided by *S-Offutt*-5, we have to consider the 14-Selective criterion, with a cost reduction over 76% (and over 75%), and a mutation score greater than the one provided by *S-Offutt*-5. Notice in this case that *N*-Selective Mutation would perform better.
- The *S-Wong* criterion determines a mutation score around 0.99. Considering the *N*-Selective criteria, the closest value is provided by the 18-Selective criterion. The cost reduction obtained with *S-Wong* is over 83% (and over 54% on the equivalent ones), and the cost reduction obtained with the 18-Selective criterion is close to 83% (and close to 89%).
- The 30%-Randomly criterion determines a mutation score over 0.99. Considering the *N*-Selective criteria, the closest value is provided by the 11-Selective criterion. The cost reduction obtained with the 30%-Randomly and 11-Selective criteria is over 67% and around 69%, respectively.

Table 4. 27-Program Suite: Selective and Randomly Mutation.

Criterion	MA Score	Generated Mutants Total	Generated Mutants Red(%)	Equivalent Mutants Total	Equivalent Mutants Red(%)
SS-27	0.9966	7048	65.0	1361	56.6
CSS-27	0.9850	4023	80.0	496	84.2
S-Offutt-27	0.9714	4409	78.1	479	84.7
S-Wong	0.9798	4082	79.7	927	70.4
10%-Randomly	0.9716	2007	90.0	NC	NC
20%-Randomly	0.9879	4119	79.6	NC	NC
30%-Randomly	0.9912	6244	69.0	NC	NC
40%-Randomly	0.9942	8189	59.4	NC	NC

NC – Not Computed

Table 5. 5-Program Suite: Selective and Randomly Mutation.

Criterion	MA Score	Generated Mutants Total	Generated Mutants Red(%)	Equivalent Mutants Total	Equivalent Mutants Red(%)
SS-5	0.9976	2304	82.0	446	46.2
CSS-5	0.9921	1383	89.2	84	89.9
S-Offutt-5	0.9907	2950	77.0	340	59.0
S-Wong	0.9919	2126	83.4	377	54.5
10%-Randomly	0.9880	1406	89.0	NC	NC
20%-Randomly	0.9950	2862	77.7	NC	NC
30%-Randomly	0.9968	4128	67.8	NC	NC
40%-Randomly	0.9972	5432	57.7	NC	NC

NC – Not Computed

It should be observed that in many cases the cost reduction on the number of equivalent mutants obtained by applying the *N*-Selective criteria is greater than the ones provided by the other criteria. This is due to the influence of the VDTR mutant operator. Only this operator weights over 20% and 35% on the total number of equivalent mutants for the 27-program and the 5-program suites, respectively.

The uniformity of the mutation scores determined by the selective criteria for all the programs is also a relevant data. Table 6(a) and Table 6(b) provide this information for the 27 and 5 programs, respectively. We take the 7-Selective and 18-Selective criteria for the 27-program and the 5-program suites, respectively, since these criteria provide a mutation score over 0.99. We notice that:

- *SS*-27 determines a mutation score equal to 1.0 for 13 programs followed by the 7-Selective and *S-Wong* criteria with 11 and 5 programs, respectively.
- *SS*-27 determines a mutation score greater than 0.99 for 25 programs followed by the 7-Selective, *CSS*-27 and *S-Wong* criteria with 20, 15 and 11 programs, respectively.
- *SS*-27 does not determine a mutation score below 0.95 for any program. The same does not happen with the *S-Offutt*-27, *S-Wong* and 7-Selective criteria.
- None of the criteria determines a mutation score equal to 1.0 for any of the 5-Unix programs.

- Only the *SS*-5 and 18-Selective-5 criteria determine mutation scores greater than 0.99 for all the 5-Unix programs.

Table 6. Distribution of Mutation Score: (a) 27-Program Suite and (b) 5-Program Suite.

(a)

Criterion	[0.00..0.95)	[0.95..0.98)	[0.98..0.99)	[0.99..1.00)	1.00
SS-27	0	1	1	12	13
CSS-27	3	1	8	11	4
S-Offutt-27	1	13	4	5	4
S-Wong	3	5	8	6	5
7-Selective	1	2	4	9	11

(b)

Criterion	[0.00..0.95)	[0.95..0.98)	[0.98..0.99)	[0.99..1.00)	1.00
SS-5	0	0	0	5	0
CSS-5	0	0	2	3	0
S-Offutt-5	0	0	3	2	0
S-Wong	0	0	2	3	0
18-Selective	0	0	0	5	0

3.2 Experiment II: Integration Testing

The same phases of Experiment I were also carried out in Experiment II. The main differences are in the testing criterion used – Interface Mutation [9] –, and in the supporting testing tool – Proteum/IM [6]. As already mentioned, Interface Mutation extends Mutation Testing to integration testing. The 33 mutant operators defined for Interface Mutation are divided into two groups [6]: 24 of Group I, and 9 of Group II.

Given a connection between units A and B (A calls B), operators in the first group apply changes to the body of function B, for example, incrementing a reference to a formal parameter. Operators in the second group apply mutations to the places unit A calls B, for example, incrementing an argument. Proteum/IM provides mechanisms for the assessment of test case adequacy for testing the interactions among the units of a given program. It is a pairwise criterion.

The programs selected were the 5 Unix-utility programs already used in Experiment I. As illustrated in Table 7, these programs have from 1825 up to 4350 interface mutants. Table 7 also provides information on the number of generated mutants per mutation group and on the number of equivalent ones. Observe that Group I is responsible for almost 95% of all the generated mutants and, in particular, for almost all of the equivalent ones. The number of executable statements (LOC) and function calls for each program are also presented. On the average, we have 26 mutants/LOC and 701 mutants/function call.

In Figure 3, we provide information on the mutant operators cost in terms of a) number of generated mutants and b) number of equivalent mutants compared with the total number of mutants and with the total number of equivalent ones. We consider the 16 most prevalent operators. All

Table 7. Experiment II: Number of LOC and Mutants.

Program	*LOC*	*Function Calls*	*Mutants Tot/Eq*	*Group I Tot/Eq*	*Group II Tot/Eq*
cal	119	4	4350 / 488	4120 / 486	230 / 2
checkeq	76	1	2954 / 12	2938 / 12	16 / 0
comm	119	7	2952 / 481	2647 / 481	305 / 0
look	107	3	1825 / 181	1743 / 180	82 / 1
uniq	103	5	1943 / 185	1833 / 183	110 / 2
Total	524	20	14024 / 1347	13281 / 1342	743 / 5

the interface operators (33) were applicable to the 5-Unix programs. Observe that the operators I-IndVarRepCon and I-IndVarRepReq weight over 30% on the total number of equivalent mutants and are the two most prevalent operators in terms of the total number of mutants.

At the integration testing phase, we tried out the N-Selective Interface Mutation approach, from 1-SelectiveIM to 32-SelectiveIM, i.e., discarding at a time each one of the 33 interface mutant operators, from the most to the less prevalent ones. Table 8 presents the average mutation score obtained w.r.t Interface Mutation, the number of interface mutants generated by applying each N-Selective Interface Mutation criterion and the cumulative cost reduction w.r.t. the total of mutants. The number of equivalent mutants and the associated cumulative cost reduction w.r.t. the total of equivalent mutants discharged are also provided.

Regarding to N-Selective Interface Mutation, from Table 8 we can observe:

- To achieve a mutation score over 0.99 we can use up to the 14-SelectiveIM criterion with associated cost reduction over 80% on the number of generated mutants and over 76% on the number of equivalent ones.
- To achieve a cost reduction over 90%, in terms of generated mutants, we would have to accept a smaller mutation score provided by the 19-SelectiveIM.

Next, we focus the comparison between N-Selective Interface Mutation and the sufficient interface mutant operators set for the 5-program suite ($SS\text{-}5_{IM}$), since the sufficient sets performed better than the N-Selective approach at the unit level. We can observe that, on the average, the $SS\text{-}5_{IM}$ set performs slightly better than N-Selective Interface Mutation:

- The $SS\text{-}5_{IM}$ determines a mutation score of 0.998. Considering the N-SelectiveIM criteria, the closest value is provided by the 6-SelectiveIM criterion. However, the cost reduction obtained with $SS\text{-}5_{IM}$, in terms of generated mutants, is around 73% (and around 71% on the equivalent ones), while the cost reduction obtained with 6-SelectiveIM is less than 55% in both cases. To obtain a cost reduction close to the one provided by $SS\text{-}5_{IM}$, we have to consider the 11-SelectiveIM criterion, that provides a mutation score of 0.992.

If we look at the mutation score uniformity (Table 9), the N-SelectiveIM and $SS\text{-}5_{IM}$ criteria perform quite well, however only $SS\text{-}5_{IM}$ determines mutation scores greater than 0.990 for all the programs. Also, none of the criteria determines a mutation score equal to 1.0 for any of the 5-Unix programs.

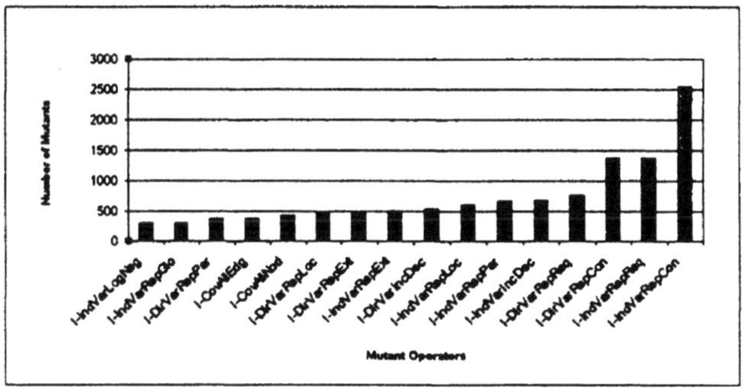

(a)

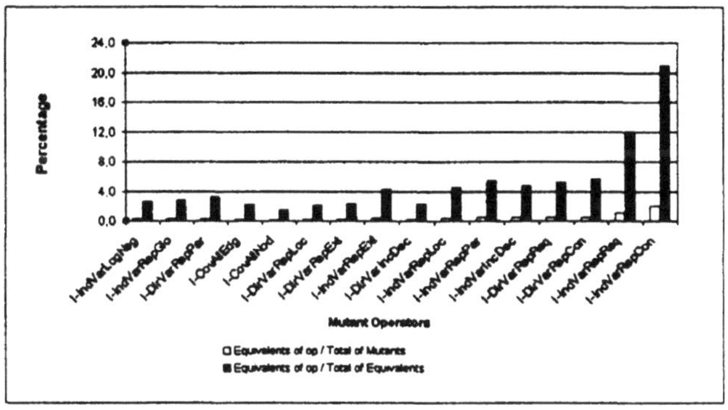

(b)

Figure 3. Experiment II: Mutant Operators Cost per Number of: (a) Generated Mutants and (b) Equivalent Mutants.

3.3 Experiment I and Experiment II: Final Remarks

In our previous work [4] we had concluded that, for the 27-program and the 5-program suites, the sufficient mutant operators sets would constitute a good choice, if not the best, amongst the other selective criteria. They presented the greatest mutation scores, empirically included the other selective criteria, presented an excellent mutation score uniformity among the programs and also determined the greatest strength against the other selective criteria. In this work, it is shown that the sufficient sets perform better than the N-Selective criteria, for both program suites of Experiment I. Concerning the Experiment II – integration testing level –, we can also conclude that the sufficient $SS\text{-}5_{IM}$ criterion performs better than the N-Selective criteria.

Table 8. Experiment II: N-Selective Interface Mutation Application.

Criterion	*IM Score*	*Generated Mutants Total*	*Generated Mutants Red(%)*	*Equivalent Mutants Total*	*Equivalent Mutants Red(%)*
1-SelIM	0.9999	11469	18.2	1064	21.0
2-SelIM	0.9997	10078	28.1	902	33.0
3-SelIM	0.9997	8698	38.0	826	38.7
4-SelIM	0.9997	7928	43.5	755	43.9
5-SelIM	0.9997	7244	48.3	691	48.7
6-SelIM	0.9990	6572	53.1	618	54.1
7-SelIM	0.9967	5954	57.5	557	58.6
8-SelIM	0.9965	5418	61.4	526	60.9
9-SelIM	0.9937	4907	65.0	469	65.2
10-SelIM	0.9928	4413	68.5	437	67.6
11-SelIM	0.9925	3925	72.0	408	69.7
12-SelIM	0.9925	3487	75.1	388	71.2
13-SelIM	0.9910	3097	77.9	358	73.4
14-SelIM	0.9905	2712	80.7	314	76.7
15-SelIM	0.9884	2400	82.9	276	79.5
16-SelIM	0.9851	2094	85.1	240	82.2
17-SelIM	0.9807	1788	87.2	213	84.2
18-SelIM	0.9600	1482	89.4	105	92.2
19-SelIM	0.9579	1228	91.2	105	92.2
20-SelIM	0.9542	1028	92.7	103	92.4
21-SelIM	0.9241	858	93.9	78	94.2
22-SelIM	0.9129	704	95.0	65	95.2
23-SelIM	0.8550	550	96.1	51	96.2
24-SelIM	0.6065	396	97.2	10	99.3
25-SelIM	0.5779	304	97.8	10	99.3
26-SelIM	0.5530	239	98.3	3	99.8
27-SelIM	0.5506	184	98.7	3	99.8
28-SelIM	0.5506	141	99.0	3	99.8
29-SelIM	0.3163	99	99.3	3	99.8
30-SelIM	0.3156	73	99.5	3	99.8
31-SelIM	0.3086	47	99.7	3	99.8
32-SelIM	0.2300	21	99.8	3	99.8

In general, if we favor the mutation score, taking a value in the same range of the one provided by the sufficient sets, the cost reductions (in terms of generated mutants) determined by the N-Selective criteria are around 28% and 63% in Experiment I, and 53% in Experiment II. For the SS sets they are 65% and 82% in Experiment I, and 73% in Experiment II. Thus, the SS sets perform better.

Table 9. Experiment II: Distribution of Mutation Score.

(b)

Criterion	[0.00..0.95)	[0.95 ..0.98)	[0.98 ..0.99)	[0.99 ..1.00)	1.00
$SS\text{-}5_{IM}$	0	0	0	5	0
14-SelectiveIM	0	0	2	3	0

In the other hand, if we favor the cost reduction (in terms of generated mutants), taking a value close to 70%, N-Selective would perform slightly worst than *SS* and *CSS* sets in Experiment I, and slightly worst than *SS* set in Experiment II. If we go further on, asking for a cost reduction close to 90%, N-Selective, again, would perform slightly worst than 10%-Randomly and *SS* criteria. For instance, N-Selective provides a mutation score around 0.93 and 0.97 for Experiment I, while the 10%-Randomly criteria provide mutation scores over 0.97 for both program suites. For Experiment II, the SS set provides a score over 0.99, greater than the ones provided by the 11-SelectiveIM and

19-SelectiveIM criteria. Thus, taking the cost reduction in terms of the number of generated mutants, the *N*-Selective approach would not constitute the best choice.

Another point that should be highlighted is the number of equivalent mutants generated per operator. Offutt *et al.* [17] define the semantic size of a fault as the relative size of the input domain for which the program is incorrect. They suggest that the main goal of Selective Mutation is to try to only use operators that tend to produce mutants that have semantically small faults. If this model holds, their expectation would be that the selective mutants should contain a high percentage of equivalent mutants, what would impose costs to determine the equivalent mutants. On the other hand, we may focus heuristic to deal with equivalent mutants just related to the selected operators. An interesting fact in this scenario is that the operators that generate the greatest percentage of the equivalent mutants, in relation to either the total number of equivalent mutants or the total number of mutants, are amongst the 16 most prevalent operators. The six most prevalent ones account approximately for 50% of the equivalent mutants in both experiments.

In the Offutt *et al.*'s experiment it turned out that the five operators in the selective set account for 57% of the equivalent mutants [17]. In our experiments we obtained similar results. In Experiment I, the SS criterion accounts for 43.4% and 53.8% of the equivalent mutants; the *N*-Selective criteria with a mutation score over 0.99 and a cost reduction of at least 50% account at maximum for 50% of the equivalent mutants in both sets of programs. In Experiment II, the *SS* criterion accounts for 28.1% while the *N*-SelectiveIM accounts for 45.9%. It should be pointed out that in this perspective, the *SS* and *N*-Selective criteria would lead to almost the same effort to analyze the equivalent mutants.

4 Conclusions and Future Work

We report in this paper two experiments aiming at investigating the application of *N*-Selective Mutation in the context of C language, considering both the unit and the integration testing phases. We also compared the results obtained by applying *N*-Selective Mutation with other alternative approaches for the Mutation Testing application: Sufficient Mutation and Randomly Selected Mutation.

In both experiments, considering mutation score, cost reduction and mutation score distribution, the sufficient operator sets determined by the application of the *Sufficient Procedure* performed better than the *N*-Selective criteria. In spite of this fact, the *N*-Selective criteria may constitute a reasonable option to establish a testing strategy comprising the unit and the integration testing phases. For instance, considering the 5-program suite, with a cost reduction close to 80% on the number of generated mutants, we would obtain a mutation score over 0.99 for the unit and the integration testing phases.

It is necessary to further investigate and refine this study, taking in consideration the operator cost, not only in terms of the number of generated mutants and equivalent ones, but also in terms of test cases required. The capability of the selective criteria to detect real faults has also to be investigated.

Based on the results presented herein we are investigating a low-cost, incremental mutation-based testing strategy comprising the unit and the integration testing levels [19]. Further studies are also been planned to investigate the scalability of these results to larger programs. We are interested on conducting the experiments in a broader selection of programs, from different application domains, in order to make the results presented so far more significant.

Finally, since we have not addressed the weak mutation approach [12], it may constitute a perspective to be investigated and complement this study.

Acknowledgments

The authors would like to thank the Brazilian funding agencies - CAPES, FAPESP and CNPq - and Telcordia Technologies (USA) for their support to this research, and the anonymous referees for their valuable comments.

References

[1] A. T. Acree, T. A. Budd, R. A. DeMillo, R. J. Lipton, and F. G. Sayward. Mutation analysis. Technical Report GIT-ICS-79/08, Georgia Institute of Technology, Atlanta, GA, Sept. 1979.

[2] H. Agrawal, R. A. DeMillo, R. Hathaway, W. Hsu, W. Hsu, E. W. Krauser, R. J. Martin, A. P. Mathur, and E. H. Spafford. Design of mutant operators for the C programming language. Technical Report SERC-TR41-P, Software Engineering Research Center, Purdue University, West Lafayette, IN, Mar. 1989.

[3] E. F. Barbosa. A contribution for the determination of a sufficient mutant operators set for C-program testing. Master's thesis, ICMC/USP, São Carlos – SP, Brazil, Nov. 1998. (in Portuguese).

[4] E. F. Barbosa, J. C. Maldonado, and A. M. R. Vincenzi. Towards the determination of sufficient mutant operators for C. In *First International Workshop on Automated Program Analysis, Testing and Verification*, Limerick, Ireland, June 2000. (Accepted for publication in a special issue of the Software Testing Verification and Reliability Journal).

[5] T. A. Budd, R. A. DeMillo, R. J. Lipton, and F. G. Sayward. Theoretical and empirical studies on using program mutation to test the functional correcteness of programs. In *7th ACM Symposium on Principles of Programming Languages*, pages 220–233, New York, NY, Jan. 1980.

[6] M. Delamaro and J. Maldonado. Interface mutation: Assessing testing quality at interprocedural level. In *19th International Conference of the Chilean Computer Science Society (SCCC'99)*, pages 78–86, Talca - Chile, Nov. 1999.

[7] M. E. Delamaro, J. C. Maldonado, and A. P. Mathur. Integration testing using interface mutation. Technical Report SERC-TR169-P, Software Engineering Research Center, Purdue University, Apr. 1996.

[8] M. E. Delamaro, J. C. Maldonado, and A. P. Mathur. Proteum - a tool for the assesment of test adequacy for C programs - user's guide. Technical Report SERC-TR168-P, Software Engineering Research Center, Purdue University, Apr. 1996.

[9] M. E. Delamaro, J. C. Maldonado, and A. P. Mathur. Interface mutation: An approach for integration testing. IEEE Transactions on Software Engineering, (accepted for publication), 2000.

[10] R. A. DeMillo, D. S. Gwind, K. N. King, W. N. McKraken, and A. J. Offutt. An extended overview of the mothra testing environment. In *Software Testing, Verification and Analysis*, Banff, Canadá, July 1988.

[11] R. A. DeMillo, R. J. Lipton, and F. G. Sayward. Hints on test data selection: Help for the practicing programmer. *IEEE Computer*, 11(4):34–43, Apr. 1978.

[12] W. E. Howden. Weak mutation testing and completeness of test sets. *IEEE Transactions on Software Engineering*, SE-8(4):371–379, July 1982.

[13] B. W. Kernighan and P. J. Plauger. *Software Tools in Pascal*. Addison Wesley Publishing Company, 1981.

[14] A. P. Mathur. Performance, effectiveness and reliability issues in software testing. In *15th Annual International Computer Software and Applications Conference*, pages 604–605, Tokio, Japan, Sept. 1991.

[15] A. P. Mathur and W. E. Wong. An empirical comparison of data flow and mutation based test adequacy criteria. *The Journal of Software Testing, Verification, and Relability*, 4(1):9–31, Mar. 1994.

[16] E. Mresa and L. Bottaci. Efficiency of mutation operators and selective mutation strategies: an empirical study. *The Journal of Software Testing, Verification and Reliability*, 9(4):205–232, Dec. 1999.

[17] A. J. Offutt, A. Lee, G. Rothermel, R. H. Untch, and C. Zapf. An experimental determination of sufficient mutant operators. *ACM Transactions on Software Engineering Methodology*, 5(2):99–118, 1996.

[18] A. J. Offutt, G. Rothermel, and C. Zapf. An experimental evaluation of selective mutation. In *15th International Conference on Software Engineering*, pages 100–107, Baltimore, MD, May 1993.

[19] A. M. R. Vincenzi, J. C. Maldonado, E. F. Barbosa, and M. E. Delamaro. Unit and integration testing strategies for C programs using mutation-based criteria. In *Symposium on Mutation Testing*, pages 56–67, San Jose, CA, Oct. 2000.

[20] E. J. Weyuker. The cost of data flow testing: an empirical study. *IEEE Transactions on Software Engineering*, SE-16(2):121–128, Feb. 1990.

[21] W. Wong, J. Maldonado, and M. Delamaro. Reducing the cost of regression test by using selective mutation. In *8th CITS – International Conference on Software Technology*, pages 11–13, Curitiba, PR, June 1997.

[22] W. Wong, J. Maldonado, M. Delamaro, and S. Souza. A comparison of selective mutation in C and fortran. In *Workshop do Projeto Validação e Teste de Sistemas de Operação*, pages 71–80, Águas de Lindóia, SP, Jan. 1997.

[23] W. E. Wong and A. P. Mathur. Reducing the cost of mutation testing: An empirical study. *The Journal of Systems and Software*, 31(3):185–196, Dec. 1995.

[24] W. E. Wong, A. P. Mathur, and J. C. Maldonado. Mutation versus all-uses: An empirical evaluation of cost, strength, and effectiveness. In *International Conference on Software Quality and Productivity*, pages 258–265, Hong Kong, Dec. 1994.

[25] H. Zhu, P. Hall, and J. May. Software unit test coverage and adequacy. *ACM Computing Surveys*, 29(4):366–427, Dec. 1997.

Mutation 2000: Uniting the Orthogonal*

A. Jefferson Offutt
ISE Department, 4A4
George Mason University
Fairfax, VA 22030-4444 USA
703-993-1654
ofut@ise.gmu.edu
www.ise.gmu.edu/faculty/ofut/

Roland H. Untch
Department of Computer Science
Middle Tennessee State University
Murfreesboro, TN 37132-0048
615-898-5047
untch@mtsu.edu
www.mtsu.edu/~untch/

Abstract

Mutation testing is a powerful, but computationally expensive, technique for unit testing software. This expense has prevented mutation from becoming widely used in practical situations, but recent engineering advances have given us techniques and algorithms for significantly reducing the cost of mutation testing. These techniques include a new algorithmic execution technique called schema-based mutation*, an approximation technique called* weak mutation*, a reduction technique called* selective mutation*, heuristics for detecting equivalent mutants, and algorithms for automatic test data generation. This paper reviews experimentation with these advances and outlines a design for a system that will approximate mutation, but in a way that will be accessible to everyday programmers. We envision a system to which a programmer can submit a program unit and get back a set of input/output pairs that are guaranteed to form an effective test of the unit by being close to mutation adequate. We believe this system could be efficient enough to be adopted by leading-edge software developers. Full automation in unit testing has the potential to dramatically change the economic balance between testing and development, by reducing the cost of testing from the major part of the total development cost to a small fraction.*

1. Introduction

Mutation analysis has a rich and varied history, with major advances in concepts, theory, technology, and social viewpoints. This history begins in 1971, when Richard Lipton proposed the initial concepts of mutation in a class term paper titled "Fault Diagnosis of Computer Programs." It was not until the end of the 1970's, however, before major work was published on the subject [1, 2, 3]; the DeMillo, Lipton, and Sayward paper [3] is generally cited as the seminal reference.

PIMS [1, 4, 5, 6], an early mutation testing tool, pioneered the general process typically used in mutation testing of creating mutants (of Fortran IV programs), accepting test cases from the users, and then executing the test cases on the mutants to decide how many mutants were killed. In 1987, this same process (of add test cases, run mutants, check results, and repeat) was adopted and extended in the Mothra mutation toolset [7, 8, 9, 10], which provided an integrated set of tools, each of which performed an individual, separate task to support mutation analysis and testing. Because each Mothra tool is a separate command, it was easy to incorporate, and thus experiment with, additional types of processing. Although a few other mutation testing tools have been developed since Mothra [11, 12, 13], Mothra is likely the most widely known mutation testing system extant.

Despite the relatively long history of mutation testing, the software development industry has failed to employ it. We posit that the three primary reasons why industry has failed to use mutation testing are the lack of economic incentives for stringent testing, inability to successfully integrate unit testing into software development processes, and difficulties with providing full and economical automated technology to support mutation analysis and testing. The first reason, the lack of economic incentives for applying highly advanced testing techniques, is beyond the scope of this paper, which is primarily technological in nature. On the other hand, software is increasingly being used to perform essential roles in applications that require high reliability, including safety-critical software (avionics, medical, and industrial control) infrastructure-critical software (telephony and networks), and commercial en-

*Supported by the National Science Foundation under awards CCR-9804011 and CCR-9707792.

terprises (e-commerce and business-to-business transactions). This increasing reliance on software implies that software must be increasingly be more reliable, thus we may expect there to be more economic incentives for applying high-end testing techniques such as mutation in the future.

The other two reasons for the lack of commercial success of mutation are primarily technological in nature. During the 1990s, a number of technological and theoretical advances were made in the application of mutation analysis and testing. Most of these advances are orthogonal, that is, they affect different aspects of mutation testing. This paper summarizes many of these advances and discusses ways to incorporate mutation into standard software development. It is thought that these advances, once united, can allow a truly practical mutation system to be built that can be used by real programmers on real software projects to greatly increase the reliability of their software products.

Before going into detail about these advances, a discussion of how mutation is used is given from a procedural point of view. Following that, a number of advances for applying mutation are discussed, which leads to a new process for how mutation can be applied. We envision a test tool that provides almost complete automation to the tester. A programmer submits a software module, and after a few minutes of computation, the tool responds with a set of test cases that are assured to provide the software with a very effective test, and a set of outputs that can be examined to find failures in the software. Furthermore, these input-output pairs can be used as a basis for debugging when failures are found. To be used by industry, this technology must be integrated with compilers, debuggers, and report generators.

1.1. The Mutation Analysis Process

Mutation analysis induces faults into software by creating many versions of the software, each containing one fault. Test cases are used to execute these faulty programs with the goal of distinguishing the faulty programs from the original program. Hence the terminology; faulty programs are *mutants* of the original, and a mutant is *killed* by distinguishing the output of the mutant from that of the original program.

Mutants either represent likely faults, a mistake the programmer could have made, or they explicitly require a typical testing heuristic to be satisfied, such as execute every branch or cause all expressions to become zero. Mutants are limited to simple changes on the basis of the *coupling effect*, which says that complex faults are coupled to simple faults in such a way that a test data set that detects all simple faults in a program will detect most complex faults The coupling effect was first hypothesized in 1978 [3], then supported empirically in 1992 [14], and has been demonstrated theoretically in 1995 [15, 16].

Mutation analysis provides a test *criterion*, rather than a test *process*. A *testing criterion* is a rule or collection of rules that imposes requirements on a set of test cases. Test engineers measure the extent to which a criterion is satisfied in terms of *coverage*; a set of test cases achieves 100% coverage if it completely satisfies the criterion. Coverage is measured in terms of the requirements that are imposed; partial coverage is defined to be the percent of requirements that are satisfied. *Test requirements* are specific things that must be satisfied or covered; for example, reaching statements are the requirements for statement coverage and killing mutants are the requirements for mutation. Thus, a test criterion establishes firm requirements for how much testing is necessary; a test process gives a sequence of steps to follow to generate test cases. There may be many processes used to satisfy a given criterion, and a test process need not have the goal of satisfying a criterion. In precise terms, mutation analysis is a way to measure the quality of the test cases and the actual testing of the software is a side effect. In practical terms however, the software is tested, and tested well, or the test cases do not kill mutants. This point can best be understood by examining a typical mutation analysis process.

When a program is submitted to a mutation system, the system first creates many mutated versions of the program. A *mutation operator*[1] is a rule that is applied to a program to create mutants. Typical mutation operators, for example, replace each operand by every other syntactically legal operand, or modify expressions by replacing operators and inserting new operators, or delete entire statements. Figure 1 graphically shows a traditional mutation process. The solid boxes represent steps that are automated by traditional systems such as Mothra, and the dashed boxes represent steps that are done manually.

Next, test cases are supplied to the system to serve as inputs to the program. Each test case is executed on the original program and the tester verifies that the output is correct. If incorrect, a bug has been found and the program should be fixed before that test case is used again. If correct, the test cases are executed on each mutant program. If the output of a mutant

[1]The terminology varies; they are also sometimes called *mutant operators*, *mutagenic operators*, *mutagens*, *mutation transformations*, and *mutation rules* [17].

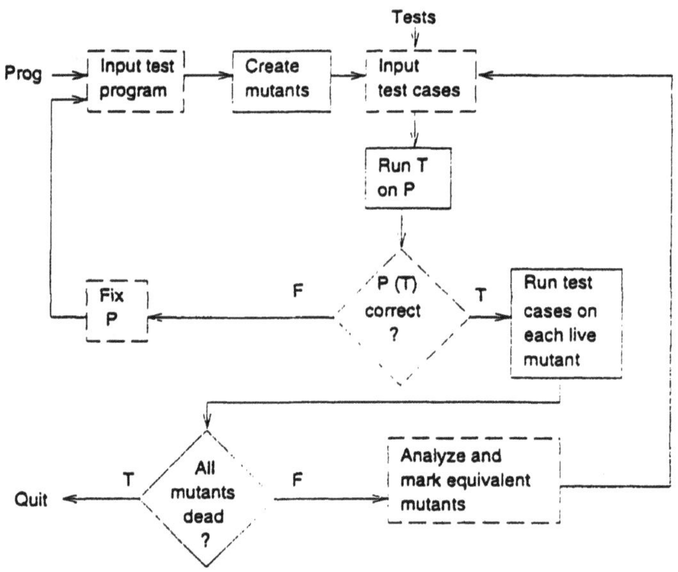

Figure 1: **Traditional Mutation Testing Process. Solid boxes represent steps that are automated and dashed boxes represent steps that are manual.**

program differs from the original (correct) output, the mutant is marked as being *dead*. Dead mutants are not executed against subsequent test cases.

Once all test cases have been executed, a *mutation score* is computed. The mutation score is the ratio of dead mutants over the total number of non-equivalent mutants. Thus, the tester's goal is to raise the mutation score to 1.00, indicating that all mutants have been detected. A test set that kills all the mutants is said to be *adequate* relative to the mutants.

If (as is likely) mutants are still alive, the tester can enhance the set of test cases by supplying new inputs. Some mutants are functionally *equivalent* to the original program. Equivalent mutants always produce the same output as the original program, so cannot be killed. Equivalent mutants are not counted in the mutation score. Note that even if the tester has not found any faults by using the previous set of test cases, the mutation score gives some indication of the extent of the testing. Moreover, the live mutants point out inadequacies in the test cases. In most cases, the tester creates test cases to kill specific live mutants. This process of adding new test cases, verifying correctness, and killing mutants is repeated until the tester is satisfied with the mutation score. A mutation score threshold can be set as a policy decision to require testers to test software to a predefined level.

2. Using Mutation Analysis to Detect Faults

Many research papers about mutation (including our own) have obscured the issue of how and when failures are found when using mutation. In standard IEEE terminology [18], a *failure* is an external, incorrect behavior of a program (an incorrect output or a runtime failure). A *fault* is the group of incorrect statements in the program that causes a failure. Failures in the software are detected when test cases are executed against the original program. The tester must decide whether the output of the program on each test case is correct. If the output is correct, the process continues as described above. If the output is incorrect, then a failure has been found and the process stops until the associated fault can be corrected. This leads to the fundamental premise of mutation testing, as coined by Geist [19]: **In practice, if the software contains a fault, there will usually be a set of mutants that can only be killed by a test case that also detects that fault.**

3. Bringing Down the Barriers

One of the barriers to the practical use of mutation testing is the unacceptable computational expense of generating and running vast numbers of mutant programs against the test cases. The number of mutants generated for a software unit is proportional to the product of the number of data references and the number of data objects [20]. Typically, this is a large number for even small software units. Because each mutant program must be executed against at least one, and potentially many, test cases, mutation analysis requires large amounts of computation. This is shown in Figure 1 in the box labeled "`Run test cases on each live mutant`". It is by far the most computationally expensive step in mutation testing.

The other barrier to more widespread use of mutation testing is the amount of manual labor involved in using this technique. For example, manual equivalent mutant detection is quite tedious and developing mutation adequate test cases can be very labor-intensive.

Recent advances show promise in bringing down both of these barriers. We first describe advances for reducing the computational expense of mutation analysis and then review research work that has been successful in partially automating much of the labor-intensive portions of mutation testing. We continue by suggesting how these advances can be combined in a manner that can lead to a practical mutation testing system in the near future.

3.1. Reducing the Computational Cost of Mutation Analysis

Recall that the major cost of mutation analysis arises from the computational expense of generating and running vast numbers of mutant programs. Approaches to reduce this computational expense usually follow one of three strategies: *do fewer*, *do smarter*, or *do faster*. The "do fewer" approaches seek ways of running fewer mutant programs without incurring intolerable information loss. The "do smarter" approaches seek to distribute the computational expense over several machines or factor the expense over several executions by retaining state information between runs or seek to avoid complete execution. The "do faster" approaches focus on ways of generating and running each mutant program as quickly as possible.

3.1.1. Selective Mutation – a "do fewer" approach

Mothra used 22 mutation operators, of which the six most populous account for 40% to 60% of all mutants. This is typical of mutation systems – the goal was to include as much testing as possible by defining as many mutants as possible. These six mutants, and others, are in some sense redundant; that is, test sets that are generated to kill only mutants generated from the other mutant operators are very effective in killing mutants generated from the six. Wong and Mathur suggested the idea of *constrained mutation* to be applying mutation with only the most critical mutation operators being used [21]. This idea was later developed by Offutt et al. as an approximation technique called *selective mutation* that tries to select only mutants that are truly distinct from other mutants [20, 22].

Results showed that of the 22 mutation operators used by Mothra, 5 turn out to be "key" operators. In experimental trials, those five operators provided almost the same coverage as non-selective mutation, with cost reductions of at least four times with small programs, and up to 50 times with larger programs. The 5 sufficient operators are ABS, which forces each arithmetic expression to take on the value 0, a positive value, and a negative value, AOR, which replaces each arithmetic operator with every syntactically legal operator, LCR, which replaces each logical connector (AND and OR) with several kinds of logical connectors, ROR, which replaces relational operators with other relational operators, and UOI, which inserts unary operators in front of expressions. Future mutation systems will have the goal of minimizing the number of mutation operators - getting as much testing strength as possible with as few mutants as possible.

3.1.2. Mutant Sampling – a "do fewer" approach

First proposed by Acree [23] and Budd [24], in sampling only a randomly selected subset of the mutant programs are run. The effects of varying the sampling percentage from 10% to 40% in steps of 5% were later investigated by Wong [25]. A 10% sample of mutant programs, for example, was found to be only 16% less effective than a full set in ascertaining fault detection effectiveness.

An alternative sampling approach is proposed by Şahinoğlu and Spafford [26] that does not use samples of some *a priori* fixed size but rather, based on a Bayesian sequential probability ratio test, selects mutant programs until sufficient evidence has been collected to determine that a statistically appropriate sample size has been reached.

3.1.3. Weak Mutation - a "do smarter" approach

Research systems such as Mothra execute mutant programs until they terminate, then compare the final output of the program with the output of the original program. Originally proposed by Howden [27], *weak mutation* is an approximation technique that compares the internal states of the mutant and original program immediately after execution of the mutated portion of the program. That is, weak mutation ensures that the necessity condition is satisfied, but not the sufficiency condition.

Weak mutation has been discussed theoretically [28, 29, 30] and studied empirically [31, 32, 33, 34]. Howden's original proposal stated that the states should be compared "after" the mutated statement, without elaborating on exactly when. Morell's concept of "extent" [28] and Woodward and Halewood's "firm" mutation [29] suggested that the comparison could be done at any point after the mutated statement.

The Leonardo system [35, 34], which was implemented as part of Mothra, did two things. It implemented a working weak mutation system that could be easily compared with strong mutation, and evaluated the extent/firm concept by allowing comparisons to be made at four different locations after the mutated component: (1) after the first evaluation of the innermost expression surrounding the mutated symbol, (2) after the first execution of the mutated statement, (3) after the first execution of the basic block that contains the mutated statement, and (4) after **each** execution of the basic block that contains the mutated statement (execution stops as soon as an invalid state is detected). Experience with Leonardo indicated that weak mutation was able to generate tests that were almost as effective as tests generated with strong mutation, and that at least 50% and usually more of the execution time was saved. Moreover, it was found that the most effective point at which to compare the program states was after the first execution of the mutated statement.

3.1.4. Other "do smarter" approaches

Using novel computer architectures to distribute the computational expense over several machines represents another " do smarter" strategy. Work has been done to adapt mutation analysis systems to vector processors [36], SIMD machines [37], Hypercube (MIMD) machines [38, 39], and Network (MIMD) computers [40]. Because each mutant program is independent of all other mutant programs, communication costs are fairly low. At least one tool was able to achieve almost linear speedup for moderate sized program functions [38].

In another "do smarter" approach, Fleyshgakker and Weiss describe algorithms that improve the run time complexity of conventional mutation analysis systems at the expense of increased space complexity [41]. By intelligently storing state information, their techniques factor the expense of running a mutant over several related mutant executions and thereby lower the total computational costs. In the best case, these techniques can improve the speed by a factor proportional to the average number of mutants per program statement.

3.1.5. Schema-based Mutation Analysis – a "do faster" approach

Most mutation systems have worked by interpreting many slightly different versions of the same program. Although interpretation-based systems make the management of the mutant executions convenient, this conventional method has significant problems. Automated mutation analysis systems based on the conventional interpretive method are slow, laborious to build, and usually unable to completely emulate the intended operational environment of the software being tested. To solve these problems, Untch developed a new execution model for mutation, the Mutant Schema Generation (MSG) method [42, 12].

Instead of mutating an intermediate form, the MSG method encodes all mutations into one source-level program, a "metamutant". This program is then compiled (once) with the same compiler used during development and is executed in the same operational environment at compiled-program speeds. Because mutation systems based on mutant schemata do not need to provide the entire run-time semantics and environment, they are significantly less complex and easier to build than interpretive systems, as well as more portable. Benchmarks show `TUMS`, an MSG-based prototype mutation analysis system, to be significantly faster than `Mothra`, with speed-ups as high as an order-of-magnitude observed.

3.1.6. Other "do faster" approaches

Another way of avoiding interpretive execution is the *separate compilation* approach, wherein each mutant is individually created, compiled, linked and run. The `Proteum` system [13] is an example of this approach. When mutant run times greatly exceed individual compilation/link times, a system based on such a strategy will execute 15 to 20 times faster than an interpretive system. When this condition is not met, however, a *compilation bottleneck* [39] may result.

To avoid compilation bottlenecks, DeMillo, Krauser, and Mathur developed a *compiler-integrated* program mutation scheme that avoids much of the overhead of the compilation bottleneck and yet is able to execute compiled code [11]. In this method, the program under test is compiled by a special compiler. As the compilation process proceeds, the effects of mutations are noted and *code patches* that represent these mutations are prepared. Execution of a particular mutant requires only that the appropriate code patch be applied prior to execution. Patching is inexpensive and the mutant executes at compiled-speeds.

3.2. Reducing Burdensome Manual Tasks

Manually developing test cases that are mutation adequate requires a great deal of effort. Additionally, determining which mutant programs are equivalent to the original program is a very tedious and error-prone activity. Progress has been made on partially automating both of these tasks and is described next.

3.2.1. Automatic Test Data Generation

One of the most difficult technical tasks in testing software is that of generating the test case values needed to satisfy the testing criterion. In his dissertation [9], Offutt developed a technique called *constraint-based test data generation (CBT)*, which creates test data that comes reasonably close to satisfying mutation. CBT is based on the observation that a test case that kills a mutant must satisfy three conditions. The first is that the mutated statement must be reached; this is called the *reachability condition*. The second condition requires the execution of the mutated statement to result in an error in the program's state; this is called the *necessity condition*. The third condition, the *sufficiency condition*, states that the incorrect state must propagate through the program's computation to result in an output failure. *Godzilla* is a test data generator that uses constraint-based testing to automatically generate test data for Mothra [10].

Godzilla describes these conditions as mathematical systems of constraints. Reachability conditions are described by constraint systems called *path expressions*. Each statement in the program has a path expression that describes all execution paths through the program to that statement. The path expression is an assertion that is true if the statement is reached. The necessity condition is described by a constraint that is specific to the mutant operator and requires that the computation performed by the mutated statement create an incorrect intermediate program state. Because expressing the sufficiency condition as a set of constraints requires knowing in advance the complete path a program will take (in general, undecidable), Godzilla does not attempt to automatically satisfy this condition directly.

Godzilla conjoins each necessity constraint with the appropriate path expression constraint. The resulting constraint system is solved to generate a test case such that the constraint system is true. Experimentation [43] has verified that constraint-based testing creates test cases that kill over 90% of the mutants for most programs. CBT uses control-flow analysis, symbolic evaluation, and information about mutants to create the constraints, and a constraint satisfaction technique called *domain reduction* to generate test values.

CBT suffers from several shortcomings that prevent it from working in some situations and hamper its applicability in practical situations. Many of these shortcomings stem from weaknesses associated with symbolic evaluation and include problems handling arrays, loops, and nested expressions. Godzilla occasionally fails to find test cases, and for some programs it fails a large percentage of the time. This is partly because of problems with the technique, partly because of insufficiently general approaches to handling expressions, and partly because Godzilla employed relatively unsophisticated search procedures.

More recently, a test data technique called the *dynamic domain reduction procedure* was developed to address most of these problems [44, 45]. The dynamic domain reduction procedure (DDR) uses part of the CBT approach, and also draws from Korel's dynamic test data generation approach [46, 47] and symbolic evaluation. It uses a direct "domain reduction" method for deriving values, rather than function minimization methods as used by Korel or linear programming-like methods as used by Clarke [48]. Korel's dynamic method [47] executes a program along one specific path by starting with a particular input. When a branching point is reached, if the current inputs will cause the appropriate branch to be taken, the inputs will remain the same. If a different branch is required, then the inputs are dynamically modified to take the correct branch using function minimization. DDR also works by choosing a specific path, but there are no initial values, and the values are derived in-process from initial input domains.

Unlike dynamic symbolic evaluation [49, 50], DDR creates sets of values that represent conditions under which a path will be executed. Thus, the results of dynamic symbolic evaluation attempt to represent all possible values that will execute a given path, while dynamic domain reduction only results in a small set of possible values. While this is more limited, it is also more practical for real programs.

The dynamic nature of DDR, which combines analysis of the software with satisfaction of constraints and test data generation, allows better handling of arrays and expressions. DDR also incorporates a sophisticated back-tracking search procedure to partially solve a problem that caused previous methods to fail. Because of the historical basis, the DDR procedure will always work when CBT does, and also in many cases when CBT does not.

The DDR procedure walks through the program control flow graph, generating test data along the way. Each input variable is initially given a large set of potential values (its *domain*) and, as branches are taken in the control flow graph, the domains for the variables involved in the predicates are reduced so that the appropriate predicates would be true for any assignment of values from the domain. When choices for how to reduce the domains must be made, a search process is initiated and choices are systematically made to try to find a choice that allows the subsequent edges on the path to be executed. When the procedure is finished, the remaining values for the variables' domains represent sets of test cases that will cause execution of the path. If any variable's domain is empty, the search process failed due to one of two possible reasons. One, the path is infeasible, so no satisfying values could be found. Two, it was very difficult to find values that execute the path; this could be because the constraints were too complicated or there are relatively few inputs that will execute the path.

3.2.2. Partial Automatic Equivalent Mutant Detection

A major problem with practically applying mutation is that of equivalent mutant programs. Equivalent mutants can be thought of as "dead-weight" in the testing process – they do not contribute to the generation of test cases, but require lots of time and attention from the tester. Equivalent mutants have traditionally been detected by hand, which is very expensive and time-consuming, and restricts the practical usefulness of mutation testing.

Although recognition of equivalent programs is in general undecidable [51], the idea of using compiler-optimization techniques to recognize some if not most equivalent mutants was suggested by Baldwin and Sayward in 1979 [52]. This technique was tried in a limited way by hand in Tanaka's 1981 thesis [53]. Offutt and Craft [54] refined, extended, and implemented the Baldwin and Sayward suggestions in a tool that was integrated with Mothra. This led directly to the idea of using constraint-based testing to detect equivalent mutants, which was implemented in a tool that detected almost 50% of the equivalent mutants [55, 56].

The constraint-based technique uses mathematical constraints to automatically detect equivalent mutants. The general idea is that if a constraint system that is created to kill a mutant is infeasible, then that mutant is equivalent. Although recognizing infeasible constraints is a difficult problem that cannot be solved in general, heuristic approximations have been developed that are quite effective. This approach also subsume all of the previous compiler-optimization techniques.

Hierons, Harman, and Danicic have gone one step further and use program slicing to detect equivalent mutants [57]. This approach in turn subsumes the constraint-based technique.

Unfortunately, no automated system will be able to detect all equivalent mutants, thus to complement the technique of recognizing equivalent mutants, we suggest that the remaining equivalent mutants can be safely ignored. Although this requires the tester to be willing to accept less than full mutation coverage, results indicate that the loss will not usually be significant, and the testing will still be more effective than testing with most other testing techniques. Although this approach is not completely satisfying from a theoretical view, it is an eminently practical engineering solution to a practically impossible problem.

3.3. Procedural Advances using Mutation

The traditional mutation testing process as shown in Figure 1 suffers from several problems. The major loop of entering test cases, running the original program, checking the output, running mutants, and marking equivalent mutants is very human intensive. The advances in automatic test data generation led to viewing test cases as throw-away items, rather than valuable resources. This in turn leads to the realization that checking whether the original program is correct on each test case does not have to be in the major loop, but can be postponed until later. This, combined with the automation of steps that were previously manual, allows us to eliminate the human tester from the main mutation loop.

Figure 2 presents a new process for applying mutation testing. Initially, a set of test cases is automatically generated and those test cases are executed against the original program, and then the mutants. The tester defines a "threshold" value, which is a minimum acceptable mutation score. If the threshold has not been reached, then test cases that killed no mutants (termed *ineffective*) are removed. This process is repeated, each time generating test cases to target live mutants, until the threshold mutation score is reached. Up to this point, the process has been entirely automatic. To finish testing, the tester will examine expected output of the effective test cases, and fix the

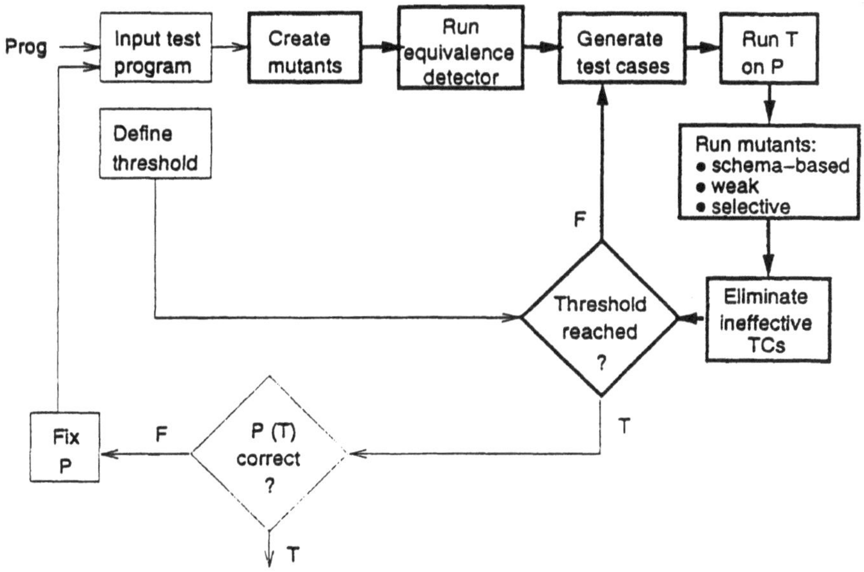

Figure 2: **New Mutation Testing Process.**
Bold boxes represent steps that are automated;
remaining boxes represent steps that are manual.

program if any faults are found.

In both the traditional and this new process, the major part of the time and effort of mutation is in the loop of generating, running, and disposing of test cases. As before, the most significant computational expense is in the mutation engine. The difference is that the new mutation engine will employ a schema-based approach (or one of the other "do faster" techniques) to execute the code, apply weak mutation to reduce the amount of execution, and use selective mutation to reduce the number of mutations. Given that the improvements given in Section 3.1 are orthogonal (rather than serial), combining these techniques will yield geometric (rather than incremental) performance boosts. Uniting these orthogonal techniques should reduce the amount of execution time for the mutation engine by **orders of magnitude**, making it possible to process moderate routines within a reasonable period of time.

A significant innovation in this new process is that the major loop (the boxes and arrows in bold in Figure 2) contains no manual steps. All manual steps are outside the loop and only need to be done once. In fact, the only significant manual step is that of deciding if the outputs of each test case is correct. Some progress on constructing automated test oracles has been made [58, 59]. However even without an automated test oracle, by disposing of ineffective test cases before checking outputs we can significantly reduce the workload of the tester. Additionally, the threshold input allows the practical tester to use approximation in the coverage criterion. This approximation heuristic does not attempt to find an exact solution to the testing problem. Software testing is an imperfect science and we see no reason for coverage to be exact. Rather, a application of a coverage criterion must be cost-effective and must always improve the situation—by providing better test cases. The use of a threshold heuristic meets this requirement.

4. A Practical and Effective Mutation Analysis System

Using these technological advances and process improvements, practical, 21st century mutation systems will be faster and more practical, and require significantly less human interaction. Figure 3 presents a high level architectural view of this type of testing system.

In this system, a program to be tested is submitted to the `schemata generator`, which produces a `metamutant` that incorporates all the mutants of the test program into one program. The `schemata generator` also produces a `mutant data store`, which is used to store statistics about the mutants such as which are alive and which have been killed. The `constraint & slicing analyzer` integrates the pre-

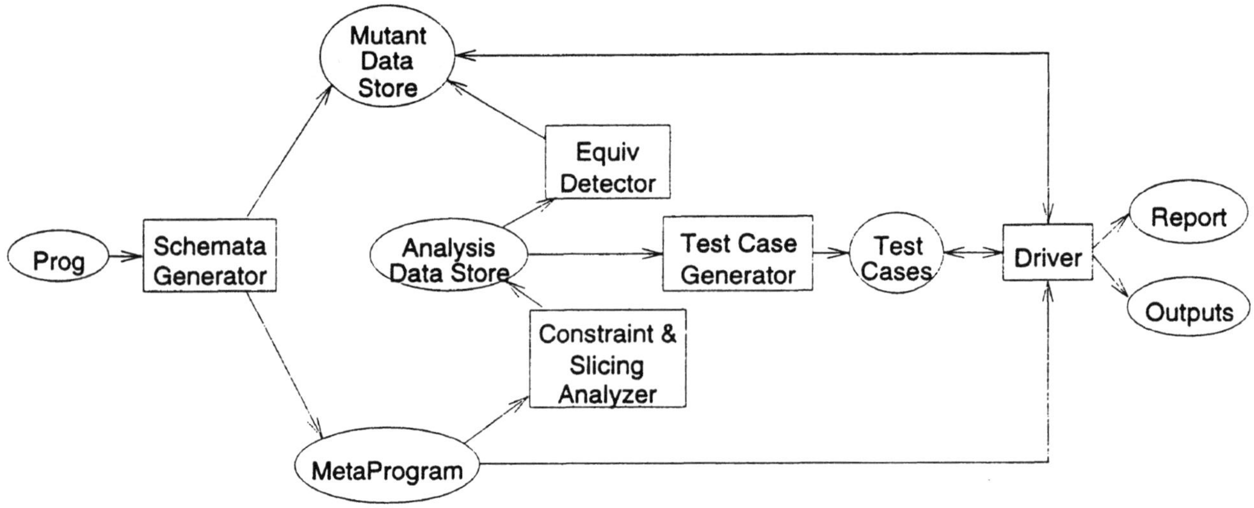

Figure 3: **Architecture of a Practical, Efficient Mutation Testing System**

processing steps for test data generation and equivalent mutant detection into one tool. It produces constraints on mutants as well as control, data flow, and slicing information about the program and its mutants. The `analysis data store` is used by the `equivalent mutant detector` to detect and mark mutants that are equivalent in the `mutant data store`. The `test case generator` uses the `analysis data store` to generate test cases to try to kill each mutant. The `driver` compiles the `metamutant`, runs each test case on the original program, then on each mutant, saving only test cases that kill at least one mutant. It continues to obtain and execute more test cases until the threshold percentage of mutants is reached. The results of running the mutants are saved in the `mutant data store`, and a report summarizing how many mutants have been killed is generated. The output of the original program on each effective test case is saved for examination by the tester.

The `schemata generator` only generates mutants using the selective operators. This consists of mutants that replace each arithmetic operator with each other arithmetic operator, replace each relational operator with each other relational operator, replace each logical connector operator with each other logical connector operator, and that modify expressions by inserting unary operations that cause each expression to be zero, negative, positive, and that modify each expression by very small amounts. The `metamutant` incorporates weak mutation semantics, so that each mutant will not execute completely, but will only execute to the end of the basic block that contains the mutated statement.

Because parallelism depends very heavily on the type of hardware available, we do not automatically assume it will be incorporated in future mutation systems. However, if it is thought to be helpful, the `driver` in Figure 3 could be modified to execute programs from the `metamutant` in parallel.

5. Conclusions

By combining the recent technological advances and an improved testing process, future mutation testing tools will be orders of magnitude faster than previous research systems and will require significantly less human involvement. Additionally, experience has shown that these systems can be built easier and faster than previous systems.

We envision a test tool that provides almost complete automation to the tester. A programmer submits a software module, and after a reasonable period of computation, the tool responds with a set of test cases that are assured to provide the software with a very effective test, and a set of outputs that can be examined to find failures in the software. Furthermore, these input-output pairs can be used as a basis for debugging when failures are found. This technology can be integrated with compilers, debuggers, and report generators.

6. Acknowledgments

We would like to thank the many students and faculty colleagues who contributed to the ideas and tool development to support the research contained in this paper, including Roger Alexander, Michael Craft, Scott Fichter, Dr. Robert Geist, Fred Harris, Dr. Mary Jean Harrold, Zhenyi Jin, Ammei Lee, Stephen Lee, Tracey Oakes, Jie Pan, Dr. Gregg Rothermel, and Christian Zapf.

References

[1] T. Budd and F. Sayward, "Users guide to the Pilot mutation system," technical report 114, Department of Computer Science, Yale University, 1977.

[2] R. G. Hamlet, "Testing programs with the aid of a compiler," *IEEE Transactions on Software Engineering*, vol. 3, pp. 279–290, July 1977.

[3] R. A. DeMillo, R. J. Lipton, and F. G. Sayward, "Hints on test data selection: Help for the practicing programmer," *IEEE Computer*, vol. 11, pp. 34–41, April 1978.

[4] T. A. Budd, R. A. DeMillo, R. J. Lipton, and F. G. Sayward, "The design of a prototype mutation system for program testing," in *Proceedings NCC, AFIPS Conference Record*, pp. 623–627, 1978.

[5] R. J. Lipton and F. G. Sayward, "The status of research on program mutation," in *Digest for the Workshop on Software Testing and Test Documentation*, pp. 355–373, December 1978.

[6] A. T. Acree, T. A. Budd, R. A. DeMillo, R. J. Lipton, and F. G. Sayward, "Mutation analysis," technical report GIT-ICS-79/08, School of Information and Computer Science, Georgia Institute of Technology, Atlanta GA, September 1979.

[7] A. J. Offutt and K. N. King, "A Fortran 77 interpreter for mutation analysis," in *1987 Symposium on Interpreters and Interpretive Techniques*, (St. Paul MN), pp. 177–188, ACM SIGPLAN, June 1987.

[8] R. A. DeMillo, D. S. Guindi, K. N. King, W. M. McCracken, and A. J. Offutt, "An extended overview of the Mothra software testing environment," in *Proceedings of the Second Workshop on Software Testing, Verification, and Analysis*, (Banff Alberta), pp. 142–151, IEEE Computer Society Press, July 1988.

[9] A. J. Offutt, *Automatic Test Data Generation*. PhD thesis, Georgia Institute of Technology, Atlanta GA, 1988. Technical report GIT-ICS 88/28.

[10] R. A. DeMillo and A. J. Offutt, "Constraint-based automatic test data generation," *IEEE Transactions on Software Engineering*, vol. 17, pp. 900–910, September 1991.

[11] R. A. DeMillo, E. W. Krauser, and A. P. Mathur, "Compiler-integrated program mutation," in *Proceedings of the Fifteenth Annual Computer Software and Applications Conference (COMPSAC' 92)*, (Tokyo, Japan), Kogakuin University, IEEE Computer Society Press, September 1991.

[12] R. H. Untch, M. J. Harrold, and J. Offutt, "Schema-based mutation analysis." In preparation.

[13] M. E. Delamaro and J. C. Maldonado, "Proteum–A tool for the assessment of test adequacy for c programs," in *Proceedings of the Conference on Performability in Computing Systems (PCS 96)*, (New Brunswick, NJ), pp. 79–95, July 1996.

[14] A. J. Offutt, "Investigations of the software testing coupling effect," *ACM Transactions on Software Engineering Methodology*, vol. 1, pp. 3–18, January 1992.

[15] K. S. H. T. Wah, "Fault coupling in finite bijective functions," *The Journal of Software Testing, Verification, and Reliability*, vol. 5, pp. 3–47, March 1995.

[16] K. S. H. T. Wah, "A theoretical study of fault coupling," *The Journal of Software Testing, Verification, and Reliability*, vol. 10, pp. 3–46, March 2000.

[17] D. Wu, M. A. Hennell, D. Hedley, and I. J. Riddell, "A practical method for software quality control via program mutation," in *Proceedings of the Second Workshop on Software Testing, Verification, and Analysis*, (Banff, Alberta, Canada), pp. 159–170, IEEE Computer Society Press, July 1988.

[18] IEEE, *IEEE Standard Glossary of Software Engineering Terminology*. ANSI/IEEE Std 610.12-1990, 1996.

[19] R. Geist, A. J. Offutt, and F. Harris, "Estimation and enhancement of real-time software reliability through mutation analysis," *IEEE Transactions on Computers*, vol. 41, pp. 550–558, May 1992. Special Issue on Fault-Tolerant Computing.

[20] A. J. Offutt, A. Lee, G. Rothermel, R. Untch, and C. Zapf, "An experimental determination of sufficient mutation operators," *ACM Transactions on Software Engineering Methodology*, vol. 5, pp. 99–118, April 1996.

[21] W. E. Wong, M. E. Delamaro, J. C. Maldonado, and A. P. Mathur, "Constrained mutation in C programs," in *Proceedings of the 8th Brazilian Symposium on Software Engineering*, (Curitiba, Brazil), pp. 439–452, October 1994.

[22] A. J. Offutt, G. Rothermel, and C. Zapf, "An experimental evaluation of selective mutation," in *Proceedings of the Fifteenth International Conference on Software Engineering*, (Baltimore, MD), pp. 100–107, IEEE Computer Society Press, May 1993.

[23] A. T. Acree, *On Mutation*. PhD thesis, Georgia Institute of Technology, Atlanta GA, 1980.

[24] T. A. Budd, *Mutation Analysis of Program Test Data*. PhD thesis, Yale University, New Haven CT, 1980.

[25] W. E. Wong, *On Mutation and Data Flow*. PhD thesis, Purdue University, December 1993. (Also Technical Report SERC-TR-149-P, Software Engineering Research Center, Purdue University, West Lafayette, IN).

[26] M. Şahinoğlu and E. H. Spafford, "A bayes sequential statistical procedure for approving software products," in *Proccedings of the IFIP Conference on Approving Software Products (ASP-90)* (W. Ehrenberger, ed.), (Garmisch-Partenkirchen, Germany), pp. 43–56, Elsevier/North Holland, New York, Sept. 1990.

[27] W. E. Howden, "Weak mutation testing and completeness of test sets," *IEEE Transactions on Software Engineering*, vol. 8, pp. 371–379, July 1982.

[28] L. J. Morell, "Theoretical insights into fault based testing," in *Proceedings of the Second Workshop on Software Testing, Verification, and Analysis*, (Banff Alberta), pp. 45–62, IEEE Computer Society Press, July 1988.

[29] M. R. Woodward and K. Halewood, "From weak to strong, dead or alive? An analysis of some mutation testing issues," in *Proceedings of the Second Workshop on Software Testing, Verification, and Analysis*, (Banff Alberta), pp. 152–158, IEEE Computer Society Press, July 1988.

[30] J. R. Horgan and A. P. Mathur, "Weak mutation is probably strong mutation," technical report SERC-TR-83-P, Software Engineering Research Center, Purdue University, West Lafayette IN, December 1990.

[31] M. R. Girgis and M. R. Woodward, "An integrated system for program testing using weak mutation and data flow analysis," in *Proceedings of the Eighth International Conference on Software Engineering*, (London UK), pp. 313–319, IEEE Computer Society Press, August 1985.

[32] B. Marick, "Two experiments in software testing," technical report UIUCDCS-R-90-1644, Department of Computer Science, University of Illinois at Urbana-Champaign, Urbana-Champaign Illinois, November 1990.

[33] B. Marick, "The weak mutation hypothesis," in *Proceedings of the Fourth Symposium on Software Testing, Analysis, and Verification*, (Victoria, British Columbia, Canada), pp. 190–199, IEEE Computer Society Press, October 1991.

[34] A. J. Offutt and S. D. Lee, "An empirical evaluation of weak mutation," *IEEE Transactions on Software Engineering*, vol. 20, pp. 337–344, May 1994.

[35] A. J. Offutt and S. D. Lee, "How strong is weak mutation?," in *Proceedings of the Fourth Symposium on Software Testing, Analysis, and Verification*, (Victoria, British Columbia, Canada), pp. 200–213, IEEE Computer Society Press, October 1991.

[36] A. P. Mathur and E. W. Krauser, "Mutant unification for improved vectorization," technical report SERC-TR-14-P, Software Engineering Research Center, Purdue University, West Lafayette IN, April 1988.

[37] E. W. Krauser, A. P. Mathur, and V. Rego, "High performance testing on SIMD machines," in *Proceedings of the Second Workshop on Software Testing, Verification, and Analysis*, (Banff Alberta), pp. 171–177, IEEE Computer Society Press, July 1988.

[38] A. J. Offutt, R. Pargas, S. V. Fichter, and P. Khambekar, "Mutation testing of software using a mimd computer," in *1992 International Conference on Parallel Processing*, (Chicago, Illinois), pp. II-257–266, August 1992.

[39] B. Choi and A. P. Mathur, "High-performance mutation testing," *The Journal of Systems and Software*, vol. 20, pp. 135–152, February 1993.

[40] C. N. Zapf, "Medusamothra – a distributed interpreter for the mothra mutation testing system," M.S. thesis, Clemson University, Clemson, SC, August 1993.

[41] V. N. Fleyshgakker and S. N. Weiss, "Efficient Mutation Analysis: A New Approach," in *Proceedings of the International Symposium on Software Testing and Analysis (ISSTA 94)*, (Seattle, WA), pp. 185–195, ACM SIGSOFT, ACM Press, Aug. 17–19 1994.

[42] R. Untch, A. J. Offutt, and M. J. Harrold, "Mutation analysis using program schemata," in *Proceedings of the 1993 International Symposium on Software Testing, and Analysis*, (Cambridge MA), pp. 139–148, June 1993.

[43] R. A. DeMillo and A. J. Offutt, "Experimental results from an automatic test case generator," *ACM Transactions on Software Engineering Methodology*, vol. 2, pp. 109–127, April 1993.

[44] J. Offutt, Z. Jin, and J. Pan, "The dynamic domain reduction approach for test data generation: Design and algorithms," technical report ISSE-TR-94-110, Department of Information and Software Systems Engineering, George Mason University, Fairfax VA, September 1994.

[45] J. Offutt, Z. Jin, and J. Pan, "The dynamic domain reduction approach to test data generation," *Software–Practice and Experience*, vol. 29, pp. 167–193, January 1999.

[46] B. Korel, "Automated software test data generation," *IEEE Transactions on Software Engineering*, vol. 16, pp. 870–879, August 1990.

[47] B. Korel, "Dynamic method for software test data generation," *The Journal of Software Testing, Verification, and Reliability*, vol. 2, no. 4, pp. 203–213, 1992.

[48] L. A. Clarke, "A system to generate test data and symbolically execute programs," *IEEE Transactions on Software Engineering*, vol. 2, pp. 215–222, September 1976.

[49] L. A. Clarke and D. J. Richardson, "Applications of symbolic evaluation," *The Journal of Systems and Software*, vol. 5, pp. 15–35, January 1985.

[50] R. E. Fairley, "An experimental program testing facility," *IEEE Transactions on Software Engineering*, vol. SE-1, pp. 350–3571, December 1975.

[51] T. A. Budd and D. Angluin, "Two notions of correctness and their relation to testing," *Acta Informatica*, vol. 18, pp. 31–45, November 1982.

[52] D. Baldwin and F. Sayward, "Heuristics for determining equivalence of program mutations," research report 276, Department of Computer Science, Yale University, 1979.

[53] A. Tanaka, "Equivalence testing for fortran mutation system using data flow analysis," Master's thesis, School of Information and Computer Science, Georgia Institute of Technology, Atlanta GA, 1981.

[54] A. J. Offutt and W. M. Craft, "Using compiler optimization techniques to detect equivalent mutants," *The Journal of Software Testing, Verification, and Reliability*, vol. 4, pp. 131–154, September 1994.

[55] A. J. Offutt and J. Pan, "Detecting equivalent mutants and the feasible path problem," in *Proceedings of the 1996 Annual Conference on Computer Assurance (COMPASS 96)*, (Gaithersburg MD), pp. 224–236, IEEE Computer Society Press, June 1996.

[56] A. J. Offutt and J. Pan, "Detecting equivalent mutants and the feasible path problem," *The Journal of Software Testing, Verification, and Reliability*, vol. 7, pp. 165–192, September 1997.

[57] R. Hierons, M. Harman, and S. Danicic, "Using program slicing to assist in the detection of equivalent mutants," *Software Testing, Verification, and Reliability*, vol. 9, pp. 233–262, December 1999.

[58] E. Mikk, "Compilation of z specifications into c for automatic test result evaluation," in *9th International Conference of Z Users (ZUM'95)*, (Limerick, Ireland), pp. 167–180, Springer-Verlag Lecture Notes in Computer Science Volume 967, J.P. Bowen and M.G. Hinchey (Eds.), September 1995.

[59] D. K. Peters and D. L. Parnas, "Using test oracles generated from program documentation," *IEEE Transactions on Software Engineering*, vol. 24, pp. 161–173, March 1998.

Unit and Integration Testing Strategies for C Programs Using Mutation-Based Criteria

Auri Marcelo Rizzo Vincenzi
José Carlos Maldonado
Ellen Francine Barbosa

Instituto de Ciências Matemáticas e de Computação
Universidade de São Paulo
{auri, jcmaldon, francine}@icmc.sc.usp.br

Márcio Eduardo Delamaro

Departamento de Informática
Universidade Estadual de Maringá
delamaro@din.uem.br

Abstract

Mutation testing, originally proposed to unit testing, has been extended to integration testing with the proposition of the Interface Mutation criterion. In this paper we analyze the results of an experiment comparing two mutation-based testing criteria for unit and integration testing phases: the Mutation Analysis and the Interface Mutation adequacy criteria, respectively. The aim is to investigate how they could be used in a complementary way during the testing activity. We attempt to establish an incremental testing strategy comprising the unit and integration testing phases and guidelines on how to obtain a high mutation score with respect to mutation testing with a lower cost, in terms of the number of mutants generated.

Mutation: Application, Effectiveness, and Test Generation

Trustable Components: Yet Another Mutation-Based Approach

Benoit Baudry, Vu Le Hanh, Jean-Marc Jézéquel and Yves Le Traon
IRISA, Campus Universitaire de Beaulieu, 35042 Rennes Cedex, France
{Benoit.Baudry, vlhanh, Jean-Marc.Jezequel, Yves.Le_Traon }@irisa.fr

Abstract

This paper presents the use of mutation analysis as the main qualification technique for:

- *estimating and automatically enhancing a test set (using genetic algorithms),*
- *qualifying and improving a component's contracts (that is the specification facet)*
- *measuring the impact of contractable robust components on global system robustness and reliability.*

The methodology is based on an integrated design and test approach for OO software components. It is dedicated to design-by-contract, where the specification is systematically derived into executable assertions called contracts (invariant properties, pre/postconditions of methods). The testing-for-trust approach, using the mutation analysis, checks the consistency between specification, implementation and tests. It points out the tests lack of efficiency but also the lack of precision of the contracts. The feasibility of components validation by mutation analysis and its usefulness for test generation are studied as well as the robustness of trustable and self-testable components into an infected environment.

1. Introduction

The *Object-Oriented* approach offers both strong encapsulation mechanisms and efficient operators for software reusability and extensibility. In a component-based approach using a *design-by-contract* methodology, the following considerations make mutation analysis useful for several analysis levels:

- in a design-by-contract approach [5,10], components integrate "contracts" that are systematically derived from the specification. Contracts behave as executable assertions that automatically check the components consistency (pre-postconditions, class invariants). Based on mutation analysis, the efficiency of contracts can thus be estimated by their capacity of rejecting faulty implementation, and the enhancement of contracts can be guided. Then, and also based on a particular application of mutation analysis, the contribution of each component to the global system robustness and reliability can be estimated.
- Components, to be reusable, are considered as an "organic" set of a specification, an implementation and embedded tests. With such self-testable component definition, all the difficulty consists of automatically improving embedded tests based on the basic test cases written by the tester/developer. Being given these basic test cases, we consider mutants programs as a population of preys and, conversely, a test set as a particular predator. This analogy leads to the application of genetic algorithms to enhance the original population of predators using as a fitness function the mutation score.
- Trustability [4] is finally the result of the global packaging of a design-by-contract approach, component self-testability and mutation analysis for both tests & contracts improvement and qualification are

In this paper, we propose a testing-for-trust methodology that helps checking the consistency of the component's three facets, i.e., specification/ implementation and tests. The methodology is an original adaptation from mutation analysis principle [1]: the quality of a tests set is related to the proportion of faulty programs it detects. Faulty programs are generated by systematic fault injection in the original implementation. In our approach, we consider that contracts should provide most of the oracle functions: the question of the efficiency of contracts to detect anomalies in the implementation or in the provider environment is thus tackled and studied (Section 4). If the generation of a basic tests set is easy, improving its quality may require prohibitive efforts. In a logical continuity with our mutation analysis approach and tool, we describe how such a basic unit tests set, seen as a test seed, can be automatically improved using genetic algorithms to reach a better quality level.

Section 2 opens on methodological views and steps for building trustable component in our approach.

Section 3 concentrates on the mutation testing process adapted to OO domain and the associated tool dedicated to the Eiffel programming language. The test quality estimate is presented as well as the automatic optimization of test cases using genetic algorithms (Section 4). Section 5 is devoted to an instructive case study that illustrates the feasibility and the benefits of such an approach. Section 6 presents a robustness measure, for a software component, based on a mutation analysis.

2. Test quality for trustable components

The methodology is based on an integrated design and test approach for OO software components, particularly adapted to a design-by-contract approach, where the specification is systematically derived into executable assertions (invariant properties, pre/postconditions of methods). Classes that serve for illustrating the approach are considered as basic unit components: a component can also be any class package that implements a set of well-defined functionality. Test suites are defined as being an "organic" part of software OO component. Indeed, a component is composed of its specification (documentation, methods signature, invariant properties, pre/ postconditions), one implementation and the test cases needed for testing it. This view of an OO component is illustrated under the triangle representation (cf. Figure 1). To a component specified functionality is added a new feature that enables it to test itself: the component is made *self-testable*. Self-testable components have the ability to launch their own unit tests as detailed in [6].

From a methodological point of view, we argue that the trust we have in a component depends on the consistency between the specification (refined in executable contracts), the implementation and the test cases. The confrontation between these three facets leads to the improvement of each one. Before definitely embedding a test suite, the efficiency of test cases must be checked and estimated against implementation and specification, especially contracts. Tests are build from the specification of the component; they are a reflection of its precision. They are composed of two independent conceptual parts: test cases and oracles. Test cases execute the functions of the component. Embedded oracles – predicates for the fault detection decision – can either be provided by assertions included into the test cases or by executable contracts. In a design-by-contract approach, our experience is that *most* of the decisions are provided by contracts derived from the specification. The fact components' contracts are inefficient to detect a fault exercised by the test cases reveals a lack of precision in the specification. The specification should be refined and new contracts added. The trust in the component is thus related to the test cases efficiency and the contracts "completeness". We can trust the implementation since we have tested it with a good test cases set, and we trust the specification because it is precise enough to derive efficient contracts as oracle functions.

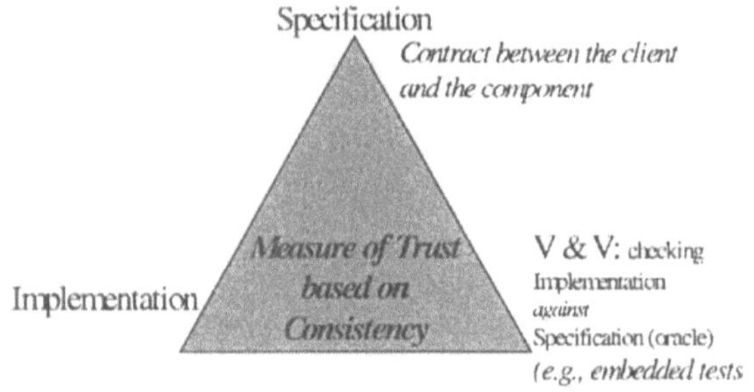

Fig. 1. Trust based on triangle consistency

The question is thus to be able to measure this consistency. This quality estimate quantifies the trust one can have in a component. The chosen quality criteria proposed here is the proportion of injected faults the self-test detects when faults are systematically injected into the component implementation. This estimate is, in fact, derived from the mutation testing technique, which is adapted for OO classes. The main classical limitation for mutation analysis is the combinatorial expense.

The global component design-for-trust process consists of 6 steps that are presented in figure 2.

1. At first, the programmer writes an initial selftest that reaches a given initial Mutation Score (MS).
2. This step aims at automatically enhancing the initial selftest. We propose to use genetic algorithms for that purpose, but any other technique could be used. The used oracle function is the comparison between the testing object states.
3. During the third step, the user has to check if the tests do not detect errors in the initial program. If errors are found, he must debug them.
4. The fourth step consists in measuring the contracts quality thanks to mutation testing. We use the embedded contracts as an oracle function here.
5. Then a non-automated step consists of improving contracts to reach an expected quality
6. At last, the process constructs a global oracle function. To do this, it executes all the tests on the initial class, and the object's state after execution is the oracle value.

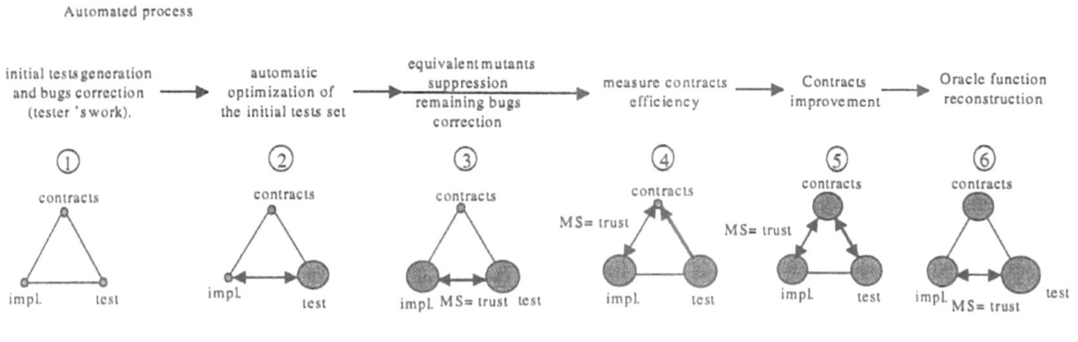

Fig. 2.The global testing-for-trust process

3. Mutation testing technique for OO domain

Mutation testing is a testing technique that was first designed to create effective test data, with an important fault revealing power [11]. It has been originally proposed in 1978 [1] , and consists in creating a set of faulty versions or *mutants* of a program with the ultimate goal of designing a tests set that distinguishes the program from all its mutants. In practice, faults are modeled by a set of *mutation operators* where each operator represents a class of software faults. To create a mutant, it is sufficient to apply its associated operator to the original program.

A tests set is relatively adequate if it distinguishes the original program from all its non-equivalent mutants. Otherwise, a *mutation score (MS)* is associated to the test set to measure its effectiveness in terms of percentage of the revealed non-equivalent mutants. It is to be noted that a mutant is considered *equivalent* to the original program if there is no input data on which the mutant and the original program produce a different output. A benefit of the mutation score is that even if no error is found, it still measures how well the software has been tested giving the user information about the program test quality. It can be viewed as a kind of reliability assessment for the tested software.

A mutation analysis seems well adapted to the Object-Oriented domain for the following reasons:

- methods body of a well designed OO component are generally shorter than for a procedural implementation, most of the control predicates being dispatched on the system dependencies: combinatorial explosion of a mutation analysis is thus limited;
- in OO paradigm, the executed program is an object with a state (attributes values and recursively states of the referenced objects): in classical mutation analysis, the oracle is obtained by comparison between the explicit outputs of the original program and the mutant. In the case of OO programming, an oracle can easily be built by comparing the states of the initial program with the state of the mutant one (a deep comparison of the object states). In fact, to avoid the problem of stateless programs (or if the injected fault does not affect the state of the object under test) the object states that will be compared are the testing programs themselves: the testing program is an object, where all queries method calls on the class under test are caught by attributes of the testing class. With this solution an efficient oracle function compares testing objects attributes. This integrated mechanism significantly enlarge the spectrum of programs concerned by a mutation analysis (no specific instrumentation of the source code is needed)

In this paper, we are looking for a subset of mutation operators

- general enough to be applied to various OO languages (Java, C++, Eiffel etc)
- implying a limited computational expense,
- ensuring at least control-flow coverage of methods.

Our current choice of mutation operators is the following:

EHF: Causes an exception when executed

AOR: Replaces occurrences of "+" by "-" and vice-versa.

LOR: Each occurrence of one of the logical operators (*and, or, nand, nor, xor*) is replaced by each of the other operators; in addition, the expression is replaced by TRUE and FALSE.

ROR: Each occurrence of one of the relational operators (<, >, <=, >=, =, /=) is replaced by each one of the other operators.

NOR: Replaces each statement by the *Null* statement.

VCP: Constants and variables values are slightly modified to emulate domain perturbation testing. Each constant or variable of arithmetic type is both incremented by one and decremented by one. Each *boolean* is replaced by its complement.

The operators introduced for the object-oriented domain are the following:

- MCP (Methods Call Replacement): Methods calls are replaced by a call to another method with the same signature.
- RFI (Referencing Fault Insertion): Stuck-at void the reference of an object after its creation. Suppress a clone or copy instruction. Insert a clone instruction for each reference assignment. Operator RFI introduces object aliasing and object reference faults, specific to object-oriented programming.

3.1. Test selection process

The whole process for generating unit test cases includes the generation of mutants and the application of test cases against each mutant. The decision can be either the difference between the initial implementation's output and the mutant's output, or the contracts and embedded oracle function. The diagnosis on alive mutants consists in determining the reason of non detection: it may be due to the tests but also to incomplete specification (and particularly if contracts are used as oracle functions). It has to be noted that when the set of test cases is selected, the mutation score is fixed as well as the test quality of the component. Moreover, except for diagnosis, the process is completely automated.

The mutation analysis tool developed, called mutants slayer or μSlayer, is suitable for the Eiffel language. This tool injects faults in a class under test (or a set of classes), executes selftests on each mutant program and delivers a diagnosis to determine which mutants were killed by tests. All the process is incremental (we do not start again the execution of already killed mutants for example) and is parameterized: the user for example selects the number and types of mutation he wants to apply at any step. The μSlayer tool is available from http://www.irisa.fr/pampa/.

3.2. Component and system test quality

The test quality of a component is simply obtained by computing the mutation score for the unit testing test suite executed with the self-test method.

The system test quality is defined as follows:

- let S be a system composed of n components denoted C_i, $i \in [1..n]$,
- let d_i be the number of dead mutants after applying the unit test sequence to C_i, and m_i the total number of mutants.

The test quality (TQ), i. e. the mutation score MS, and the System Test Quality (STQ) are defined as follows :

$$TQ(C_i,T_i) = \frac{d_i}{m_i} \qquad STQ(S) = \frac{\sum_{i=1}^{n} d_i}{\sum_{i=1}^{n} m_i}$$

These quality parameters are associated to each component and the global system test quality is computed and updated depending on the number of components actually integrated to the system.

In this paper, such a test quality estimate is considered as the main estimate of component's trustability.

4. Test cases generation : genetic algorithms for test generation

In this section we present the results obtained after using a genetic algorithm as a way to automatically improve the basic test cases set in order to reach a better Test Quality level with limited effort. We begin with a population of mutant programs to be killed and a test cases pool. We randomly combine those test cases (or "gene pool") to build an initial population of test sets which are the predators of the mutant population. From this initial population, how can we mutate the "predators" test cases and cross them over in order to improve their ability to kill mutants programs? One of the major difficulties in genetic algorithms is the definition of a fitness function. In our case, this difficulty does not exist: the mutation score is the function that estimates the efficiency of a test case.

Genetic algorithms [2] have been first developed by John Holland [3], whose goal was to rigorously explain natural systems and then design artificial systems based on natural mechanisms. So, genetic algorithms are optimization algorithms based on natural genetics and selection mechanisms. In nature, creatures which best fit their environment (which are able to avoid predators, which can handle coldness...) reproduce and, due to crossover and mutation, the next generation will fit better. This is just how a genetic algorithm works: it uses an objective criterion to select the fittest individuals in one population, it copies them and creates new individuals with pieces of the old ones.

For test optimization, the problem is modeled as follows:

Test: 1 test = 1 gene

Gene: G = [an initialization sequence, several method calls] = [I , S]

Individual: An individual is defined as a finite set of genes = $\{G_1,\ldots,G_m\}$

The function we want to maximize is the one we use as the fitness function; in our problem, it is the mutation score.

Here are the three operators that manipulate the individuals and genes in our problem:

- Reproduction: selection of individuals that will participate to the next generation guided by the individuals' mutation score.
- Crossover: we select at random an integer i between 1 and individual's size, then from two individuals A and B, we can create two new individuals A' and B'. A' is made of the i first genes of A and the m-i last genes of B, and B' is made of the i first genes of B and (m-i) last genes of B.
- Mutation: we use two mutation operators. The first one changes the method call parameters values in one or several genes. This mutation operator is important, for example if there is an if-then-else structure in a method, we need one value to test the if-branch and another one to test the else-branch, in this case it is interesting to try different parameters for the call. Moreover, in practice, we can use μSlayer's Variable and Constant Perturbation operator to implement this operator.

  The second mutation operator makes a new gene with two genes either by adding, at the end of a gene, the method calls of the other gene, or by switching the genes initialization sequences.

The genetic algorithm is applied until the Quality Test (i. e. the mutation score of the whole set of individuals) level is no more improved.

5. Case study

In this case study, the class package of the Pylon library (http://www.eiffel-forum.org/archive/arnaud/pylon.htm) relating to the management of time was made self-testable. These classes are complex enough to illustrate the approach and obtain interesting results. The main class of this package is called p_date_time.e.

This study proceeds in two stages to help isolating the efforts of test data generation compared to those of oracle production. In real practice, the contracts - that should be effective as embedded oracle functions - can be improved in a continuous process: in this study, we voluntarily separate test generation stage from contract improvement one to compare the respective efforts. The last stage only aims to test the capacity of contracts to detect faults coming from provider classes. We call that capacity the "**robustness**" of the component against an infected environment.

The aims of this case study were:

1. estimating the test generation with genetic algorithms for reaching 100% mutation score,
2. appraising the initial efficiency of contracts and improve them using this approach,
3. estimating the robustness of a component embedded selftest to detect faults due to external infected provider classes.

The last point aims at estimating whether a self-testable system, with high quality tests, is robust enough to detect new external faults due to integration or evolution. Indeed, each component's selftest checks its own correctness but also some of its neighboring provider's components. These crosschecking tests between dependent components increase the probability to detect faults in the global system. So the intuition is that 100 tests method calls per class in a 100 classes system make a high fault revealing power test of 10 000 tests for the whole system. The question is thus to estimate whether a selftest has or not a good probability to detect a fault due to one of its infected provider.

The analysis focuses on three classes: **p_date_time.e**, **p_date.e** and **p_time.e.**

For the classes that are studied here, this first stage of generation allowed to eliminate approximately 60 to 70% of the generated mutants. It corresponds to the test seed that can be used for automatic improvement through genetic algorithm optimization (see Section III.3). Figure 3 presents the curves of the mutation score growth as a function of the number of generated predators (one plot represents a generation step). To avoid the combinatorial expense, we limit the new mutated generation to the predators that have the best own mutation score (good candidates). The new generation of predators was thus target-guided (depends on the alive mutants) and controlled by the fitness function. Results are encouraging even if the CPU time remains important (2 days of execution time for the three components to reach more than 90 percent mutation score on a Pentium II). The main interest is that the test improvement process is automated.

Table 1. Main results

	p_date	p_time	p_date_time
# generated mutants	673	275	199
# equivalents mutants	49	18	15
% mutants killed (initial contracts)	**10,3%**	**17,9%**	**8,%**
% mutants killed after contracts improvement	**69,4%**	**91,4%**	**70,1%**

Then, the mutation score has been improved by analyzing the mutants one by one: equivalent mutants were suppressed and specific test cases were written for alive mutants to reach 100% mutation score. Concerning the improvement of contracts, the results on the initial quality of contracts used as oracles are given in Table 1. The table recapitulates the initial efficiency of contracts and then the final level they reached after improvement.

Table 2. p_date_time robustness in an infected environment

Infected component	P_date	p_time
Total number of methods	19	12
Number of used/infected methods	14	11
# generated mutants	350	161
# equivalents	33	8
# killed mutants	195	114
% killed mutants	**61%**	**74%**

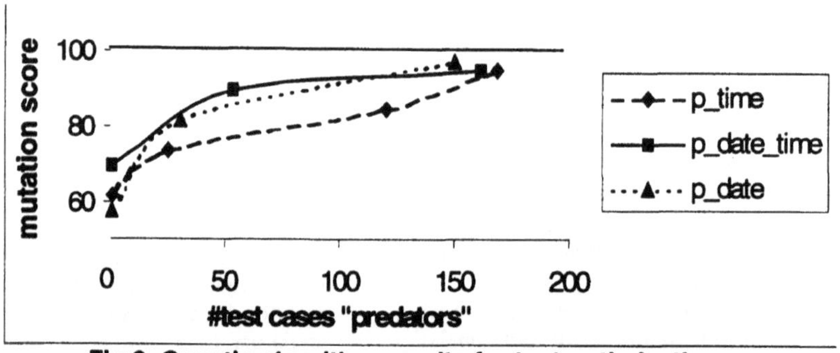

Fig.3. Genetic algorithm results for test optimization

The addition of new contracts thus improves significantly their capacity to detect internal faults (from 10 to 70 % for p_date, from 18 to 91 for p_time and from 9 to 70 for p_date_time). The fact that all faults are not detected by the improved contracts reveals the limit of contracts as oracle functions. The contracts associated with these methods are unable to detect faults disturbing the global state of a component. For example, a *prune* method of a stack cannot have trivial local contracts checking whether the element removed had been previously inserted by a put. In that case, a class invariant would be adapted to detect such faults.

Concerning the robustness of a component against an infected component, **p_date.e** and **p_time.e** have been infected and **p_date_time** client class selftest launched. Table 2 gives the percentage of mutants detected by the client class selftest **p_date_time**. It gives an index of the robustness of **p_date_time** against its infected providers. The numbers of methods used by **p_date_time**, and thus infected by our mutation tool, are given as well as number of generated mutants for each provider class. The results show however that 60-80% of faults related to the external environment is locally detected by the selftest of a component.

6. Reliability and Robustness of a designed by contract system

Based on mutation analysis, we propose a first approximation of the initial failure rate that could be used in a reliability model for initializing some of the initial constant parameters [8,9]. We do not look for a new reliability model but the argumentation aims at bridging the gap between testing and initial reliability/robustness of a system in a design-by-contracts approach, with self-testable components.

Embedded contracts, as executable assertions derived from a specification, provide a mechanism to detect faults before they provoke a failure. We analyze the initial reliability of a system, tested using mutation analysis, and the robustness reached by a system using contractable components versus no contractable ones.

Let C_i, $i \in [1..n]$ be the n components of a system.

Let F_i^0, the initial failure rate (after validation steps), i.e., the probability that a failure occurs in the component in the next statement execution. The initial reliability R_i^0 of the component is thus: $R_i^0 = 1 - F_i^0$

In a mutation analysis approach, the test cases have been executed against all the mutant programs. Recall that we consider a component as an organic set of a specification (contracts), an implementation and the embedded test sets. A component has a good behavior if its tests are able to detect failure coming from the implementation. So, the number of killed mutants represents a number of successful behavior of the component, since the known injected faults have been successfully detected by the selftest. To measure the initial reliability, the assumption is the following: we assume that if a new test case is executed, then a failure will certainly occur. With such an assumption if the number of statements executed before the faulty code is infected is $Nstat_i$, then the initial failure probability is $F_i^0 = 1/Nstat_i$.

In this paper, we estimate $Nstat_i$ by multiplying the number of statements executed in the correct program by the number of killed mutants. It provides a satisfying approximation of the number of executed statements. So we have: $Nstat_i \cong \#killed\_mutants_i \times K_i$, where K is the number of statements executed by the test set on the program.

The global initial reliability of a system composed of n components can thus be estimated in two ways depending on fault independence assumption. First, we can approximate the reliability by considering that failure events occurring in the system are independent. With such a (pessimistic) assumption, the initial reliability R^0 of a system is equal to : $R^0 = \prod_{i=1}^{n} R_i^0$.

Another consideration would lead to a more realistic model, by considering that one statement will be executed at a time (indeed this no more true for parallel and distributed software). Under that optimistic assumption, we have the following initial reliability and failure rate:

$$R^0 = 1 - F^0 = 1 - \frac{1}{\sum_{i=1}^{n} Nstat_i} = 1 - \frac{1}{\sum_{i=1}^{n} \frac{1}{F_i^0}}$$

Both models provide boundaries of the initial reliability and failure rates.

Independently of the way these factors are measured, the robustness Rob_i of a component C_i is defined here as the probability that a fault is detected, assuming that this fault would provoke a failure if not detected by a contract or an equivalent mechanism. Conversely, the "weakness" $Weak_i$ of the component is equal to the probability that the fault is not detected. This probability corresponds to the percentage of faults detected by contracts. Indeed, if the component has been designed by contracts, then the detected fault can be retrieved, and a mechanism (such as exception handling and processing) will prevent a failure to occur. In the case of a component C_i with no contracts, its robustness is equal to 0: $Rob_i = 1 - Weak_i = 0$.

A component isolated from the system has a basic robustness corresponding to the strength of its embedded contracts. A component plugged into a system has robustness enhanced by the fact that its clients will add their contracts to the fault detection. The notion of Test Dependency is thus introduced for determining the relation between a component and its client and heirs in a system.

Test dependency : A component class C_i is *test-dependent* from C_j if it uses some objects from C_j or inherits from C_j. This dependency relation is noted:

$$C_i \, R_{TD} \, C_j$$

If $C_i \, R_{TD} \, C_j$, then the probability that C_i contracts detect a fault due to C_j is noted Det_j^i. To estimate this probability, one can use the proportion of mutants detected by C_i while C_j is infected. Even though the test dependency relation is transitive, we only consider faults that are detected by a components directly dependent from the faulty one.

The robustness $Rob\_intoS_i (= 1 - Weak\_intoS_i)$ of the component into the system S –and so enhanced by the client components contracts- is thus :

$$Rob\_intoS_i = 1 - (Weak_i \cdot \prod_k (1 - Det_i^k)), \quad k / C_k \, R_{TD} \, C_i$$

Finally, the robustness Rob of the system is thus equal to:

$$Rob = 1 - Weak = 1 - \sum_{i=1}^{n} Prob\_failure(i) \times Weak\_intoS_i$$

where *Prob_failure(i)* is the probability the failure comes from the component C_i knowing that a failure certainly occurs. This probability is approximated by the component's complexity.

To conclude, considering that a fault detected by a contract allows the service continuity, the initial reliability of the system is also enhanced as follows: $R_{new}^0 = 1 - F_{new}^0 = 1 - (F^0 \cdot Weak) = R^0 + F^0 \cdot Rob$.

Fixing the values

The parameters of this model of robustness and initial reliability are easily fixed using mutation analysis.

$R_i^0 = 1 - F_i^0$ with $F_i^0 = 1/Nstat_i$

$Rob_i = 1 - Weak_i =$ percentage of mutants detected by contracts.

$Det_i^j =$ percentage of mutants in C_j detected by C_i contracts.

$Prob\_failure(i) = 1/n$

Illustration

To estimate (roughly) the gain in robustness of a system, we consider the SMDS system composed of 37 components, already studied in [7] for optimizing integration testing. Here, we apply our robustness estimator for this system. The detailed model is not needed to understand the application to robustness. We fix the values as follows to appraise the global improvement in robustness of the system due to a systematic use of contracts:

$Rob_i = 1 - Weak_i = 0.85$, $Det_i^j = 0.7$ and $Prob\_failure(i) = 1/n = 1/37$.

As a mean estimator, we consider that a test case is composed of mean 100 tests and that 200 mutants are generated for each of the component. A test approximately executes 10 statements.

The initial failure rate of the system composed of 37 components is thus equal to $F^0 = 1.35 \cdot 10^{-7}$.

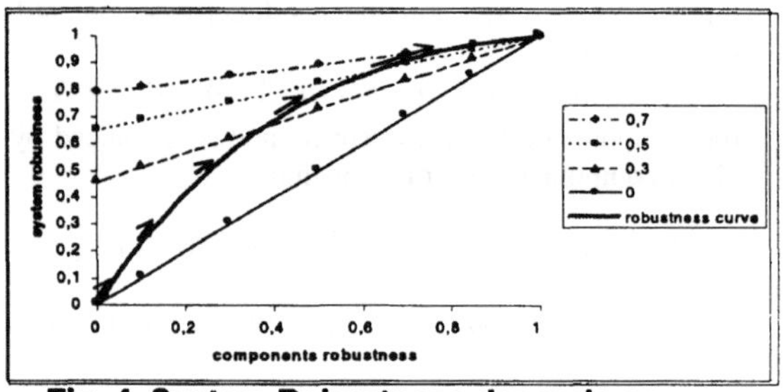

Fig. 4. System Robustness depends on Components Robustness

Figure 4 first shows four evolutions of the SMDS system robustness depending on the components robustness. The four curves correspond to four different Det_i^j values. This figure shows that contracts, by enhancing a component's robustness and by enhancing the Det_i^j value, improve the global system's robustness.

Since it is obvious that a relationship exists between Det_i^j and the robustness, the figure 4 also displays the "robustness curve". To draw this curve, we have considered that Det_i^j is related to the robustness by a linear function such as: $Det_i^j = K \cdot Rob$. Here we have taken K equal to 0.8. So this curve really corresponds to the real global robustness evolution: during the development phase, the programmer will start with basic weak contracts and then enhance them. So during this period, the robustness of components and Det_i^j will grow together and so will the system's robustness.

7. Conclusion

The feasibility of components validation by mutation analysis and its utility to test generation have been studied as well has the robustness of trustable and self-testable components into an infected environment. The approach presented in this paper aims at providing a consistent framework for building trust into components. By measuring the quality of test cases (the revealing power of the test cases [12]) we seek to build trust in a component passing those test cases. The analysis also shows that a design-by-contract approach associated to the notion of embedded selftest significantly improves the robustness, and indirectly the reliability, of a final-product.

References

[1] R. DeMillo, R. Lipton, and F. Sayward, "Hints on Test Data Selection : Help For The Practicing Programmer", *IEEE Computer*, Vol. 11, pp. 34-41, 1978.

[2] D. E. Goldberg, "Genetic Algorithms in Search, Optimization and Machine Learning", Addison Wesley, 1989. ISBN 0-201-15767-5.

[3] J. H. Holland, "Robust algorithms for adaptation set in general formal framework", Proceedings of the 1970 IEEE symposium on adaptive processes (9th) decision and control, 5.1 –5.5, December 1970.

[4] William E. Howden and Yudong Huang, "Software Trustability", In proc. of the IEEE Symposium on Adaptive processes- Decision and Control, XVII, 5.1-5.5, 1970.

[5] J-M. Jézéquel, M. Train and C. Mingins, "Design-Patterns and Contract" Addison-Wesley, October 1999. ISBN 0-201-30959-9.

[6] Yves Le Traon, Daniel Deveaux and Jean-Marc Jézéquel, "Self-testable components: from pragmatic tests to a design-for-testability methodology", In proc. of TOOLS-Europe'99, TOOLS, Nancy (France), pp. 96-107, June 1999.

[7] Yves Le Traon, Thierry Jéron, Jean-Marc Jézéquel and Pierre Morel, "Efficient OO Integration and Regression Testing", *IEEE Transactions on Reliability*, March 2000.

[8] M. Lyu, "Handbook of Software Reliability Engineering", McGraw Hill and IEEE Computer Society Press, 1996, ISBN 0-07-0349400-8.

[9] J. D. Musa, A. Iannino, K. Okumoto, "Software Reliability: Measurement, Prediction, Application", McGraw Hill, 1987, ISBN 0-07-044093-X.

[10] B. Meyer, "Applying design by contract", *IEEE Computer*, Vol. 25, No. 10, pp. 40-52, October 1992.

[11] J. Offutt, J. Pan, K. Tewary and T. Zhang, "An experimental evaluation of data flow and mutation testing", *Software Practice and Experience*, Vol. 26, No. 2, pp. 165-176, February 1996.

[12] J. Voas, "PIE: A Dynamic Failure-Based Technique", *IEEE Transactions on Software Engineering*, Vol.18, pp. 717-727, 1992.

Parallel Firm Mutation of Java Programs

David Jackson and Martin R. Woodward
Computer Science Department,
University of Liverpool,
Chadwick Building, Peach Street,
Liverpool L69 7ZF, U.K.

Email: {d.jackson, m.r.woodward}@csc.liv.ac.uk

Abstract

Firm mutation was introduced as an intermediate form of mutation testing representing the middle ground between weak and strong mutation. In firm mutation, components may be groups of statements and partial program executions may be considered rather than each separate component execution as in weak mutation or the complete program execution as in strong mutation. Despite its flexibility and its potential for combining the reduced expense of weak mutation with the greater transparency of strong mutation, firm mutation has remained largely unexplored. One of the difficulties with firm mutation is that there has been no obvious systematic basis on which to select the areas of program code as candidates for firm mutation testing. The advent of object-oriented languages has, in a sense, provided a natural solution to this problem. The individual methods that form part of object classes tend to be small but cohesive components that lend themselves ideally to firm mutation. This paper considers such application of firm mutation to Java methods by exploiting the use of Java threads to perform mutant execution. The potential parallelism that this affords is another factor in the cost reduction envisaged.

Keywords: Firm mutation, object-oriented methods, Java threads, parallelism.

1. Introduction

Mutation testing has been perceived as computationally expensive ever since its first introduction [7, 12]. This may account, in part, for its poor uptake outside the realms of academia. A major factor in the cost is the sheer number of mutant versions of the program under test that could be generated, each of which then needs executing to completion with a number of test cases. It has been suggested that for a program with n statements that the number of mutants is $O(n^2)$ and if a proposed test set contains k test cases the number of program executions could be $O(k \times n^2)$ [13].

One of the earliest suggestions for lessening the computational impact of mutation testing was to demand that a mutant program component gives a different outcome from its corresponding original program component *on at least one execution* of that component [13]. This form of mutation testing was labelled 'weak mutation' and henceforth the original form became known as 'strong mutation'. By focussing on components at a fine level of granularity, e.g. variable references and variable definitions, and requiring that just one execution of such a mutated component gives a different outcome from the component it replaces, several advantages ensue. First it is often possible to determine *in advance* the necessary conditions for such a difference in outcome, meaning that the actual mutant may not need to be physically created. Secondly a number of such mutants can be considered in the *same* program execution. These advantages must be balanced against the disadvantage of the weaker conclusions that can be drawn from such testing.

Following on from the weak mutation notion of, in effect, altering low-level components for just one execution, it became apparent that the following could be considered: (1) bigger program components; and (2) partial executions that are more than a single statement execution, but less than the complete program execution. This intermediate ground between strong mutation and weak mutation has been termed 'firm mutation' [24]. However, its benefits or otherwise still remain largely unexplored.

Weak and firm mutation both aim to make the mutation idea more tractable by altering the parameters of the strong mutation process. A whole variety of other techniques have been suggested which preserve the strong mutation concept but seek either more efficient ways of applying it or more efficient means of implementing it. Work in the first of these two categories includes: selective mutation [18, 20, 21]; ordered mutation [8]; and parameterized mutation [9]. Work in the second category, i.e. more efficient implementations, includes: exploitation of parallel and other novel machine architectures [3, 4, 16, 17]; utilisation of close compiler co-operation to introduce object-level patches [6]; encoding of all mutants in one meta-mutant version [22]; and improvements to the existing serial algorithms [10, 23].

One of the attractions of the mutation approach to testing is that it is a generic technique that can be applied to all languages and language paradigms. Despite this fact, most of the work that has been undertaken on mutation has involved high-level imperative languages such as Fortran [5, 15], C [1] and Pascal [22]. Exceptions to this include work on mutation of specifications in predicate logic [2], in an algebraic form [25] and in the form of UML state diagrams [26].

This paper describes work in progress aimed at moving mutation testing forward in three ways simultaneously.

1. *Object-oriented target language.* As just discussed the principal applications of mutation testing to date, have been to imperative languages. It seems timely therefore to apply the ideas to a modern and widespread object-oriented language, namely Java. It is noted that recently a Java mutation operator set has been proposed by Kim *et al.* [14].
2. *Parallelism.* The target language contains built-in features for multiple threads of execution that can be utilised for concurrent execution of mutants.
3. *Firm mutation.* It is intended to be a practical application of the firm mutation concept so that the benefits or otherwise of this particular mutation regime can be determined.

Besides having these three research directions, the principal aims of the intended approach, as far as the user is concerned, are flexibility and efficiency.

The rest of the paper is organised as follows. Section 2 briefly reviews the nature and status of firm mutation testing. Section 3 outlines the proposed system for mutation of Java and illustrates the system by means of an example. Finally, Section 4 makes some concluding remarks and provides pointers to future work.

2. Firm Mutation

Firm mutation [24] was proposed as an intermediate form of mutation testing between the two extremes of strong and weak mutation. The essential idea is to focus on some program component and introduce a mutant change to that component at some point t_{change} in the execution of the program. Then at point t_{undo} in program execution, the effect of executing the mutated component over the designated slice of execution time is compared with the effect of executing the original version of the component over the same time slice. The precise nature of what is compared, e.g. program output, defined variables, etc, can have a significant impact on whether the mutant is deemed to be 'live' or 'dead' and the decision over what comparison mechanism should be used is considered to be part of the firm mutation process. When t_{change} and t_{undo} are respectively immediately before and immediately after each single execution of some fine-grained component such as variable reference or variable definition, the mutation regime described corresponds to weak mutation. When t_{change} and t_{undo} correspond to the start and end of the whole program execution, the mutation regime corresponds to strong mutation.

The original paper on firm mutation discussed the practical considerations of how such a mechanism could be implemented. Basically two approaches were envisaged.

1. *Parallel execution.* A copy of the original component that incorporates the mutant change is made and this mutant copy can then be executed in parallel with the original non-mutated component. On exit from the component a rendezvous is required to enable comparison of outcomes.
2. *Sequential execution.* The state of the program at t_{change} is stored and the mutant component is executed until t_{undo} is reached whereupon the result is saved. Reverse execution is then performed, by restoring the state as it was at t_{change}, and the original non-mutated component is executed. On arrival at t_{undo}, the result of the original component needs to be compared with the saved result of the mutated component.

In both approaches the execution can proceed normally after t_{undo} and further mutation changes could be countenanced in the same program run. Detailed plans were made for incorporating firm mutation using the sequential approach of saving and restoring the state in an interpreted and highly interactive environment called GRIPSE [11]. The GRIPSE project successfully utilised a uniform graphical view for the development of Pascal programs, but the project terminated before a full implementation of the firm mutation aspect could be achieved. The current work results from a renewed attempt to discover the potential of the firm mutation approach.

In their work on the empirical evaluation of weak mutation testing, Offutt and Lee [19] in effect developed a firm mutation system. The Leonardo system, which was based on the earlier Mothra system [5, 15], incorporated four variants of weak mutation with comparison of states: (1) after the first execution of the innermost expression surrounding the mutant; (2) after the first execution of the mutated statement; (3) after the first execution of the basic block containing the mutant; and (4) after each execution of the basic block containing the mutant. The last three variants can be considered as an application of firm mutation with point t_{change} fixed to be the start of program execution.

One of the problems envisaged with firm mutation in the GRIPSE project, was the development of a strategy for selection of appropriate components as targets for firm mutation. A scheme was devised for identification of coherent code fragments which were likened to *headerless procedures* capable of being encapsulated in a `begin...end` block for which the inputs and outputs could be determined by data flow considerations. With the advent of object-oriented languages such as C++ and Java, the methods that form part of object classes make natural, coherent, and often small, code fragments that are ideally suited to firm mutation. What is more, the notion of 'threads' in Java permits the possibility of implementation based on the first approach identified above, i.e. parallel execution of mutant and original components. The following section explains in more detail how this can be achieved.

3. Mutation of Java

The process of creating multiple mutations of a Java program involves the translation of the original code to a form incorporating a number of threads of control running in parallel. Although the system for effecting this is still under development we can still describe this translation process in some detail, showing how it applies to example programs.

Execution of the proposed system proceeds in three main stages:

1. *Mutant specification.* The system offers a view of the program code, and enables a user to select where and in what ways the code is to be mutated. During this phase, the user also specifies the elements that are to be compared by the system in determining whether mutants are dead or alive.
2. *Mutant generation.* Based on the user's specification, the system creates mutant versions of the appropriate object methods. Each mutant exists as a separately executing thread of control, running in parallel with the original, unmodified code.
3. *Comparison and reporting.* Once all the mutant threads have terminated, the system examines the results produced and compares them with those generated in the original method in order to discover which mutants have been killed.

To understand how these work, suppose we have a program that has the following outline:

```
class TestApp {

  static int f(...) {
    ...
  }

  public static void main(String [] args) {
    ...
    x = f(...);  // make call to f()
    ...
  }
}
```

In the first phase, the user might specify several mutations of the method `f()`. The subsequent stage would then use this information to create a new class for each mutant:

```
class Mutant extends Thread {

  public Mutant(...) {
      // Constructor to make local copy of
      // args to f
      ...
  }

  private static int f(...) {
     // Mutated version of f
     ...
  }

  public void run() {
     // Execute mutant and store result
     ...
  }
}
```

This new class, here called `Mutant`, extends the `Thread` class and is thus capable of running in parallel with the original code. As well as holding the mutated version of the method `f`, it also holds a constructor method, which creates local copies of the arguments to `f` when it is invoked, and a `run()` method, used to start execution of the thread and to record the results produced by the mutated method.

At the point in the program where the call to `f()` is made, the system inserts a number of additional statements, as can be seen in the program outline below.

```
class TestApp {

  static int f(...) {
    ...
  }

  private static void compare(...) {
    // Function to compare results of
    // original and mutant
    ...
  }


  public static void main(String [] args) {
    ...
    // Create threads
    Mutant1 mutThread1 = new Mutant1(...);
    Mutant2 mutThread2 = new Mutant2(...);
    // and so on for all threads
```

```
        // Now start threads running
        mutThread1.start();
        mutThread2.start();
        ...

        // make call to f(), as before
        x = f(...);

        // Wait for threads to finish
        try { mutThread1.join();
              mutThread2.join();
        }
        catch (InterruptedException e) {
              // Handle exception
        }
        ...
        // Now compare results
        compare(...);
        ...
    }
}
```

Firstly, the altered code creates a new thread for each function by calling the constructor methods, passing to them precisely the same arguments that will be passed in the call to `f()`. Next, it calls the `start()` method of each thread. This allocates necessary memory, initializes the thread and then calls the `run()` method shown in the Mutant class earlier. The `run()` method in turn calls the mutated version of `f()`, passing across the local copy of `f`'s arguments. Once all mutant threads have begun execution, the call to `f()` proper can be made, to run concurrently with the mutants.

When the call to `f()` has completed, comparison cannot proceed until all the mutant threads have finished executing; this is achieved by calling their `join()` methods. Finally, the results produced by each thread can be compared with those of the original code. The system implements this by generating and calling a new `compare()` method, tailored according to the number and types of the data items being compared.

A more specific example of the system's use is in relation to the small program shown below. It is an adaptation of an example originally used by DeMillo *et al.* [7].

```
class MaxOrig {

  static int max (int [] a, int n) {
    int r = 0;
    for (int i = 1; i < n; i++)
        if (a[i] > a[r])
            r = i;
    return r;
  }

  public static void main(String [] args) {
    int [] test1 = {0,1,2};
    int size = 3;
    int maxindex;

    System.out.print("Array= "+test1[0]
           +' '+test1[1]+' '+test1[2]);
    maxindex = max(test1,size);
    System.out.println("\tMax element="
                             + maxindex);
  }
}
```

This program finds the first occurrence of the largest element in a vector of integers, and prints out the index of that element. In using our system to experiment with various mutations of the `max()` method, the user might, say, specify that the '>' operator in the predicate '`if (a[i] > a[r])`' be changed to a '>=' operator, and that the mutant be declared dead or alive according to the value returned by `max()`. In that case, the new version of the program generated by our system would then look as follows:

```
class Mutant extends Thread {

  private int [] thisa;
  private int thisn;
  public int res;

  public Mutant(int [] acopy, int ncopy) {
    thisa = acopy;
    thisn = ncopy;
  }

  private static int max (int[] a, int n) {
    int r = 0;
    for (int i = 1; i < n; i++)
        if (a[i] >= a[r])
            r = i;
    return r;
  }


  public void run() {
     res=max(thisa,thisn);
  }
}

public class MaxOrigMut1 {
  static int max (int [] a, int n) {
    int r = 0;
    for (int i = 1; i < n; i++)
        if (a[i] > a[r])
            r = i;
    return r;
  }

  private static void compare(int m1,
                              int m2) {
    if (m1 != m2)
         System.out.println(
                    "\nMutant 1 Dead");
    else System.out.println(
                    "\nMutant 1 Alive");
  }
```

```
public static void main(String [] args) {
    int [] test1 = {0,1,2};
    int size = 3;
    int maxindex;
    System.out.print("Array= "+test1[0]
              +' '+test1[1]+' '+test1[2]);
    Mutant mutThread =
                    new Mutant(test1,size);
    mutThread.start();
    maxindex = max(test1,size);
    try { mutThread.join();
    }
    catch (InterruptedException e) {
          System.out.println(e);
    }
    compare(maxindex,mutThread.res);
    System.out.println("\tMax element="
                               + maxindex);
  }
}
```

The role of most of the code shown above should be apparent from our previous discussion. Although here it simply prints out whether a mutant remains dead or alive after execution, this could be altered to perform more sophisticated actions.

All of the above pre-supposes that a mutated method makes no changes to the state space of other objects; in practice, of course, things may not be as straightforward. Consider the following program outline:

```
class SomeObj {
  public SomeObj(...) {
    // Constructor
    ...
    z = 0;
  }

  public void addone() {
    ++z;
  }

  private int z;
}

class TestApp {
  static int f(SomeObj any) {
    ...
    any.addone();
  }

  public static void main(String [] args) {
    ...
    // create new object
    SomeObj obj = new SomeObj(...);
    ...
    // make call to f()
    x = f(obj);
    ...
  }
}
```

Suppose, as before, that `f()` is the method to be mutated. The problem arising now is that it is not sufficient merely to make a mutated copy of `f()`, because then both threads will update the state variable `z` defined in the `SomeObj` class. To solve this, the mutant must be able to operate on its own private version of `obj`, and this must have an internal state that is identical to the original. To ensure this, we must clone the internal state of `obj` at the time `f()` is called. However, a more general problem is that class attributes tend to be marked as private to the class. Our solution is to introduce a couple of extra methods to the class of the object to be cloned: one which moves the state space into public variables, and another which works in the opposite direction. Hence, for the code above, the output of our system might be as follows:

```
class SomeObj {

  public SomeObj(...) {
    // Constructor
    ...
    z = 0;
  }

  public void addone() {
    ++z;
  }

  private int z;

  public int zstate;

  public void getstate() {
    zstate = z;
  }

  public void putstate() {
    z = zstate;
  }

}

class TestApp {

  static int f(SomeObj any) {
    ...
    any.addone();
  }

  public static void main(String [] args) {
    ...
    // create new object
    SomeObj obj = new SomeObj(...);

    // create duplicate
    SomeObj obj2 = new SomeObj(...);
    ...
    // make state vars public
    obj.getstate();

    // copy state vars to duplicate
    obj2.zstate = obj.zstate;
```

```
        // update state vars of duplicate
        obj2.putstate();

        //create mutant to act on duplicate
        Mutant mutThread = new Mutant(obj2);
        MutThread.start();

        x = f(obj);   // make call to f()
        ...
    }
}
```

Clearly, the analysis required to determine which objects require cloning is fairly demanding, and in the worst case it may be necessary to clone everything. However, the approach does allow us to cope with any number of mutations of any method. Moreover, it is no more difficult to cope with multiple mutations of other methods within the same program. All mutations simply co-exist as independently executing Java threads, created as and when calls to the original methods are made.

4. Conclusions

We have described in some detail in this paper the translation process associated with a proposed system for firm mutation testing of Java programs. By concentrating on mutations to individual methods within such an object-oriented language we attain a level of focus that has been shown to be capable of providing insights into test data adequacy that are not always revealed by the extremes of weak and strong mutation. Moreover, by using Java threads to encapsulate each of the mutants of a program we pave the way to executing these mutants in parallel, thereby offering the potential for drastically reducing the computation time required. As with any thread-based solution, of course, execution on appropriate multi-processor architectures would be necessary for these gains to be realised.

As already mentioned, the proposed system is currently under construction. Once it is complete we aim to do some performance measurement and analysis. In particular, it will be important to discover the extent to which the need to save and restore object states will affect the efficiency of the approach.

We already have in mind a number of ways in which we hope to extend the project in the future. One next step we are considering is to further the firm mutation theme by introducing the ability to select code fragments that are even smaller than complete methods, and then encapsulate these fragments in their own threads. Another objective is to investigate the ways in which we can exploit the Internet: Java was always intended as a network programming language, and it will be interesting to see how well this facilitates making our parallel mutation system truly distributed.

References

[1] Agrawal, H., DeMillo, R.A., Hathaway, R., Hsu, Wm., Hsu, W., Krauser, E., Martin, R.J., Mathur, A. and Spafford, E., 'Design of mutant operators for the C programming language', Technical Report SERC-TR-41-P, Software Engineering Research Center, Purdue University (March 1989).

[2] Budd, T.A. and Gopal, A.S., "Program testing by specification mutation", *Computer Languages*, **10**(1), 63-73 (1985).

[3] Choi, B.J. and Mathur, A.P., "High performance mutation testing", *Journal of Systems and Software*, **20**(2), 135-152 (Feb. 1993).

[4] Choi, B.J., Mathur, A.P. and Pattison, B., "pMothra: scheduling mutants for execution on a hypercube", *Proc. ACM SIGSOFT '89 Third Symp. on Software Testing, Analysis and Verification (TAV3)*, Key West, FL, U.S.A., ACM Press, pp. 58-65 (Dec. 1989).

[5] DeMillo, R.A., Guindi, D.S., McCracken, W.M., Offutt, A.J. and King, K.N., "An extended overview of the Mothra software testing environment", *Proc. Second Workshop on Software Testing, Verification and Analysis*, Banff, Canada, IEEE Computer Society Press, pp. 142-151 (July 1988).

[6] DeMillo, R.A., Krauser, E.W. and Mathur, A.P., "An approach to compiler-integrated software testing", Technical Report SERC-TR-71-P, Software Engineering Research Center, Purdue University (April 1990).

[7] DeMillo, R.A., Lipton, R.J. and Sayward, F.G., "Hints on test data selection: help for the practicing programmer", *IEEE Computer*, **11**(4), 34-41 (April 1978).

[8] Duncan, I.M.M. and Robson, D.J., "Ordered mutation testing", *ACM SigSoft Software Engineering Notes*, **15**(2), 29-30 (April 1990).

[9] Duncan, I.M.M. and Robson, D.J., "Parametrized mutation testing", *Software Testing, Verification and Reliability*, **1**(4), 3-16 (Jan.-March 1992).

[10] Fleyshgakker, V.N. and Weiss, S.N., "Efficient mutation analysis: a new approach", *Proc. Int. Symp. on Software Testing and Analysis (ISSTA '94)*, Seattle, WA, U.S.A., ACM Press, pp. 185-195 (Aug. 1994).

[11] Halewood, K. and Woodward, M.R., "A uniform graphical view of the program construction process: GRIPSE", *Int. Journal of Man-Machine Studies*, **38**(5), 805-837 (May 1993).

[12] Hamlet, R.G., "Testing programs with the aid of a compiler", *IEEE Trans. Soft. Eng.*, **3**(4), 279-290 (July 1977).

[13] Howden, W.E., "Weak mutation testing and completeness of test sets", *IEEE Trans. Soft. Eng.*, **8**(4), 371-379 (July 1982).

[14] Kim, S., Clark, J.A. and McDermid, J.A., "The rigorous generation of Java mutation operators using HAZOP", *Proc. 12th Int. Conf. on Software & Systems Engineering and their Applications (ICSSEA '99)*, Paris, France (Dec. 1999).

[15] King, K.N. and Offutt, A.J., "A Fortran language system for mutation-based software testing", *Software – Practice and Experience*, **21**(7), 685-718 (July 1991).

[16] Krauser, E.W., Mathur, A.P. and Rego, V.J. "High performance software testing on SIMD machines", *IEEE Trans. Soft. Eng.*, **17**(5), 403-423 (May 1991).

[17] Mathur, A.P. and Krauser, E.W., "Modeling mutation on a vector processor", *Proc. 10th Int. Conf. on Software Engineering (ICSE-10)*, Singapore, IEEE Computer Society Press, pp. 154-161 (April 1988).

[18] Mresa, E.S. and Bottaci, L., "Efficiency of mutation operators and selective mutation strategies: an empirical study", *Software Testing, Verification and Reliability*, **9**(4), 205-232 (Dec. 1999).

[19] Offutt, A.J. and Lee, S.D., "An empirical evaluation of weak mutation", *IEEE Trans. Soft. Eng.*, **20**(5), 337-344 (May 1994).

[20] Offutt, A.J., Lee, A., Rothermel, G., Untch, R.H. and Zapf, C., "An experimental determination of sufficient mutant operators", *ACM Trans. on Software Engineering and Methodology*, **5**(2), 99-118 (April 1996).

[21] Offutt, A.J., Rothermel, G. and Zapf, C., "An experimental evaluation of selective mutation", *Proc. 15th Int. Conf. on Software Engineering (ICSE-15)*, Baltimore, MD, U.S.A., IEEE Computer Society Press, pp. 100-107 (May 1993).

[22] Untch, R., Offutt, A.J. and Harrold, M.J., "Mutation analysis using mutant schemata", *Proc. Int. Symp. on Software Testing and Analysis (ISSTA '93)*, Cambridge, MA, U.S.A., ACM Press, pp. 139148 (June 1993).

[23] Weiss, S.N. and Fleyshgakker, V.N., "Improved serial algorithms for mutation analysis", *Proc. Int. Symp. on Software Testing and Analysis (ISSTA '93)*, Cambridge, MA, U.S.A., ACM Press, pp. 149-158 (June 1993).

[24] Woodward, M.R. and Halewood, K., "From weak to strong, dead or alive? An analysis of some mutation testing issues", *Proc. Second Workshop on Software Testing, Verification and Analysis*, Banff, Canada, IEEE Computer Society Press, pp. 152-158 (July 1988).

[25] Woodward, M.R., "Errors in algebraic specifications and an experimental mutation testing tool", *Software Engineering Journal*, **8**(4), 211-224 (July 1993).

[26] Yoon, H., Choi, B. and Jeon, J.-O., "Mutation-based inter-class testing", *Proc. 1998 Asia Pacific Soft. Eng. Conf.*, IEEE Computer Society Press, pp. 174-181 (Dec. 1998).

Theoretical Insights into the Coupling Effect

K. S. How Tai Wah
CSSE
School of Computing, Information Systems and Mathematics
South Bank University
London SE1 0AA
howtair@sbu.ac.uk

Abstract

It is shown that there is indeed a coupling effect such that a test set that kills all first-order mutants would prove able to kill the great majority of higher-order mutants too. The basis of the approach is that programs are modelled as compositions of finite functions, the domain of which is assumed to be large.

A heuristic approach is adopted, and attention is focused on the various insights into the nature of the coupling effect revealed by such an approach. These insights are helpful in determining in a rough-and-ready fashion whether the testing is as effective in killing higher-order mutants as one would wish.
Key Words / Phrases : *coupling effect, single-fault (multi-fault) alternate, proper test set, survival ratio, fault size, domain-to-range ratio (DRR).*

1 Introduction

The *coupling effect hypothesis* plays a crucial role in mutation testing [1, 2, 6]. It asserts that a test set that kills all first-order mutants would prove able to kill all higher-order mutants as well; it therefore provides justification for the usual focus of mutation testing on first-order mutants. There is strong empirical support for the hypothesis [7, 8]; however, while most higher-order mutants do get killed, a few manage to survive.

The present paper, for its part, provides strong theoretical support for the hypothesis. It is based on two other papers [4, 5], which together demonstrate that there is indeed an approximate coupling effect operating in such a manner that only a very small proportion of higher-order mutants would be expected to survive a mutation-adequate test set (one that kills all first-order mutants).

This is not quite the whole story, however. The aim of mutation testing is to ensure that all mutants, whether first-order or higher-order, are killed; the focus on first-order mutants is primarily due to a lack of resources. The fact that some higher-order mutants manage to survive is therefore an adverse reflection on the reliability of the program being tested. This suggests that there is some kind of link between software reliability and the number of higher-order mutants surviving detection; the fewer the number of such mutants, the more reliable the testing, and vice versa.

Different programs have different testing requirements. For instance, a program designed for a safety critical system needs to be tested more stringently than the ordinary run of programs. It is probably not enough in such a case to simply assume that a coupling effect operates to such good effect that the great majority of higher-order mutants get killed; one would also like to be assured that the number of surviving mutants is appropriately small. It is thus of vital importance, when testing a program, to obtain an estimate of the number of higher-order mutants likely to survive.

The present paper attempts to do precisely that within the context of a simple, but not unrealistic, model. The basis of the approach is to model programs as compositions of finite functions, each of which is susceptible to one or more faults; the number of functions q can be large, but it must be small relative to n, the size of the underlying domain. The approach is probabilistic: all possible combinations of compositions, faults and test sets are to be taken into account when solving the model.

The solution of the model for values of q greater than 3 involves mathematical computations of great complexity. A more heuristic approach is adopted in this paper; this consists in the formulation of simple rules for dealing with the various cases of interest. While heuristic arguments are sometimes advanced in support of these rules, no attempt will be made to prove them here; however such proofs can be found in the two papers mentioned above. One great advantage of the heuristic approach is that the rules can be applied to the general q-function model, where q is arbitrary. It is worth adding that the rules are only valid to leading order in n; this requires not only that n be large, but also that q be small relative to n.

The coupling effect is said to be strong if few higher-order mutants survive, and weak otherwise. It will be shown that the strength of the coupling effect depends on a number of factors : the number of test data, whether test outputs are distinct or identical, and whether each test data kills few or many of the first-order mutants. Though these results are derived within the context of a simple theoretical model, it is argued that they are applicable to practical programs too, if only qualitatively; the heuristic approach turns out to be particularly helpful in the transition from model to reality.

Three main cases will be considered. Test sets of order 1 are dealt with in section 3, *efficient test sets* of order 2 (those in which each of the test data individually kills all the first-order mutants) in section 4, and other types of test sets of order 2 in section 5; the treatment of test sets of order 2 covers both distinct and identical outputs. The discussion is quantitative in the first two cases, but only qualitative in the third case.

It is worth noting that, though only test sets of order 1 and 2 are considered in this paper, there is no difficulty in principle in generalising to test sets of order r, though the heuristic rules do require that r be much less than n. The picture that emerges can be described qualitatively as follows. Test sets are efficacious to the extent that each test data kills as many first-order mutants as possible and that test outputs are distinct; it is also advantageous if test data kill more or less equal numbers of first-order mutants.

These general conclusions follow more or less directly from the model. It is possible, however, to go some way beyond the model and arrive at qualitative conclusions about specific programs and test sets. In particular, it is argued in section 6 that the coupling effect is stronger if faults are small in size and the program is close to being bijective (other things remaining equal).

2 Description of the Model

The *q-function model* is now introduced; this is a fairly straightforward generalisation of the simple model studied in a previous paper [3]. In the latter, programs were viewed as compositions of just two functions; the generalisation is to compositions of q functions, where q can be large. The domain N consists of n points, which are denoted by $0, \ldots, n-1$; there are thus n^n functions in all.

Consider the following composition of q functions (the convention is that function application proceeds from right to left) :

$$f_{ts \ldots ji} = f_t \circ f_s \ldots f_j \circ f_i$$

where $f_i, \ldots, f_t$ are functions from N to N. It is assumed that each function in the composition is susceptible to just one fault; the case where there are more than one fault per function is briefly treated elsewhere [4]. There are then q *single-fault alternates* (first-order mutants); the one with the fault in the first function is denoted thus :

$$f_{t \ldots ji'} = f_t \circ \ldots \circ f_j \circ f_{i'}$$

where the location of the fault is indicated by the prime. There are $q(q-1)/2$ *double-fault alternates* (second-order mutants), the one with the faults in the first two functions being denoted by :

$$f_{t \ldots j'i'} = f_t \circ \ldots \circ f_{j'} \circ f_{i'}$$

There are also $q(q-1)(q-2)/6$ *triple-fault alternates* (third-order mutants), ..., and one *q-fault alternate.* Note the change in terminology from 'mutant' to 'alternate' when discussing the model.

A *test situation* is defined to be the set consisting of the correct function (i.e., the original composition) and its various faulty alternates; it is most conveniently denoted by $[f_t, \ldots, f_i, f_{t'}, \ldots, f_{i'}]$. A *proper test set* is one that kills all the single-fault alternates; it is thus the equivalent of a mutation-adequate test set. The question arises as to whether such a test set would be able to kill all the multi-fault alternates as well; it will probably succeed in some cases, but fail in others. In view of this, a probabilistic approach seems the most reasonable one to adopt; in other words, it is proposed that one take an average over all the possible cases, i.e., over all compositions, faults and test sets (of a specific size or type).

The case of test sets of order 1 is considered in some detail to illustrate the discussion. The total number of proper test cases, as one ranges over all the different possibilities, is formally given by (the superscript indicates the size of the test set, and the subscript the number of functions in the composition) :

$$P^1_q(n) = \sum \rho(t, \ldots, i, t', \ldots, i', a)$$

where the single summation sign actually stands proxy for the following set of summations :

$$\sum \equiv \sum_{t=0}^{n^n-1} \cdots \sum_{i=0}^{n^n-1} \sum_{t'=0}^{n^n-1} \cdots \sum_{i'=0}^{n^n-1} \sum_{a=0}^{n-1}$$

and $\rho(t, \ldots, i, t', \ldots, i', a)$ is 1 or 0 according as to whether $\{a\}$ is a proper test set for the test situation $[f_t, \ldots, f_i, f_{t'}, \ldots, f_{i'}]$ or not. The total number of test cases in which the double-fault alternate $f_{t \ldots kj'i'}$ survives is similarly given by :

$$S^1_{t \ldots j'i'}(n) = \sum \sigma_{t \ldots j'i'}(t, \ldots, i, t', \ldots, i', a)$$

where $\sigma_{t \ldots j'i'}(t, \ldots, i, t', \ldots, i', a)$ is 1 if $\{a\}$ is a proper test set and yet fails to kill the double-fault alternate $f_{t \ldots kj'i'}$, and 0 otherwise (the single summation actually stands for a whole set of summations as above). Note that, since there are q subscripts in all, there is no need for a special subscript to denote the number of functions. Similar formulae can be written for the other multi-fault alternates.

The *survival ratio* of a multi-fault alternate is defined to be the probability that the alternate survives detection; the survival ratio of the double-fault alternate $f_{t \ldots j'i'}$, for instance, is obtained by dividing the number of surviving test cases $S^1_{t \ldots j'i'}(n)$ by the number of proper test cases $P^1_q(n)$ (the phrase 'coupling ratio' used in previous papers has been discontinued to avoid confusion). The sum of survival ratios gives the *expected number of survivors*; if this number is high, the coupling effect is weak. Note that, while a survival ratio, being a probability, is always less than one, the sum of survival ratios can be greater than one; if such is the case, its interpretation as a probability fails, thus favouring the alternative interpretation as the number of multi-fault alternates expected to survive.

Another measure of the strength of the coupling effect is the *average survival ratio* of multi-fault alternates; this is obtained by dividing the expected number of survivors by the number of multi-fault alternates. This measure is the one preferred here since it is equivalent to the one used in the literature. Note that one can also talk of the expected number of double-fault survivors or the average survival ratio of triple-fault alternates, and so on.

The q-function model can be solved mathematically if q is small enough; in other words, it becomes possible in such cases to derive explicit formulae for the number of proper test cases as well as the number of surviving test cases of each of the multi-fault alternates. In the case of the two-function model, mathematical solutions are available for both test sets of order 1 and 2 [3]; in the case of the three-function model, on the other hand, a mathematical solution is only available for test sets of order 1 [4]. These solutions are approximate in the sense that the problem of equivalent alternates has been ignored; however, it can be shown that this is justified, provided that n is large.

A complete mathematical solution becomes increasingly difficult as q grows larger. If all but the leading-order terms in n are ignored, however, the q-function model becomes solvable in the two cases of test sets of order 1 and efficient test sets of order 2; in the case of the other types of test sets of order 2, however, only a qualitative solution is available. These solutions are valid only if n is large and q is small relative to n; this is because only then are the leading-order terms the dominant ones.

These solutions are more easily derived using a heuristic approach. This involves the formulation of heuristic rules that are valid to leading order in n; these rules can be proved mathematically [4, 5], but no attempt will be made to do so in this paper.

3 Test Sets of Order 1

The two-function model has been solved explicitly in the case of test sets of order 1 [3]; the survival ratio of the sole double-fault alternate $f_{j'i'}$ is $1/n$. The three-function model has also been solved explicitly [4]; the survival ratios of the three double-fault alternates $f_{kj'i'}$, $f_{k'ji'}$ and $f_{k'j'i}$ are $2/n$, $1/n$ and $1/n$ respectively, while that of the sole triple-fault alternate $f_{k'j'i'}$ is $1/n$. Note that these survival ratios are all correct to leading order in n.

It is interesting to observe that, in the three-function model, three of the multi-fault alternates, i.e., $f_{k'ji'}$, $f_{k'j'i}$ and $f_{k'j'i'}$, each have a survival ratio of $1/n$; they share the property that the last function to be executed is faulty. The odd one out is $f_{kj'i'}$, which has a survival ratio of $2/n$; its distinctive feature is that the last function is free of faults. Moreover, the double-fault alternate $f_{j'i'}$ in the two-function model also has a survival ratio of $1/n$; as it happens, its last function is faulty too. The following heuristic rule suggests itself : the survival ratio of a multi-fault alternate is $1/n$ if the last function to be executed is faulty.

The following argument explains why the survival ratio is $1/n$ in this case. Consider the double-fault alternate $f_{j'i'}$ in the two-function model, and let the test set be $\{a\}$. The double-fault alternate survives if and only if $f_{j'i'}(a)$ and $f_{ji}(a)$ both have the same value; the probability that this occurs is $1/n$ (recall that the model requires an averaging over all possible compositions, faults and test sets). In most cases, though not this one, this probability is not precisely $1/n$; this is because of the restriction that $\{a\}$ be a proper test set, which rules out some test cases, but this does not actually affect the leading-order term.

It remains to deal with the case of multi-fault alternates whose last functions are not faulty. Consider the double-fault alternate $f_{kj'i'}$ in the three-function model and let the test set be $\{a\}$. One can use the same argument as above to show that the probability that $f_{kj'i'}$ and f_{kji} have the same value after the execution of the first two functions is $1/n$; this means that the probability that the two intermediate values differ is $1 - 1/n$. There still remains one function to be executed; this is f_k for both $f_{kj'i'}$ and f_{kji}. Observe now that, though the two intermediate values are different, there is no guarantee that the final values would also be different, unless f_k is bijective, which it is not since an average over all f_k's is implied.

The probability that two distinct inputs a and b to an arbitrary function f lead to the same output is easily found to be $1/n$; it is enough to observe that $f(a)$ has one chance in n to be any of the points of the domain, and so has $f(b)$. Since the case of identical intermediate values necessarily leads to identical final values, one naturally concludes that the survival ratio of the alternate $f_{kj'i'}$ is $2/n$ (to leading order in n), which is in agreement with the result obtained by explicit computation.

The above heuristic rule can now be enhanced to include those cases in which the last function is fault-free. If the last fault to be executed occurs in the last function, the survival ratio is $1/n$; if it occurs in the penultimate function, it is $2/n$, and so on. In general, if there are still p functions to be traversed after the execution of the last fault, the survival ratio is $(p+1)/n$ (to leading order in n). It is important to note that this rule is valid only if the test set is proper, i.e., it kills all the single-fault alternates.

The q-function model can now be solved. Observe first that there is one multi-fault alternate in which the last fault occurs in the second function, three multi-fault alternates in which it occurs in the third function, and seven multi-fault alternates in which it occurs in the fourth function; in general, there are $(2^{p-1}-1)$ multi-fault alternates in which the last fault occurs in the pth function. The expected number of survivors (the sum of survival ratios) is thus given by :

$$< s(n,q) >_1 \; = \frac{1}{n} \sum_{p=1}^{q} (2^{p-1}-1)(q-p+1)$$

where the subscript denotes test sets of order 1. This sum is easily evaluated; one obtains :

$$< s(n,q) >_1 \; = \frac{1}{n}\left(2^{q+1} - \frac{1}{2}q^2 - \frac{3}{2}q - 2\right) \qquad (1)$$

It is clear that the expected number of survivors increases exponentially with q, but then so does the number of multi-fault alternates; the average survival ratio is thus $2/n$ (if q is large).

If, on the other hand, one restricts attention to the class of double-fault alternates, one finds that the average survival ratio is $(q+1)/3n$; similarly, one finds that the average survival ratio of triple-fault alternates is $(q+1)/4n$, that of quadruple-fault alternates is $(q+1)/5n$, and so on. One therefore concludes that double-fault alternates are more likely to survive than triple-fault ones, triple-fault alternates more likely to survive than quadruple-fault ones, and so on; this phenomenon has previously been observed empirically by Offutt [7, 8].

The reason for this phenomenon is as follows. The last fault to be executed is more likely to occur early in the composition if there are few faults than if there are many; as the heuristic rule indicates, the survival ratio is large if the last fault occurs early. The same explanation holds in the case of efficient test sets of order 2 if the outputs are distinct (subsection 4.2); different explanations, however, are required in other cases.

Incidentally, the reason why q is required to be smaller than n is as follows. Suppose that q is actually larger than n; applying the above heuristic rule to the double-fault alternate $f_{t\ldots j'i'}$, one finds that its survival ratio is negative, which is patently absurd. One concludes that q must be smaller than n for the rule to be valid; unfortunately, however, it is not clear how much smaller q must be relative to n.

4 Efficient Test Sets of Order 2

There are two main problems when dealing with test sets of order 2. One is that such test sets come in several varieties, depending on precisely how the two test data kill the single-fault alternates. The other problem is that the two outputs can be either distinct or identical (note that one is referring here to the outputs of the original composition or program). This section considers the second problem with respect to efficient test sets; recall that these are such that each test data individually kills all the single-fault alternates.

4.1 Decoupling of Test Data

If the two test outputs are distinct, the test data can be regarded as being decoupled from each other; this means that each test data can be treated independently of the other. This heuristic rule is valid to leading order in n, and applies to all types of test sets of order 2, whether efficient or not; indeed, it applies generally to test sets of order r, where r is small relative to n (provided that all r outputs are distinct).

A proof of this rule is sketched in the second of the two papers mentioned in the introduction [5]. Unfortunately, no simple argument can be given here in support of the rule. Suffice it to say that the two test data are not truly independent of each other; the effects of the dependence, however, first manifest themselves not in the leading-order term, but in the one after that.

The decoupling rule is applied in the following way. Consider the double-fault alternate $f_{j'i'}$ in the two-function model, and let the test set $\{a,b\}$ be efficient; suppose the two outputs are distinct, i.e., $f_{ji}(a) \neq f_{ji}(b)$. The double-fault alternate survives only if $f_{j'i'}(a) = f_{ji}(a)$ and $f_{j'i'}(b) = f_{ji}(b)$ simultaneously. The probability that either condition holds is $1/n$ (recall that a and b are each able to kill all the single-fault alternates and thus act as proper test sets of order 1), so the probability that both hold together is $1/n^2$. The survival ratio is thus $1/n^2$, which is in agreement with the results of a previous paper [3].

4.2 Distinct Outputs

The q-function model can now be solved in the case of efficient test sets and distinct outputs. The survival ratio of a multi-fault alternate whose last function is faulty is easily seen to be $1/n^2$ (i.e., $1/n \times 1/n$); that of a multi-fault alternate whose last fault occurs in the penultimate function is $4/n^2$ (i.e., $2/n \times 2/n$), and so on. The expected number of survivors is thus given by :

$$< s(n,q) >_{2(d)} = \frac{1}{n^2} \sum_{p=1}^{q} (2^{p-1} - 1)(q - p + 1)^2$$

where the subscript indicates that there are two test data and the outputs are distinct (it is implicitly assumed that the test sets are efficient). The evaluation of this sum yields :

$$< s(n,q) >_{2(d)} = \frac{1}{n^2} (6 \times 2^q - \frac{1}{3} q^3 - \frac{3}{2} q^2 - \frac{25}{6} q - 6) \quad (2)$$

It again turns out that the expected number of survivors increases exponentially with q; there are $(2^q - q - 1)$ multi-fault alternates in all, so the average survival ratio is $6/n^2$ (assuming q is reasonably large).

If one restricts attention to the class of double-fault alternates, one finds that the average survival ratio is $q(q+1)/6n^2$; similarly, the average survival ratio of triple-fault alternates is $(q - \frac{1}{2})(q+1)/10n^2$, that of quadruple-fault alternates is $(q-1)(q+1)/15n^2$, and so on. One again finds that double-fault alternates are more likely to survive than triple-fault ones, triple-fault alternates more likely to survive than quadruple-fault ones, and so on; in other words, the more faults there are, the stronger the coupling effect. The explanation is identical to the one given in the case of test sets of order 1.

4.3 Identical Outputs

In the q-function model, there are q distinct ways in which the final outputs turn out to be identical. The first occurs when, after the first function is executed, the two intermediate values turn out to be the same, the second when this happens after the first two functions are executed, and so on. It is not difficult to see that, to leading order in n, the number of proper test cases corresponding to each of these possibilities is the same; incidentally, this number is also $1/n$ of the number of proper test cases in which the final outputs are distinct.

The appropriate heuristic rule to use here is as follows. Once the intermediate values become identical, the two test data effectively act as one for the remainder of the program. Not all the multi-fault alternates are affected, however, only those whose faults all lie after the two values become one. The survival ratios of the latter are $O(n^{-1})$, but those of the others are $O(n^{-2})$.

Consider the three-function model for simplicity, and suppose that, after the first function is executed, the two intermediate values are the same, i.e., $f_i(a) = f_i(b)$. There are four multi-fault alternates, of which only one is such that all its faults lie after the first function, namely $f_{k'j'i}$. The survival ratio of the latter is $1/n$ if test sets are such that $f_i(a) = f_i(b)$; the survival ratios of the other multi-fault alternates, on the other hand, are $O(n^{-2})$.

The case where the two intermediate values only become identical after the first two functions have been executed yields no example of a multi-fault alternate having a survival ratio of $O(n^{-1})$; neither does the last case where the outputs become identical only after all three functions have been executed. It follows that, if test sets are restricted only by the condition that the final outputs be identical, the expected number of survivors is $1/3n$ while the average survival ratio is $1/12n$.

It is important to realise that the three-function mode for efficient test sets of order 2 conceals a version of the two-function model for test sets of order 1, which is revealed only when test sets are required to obey the condition that $f_i(a) = f_i(b)$. One can similarly show that the q-function model conceals versions of the $(q-1)$-function $(q-2)$-function, ..., two-function models, which ar revealed only when test sets are such that the intermedi ate values become identical after the first, second, ... $(q-2)$th function has been executed. It follows that th expected number of survivors is given by :

$$< s(n,q) >_{2(i)} = \frac{1}{qn} \sum_{p=1}^{q-1} (2^{p+1} - \frac{1}{2} p^2 - \frac{3}{2} p - 2)$$

Note that the $p = 1$ term is trivial and does not actuall add to the sum. The evaluation yields :

$$< s(n,q) >_{2(i)} = \frac{1}{qn} (2^{q+1} - \frac{1}{6} q^3 - \frac{1}{2} q^2 - \frac{4}{3} q - 2) \quad (3)$$

One thus finds that the expected number of survivo still increases exponentially with q, but the denominat is now qn rather than n^2; the average survival ratio $2/qn$. It is clear that identical outputs should be avoide if this is at all possible.

It should come as no surprise that double-fault alte nates are more likely to survive than triple-fault one and so on; however, the explanation is quite differe in the present case. Consider the sole q-fault alterna $f_{t' \ldots i'}$; its survival ratio is $O(n^{-2})$ since it never happe that all its faults lie after the two intermediate valu become identical. Only $f_{t' \ldots j' i}$ of the $(q-1)$-fault alte nates (there are q of them) has a survival ratio of $O(n^{-1}$ this is because all its faults lie after the execution of t first function. Most double-fault alternates, on the oth hand, have survival ratios of $O(n^{-1})$; only those th have faults in the first function have survival ratios

$O(n^{-2})$. It is clear that, the fewer faults there are, the more likely is the multi-fault alternate to have a survival ratio of $O(n^{-1})$, and thus to survive.

4.4 Arbitrary Outputs

The case where there is no restriction on the outputs that they be distinct or identical is now considered. The details are omitted, but the expected number of survivors is :

$$< s(n, q) >_2 = \frac{1}{n^2}(8 \times 2^q - \frac{1}{2}q^3 - 2q^2 - \frac{11}{2}q - 8) \quad (4)$$

where the subscript 2 has been left unadorned. The average survival ratio is $8/n^2$, which is larger than if the outputs were distinct.

5 Other Types of Test Sets of Order 2

There is only one type of proper test set of order 1; the sole test element must be such as to kill all the single-fault alternates. Proper test sets of order 2, on the other hand, come in a variety of types, depending on how the two test data manage to kill the single-fault alternates. Efficient test sets, for instance, are such that each test data individually kills all of them; other types, however, are such that one or both of the test data fail to kill one or more of them. It turns out that there are five types of proper test sets of order 2 if q is 2, and fourteen if q is 3; the number increases exponentially with q.

This section deals with non-efficient test sets of order 2; both distinct and identical outputs are considered, though the emphasis is on the former. Unlike the case of efficient test sets of order 2, however, the discussion is wholly qualitative.

5.1 Distinct Outputs

One can invoke the decoupling rule if the two test outputs turn out to be distinct; this states that the two test data act independently of each other (to leading order in n). It is only in the case of efficient test sets, however, that both test data act as proper test sets of order 1, so one is able to apply the results of section 3; in the case of other types of test sets, one or both test data fail to be proper test sets. The behaviour of non-proper test sets of order 1 thus becomes of pressing importance; unfortunately, however, this behaviour is mostly unknown. The little that is known is of a qualitative nature and is now described.

Each multi-fault alternate has associated with it a set of single-fault alternates in which the faults of the former occur singly. One can now state the following heuristic rule governing the qualitative behaviour of test sets of order 1, whether proper or not. The survival ratio of a multi-fault alternate is $O(n^{-1})$ or $O(1)$ according to whether the test set kills at least one of the associated single-fault alternates or not. For instance, a proper test set of order 1 is able to kill all the single-fault alternates, whether associated or not, so the survival ratio of any multi-fault alternate is $O(n^{-1})$, in line with the results of section 3.

It is now possible to infer the order of magnitude (in terms of n) of any survival ratio for any type of test set of order 2. The survival ratio of a multi-fault alternate is $O(n^{-1})$ or $O(n^{-2})$ according to whether only one or both test data succeed in killing at least one of the associated single-fault alternates (note that both test data cannot fail to do so if the test set is proper). It is on this observation that the following discussion is based.

Efficient test sets are such that all the survival ratios are $O(n^{-2})$. The same is true of test sets in which the two test data each fail to kill at most one of the single-fault alternates; one can refer to such test sets as *near-efficient test sets.* It turns out that some of these near-efficient types are actually more effective than the pure efficient one, but this is of little interest here; what is of interest is that this group of types represents one pole in the behaviour of proper test sets of order 2.

Consider test sets in which one test data kills all the single-fault alternates; suppose the other kills all but two of them. The survival ratio of one double-fault alternate is then $O(n^{-1})$, while those of the remaining multi-fault alternates are still $O(n^{-2})$. It does not necessarily follow, however, that the former dominates the sum of survival ratios; this really depends on the number of multi-fault alternates. If q is such that this number is around n, the two contributions are comparable; if, however, q is such that the number of multi-fault alternates is around n^2, whether one survival ratio is $O(n^{-1})$ or not is neither here nor there.

Consider now the case where the second test data fails to kill three of the single-fault alternates; there are now four multi-fault alternates whose survival ratios are $O(n^{-1})$. As the second test data fails to kill more and more single-fault alternates, more and more multi-fault alternates have survival ratios of $O(n^{-1})$, and their influence gradually becomes dominant. In the limit that the second test data fails to kill any of the single-fault alternates, all the survival ratios are $O(n^{-1})$ (it is assumed that the first test data continues to kill all the single-fault alternates). Such test sets are said to be *inefficient*; they represent the opposite pole of behaviour to that displayed by efficient and near-efficient test sets.

Suppose now that each single-fault alternate is killed by just one of the test data. If the test sets are inefficient, all the survival ratios are $O(n^{-1})$. Consider next the case where the first test data fails to kill just one single-fault alternate, and the second succeeds in killing only this one. One then finds that approximately half of the multi-fault alternates have survival ratios of $O(n^{-1})$, while the other half have survival ratios of $O(n^{-2})$. As the second test data kills more and more single-fault alternates (and the first one fewer and fewer), more and more multi-fault alternates have survival ratios of $O(n^{-2})$ until an equilibrium is reached when each test data kills the same numbers of single-fault alternates, and the trend reverses. The point being made here is that, for maximum effectiveness, the kills should be evenly distributed between the two test data.

It only remains to make one final point. A double-fault alternate has two associated single-fault alternates, a triple-fault alternate three, and so on. It is clear that the larger the number of associated single-fault alternates, the higher the probability that each of the test data manages to kill at least one of them. It follows that triple-fault alternates have a higher probability than double-fault ones that the survival ratio is $O(n^{-2})$, and not $O(n^{-1})$, quadruple-fault alternates a higher probability than triple-fault ones that this is the case, and so on; in other words, the more faults there are, the less likely is the multi-fault alternate to survive, and so the stronger the coupling effect.

5.2 Identical Outputs

As shown in subsection 4.3, there are q distinct ways in which two final outputs turn out to be identical, depending on precisely when the intermediate values become the same. For most types of test sets, however, only a few of these ways are of relevance; this is because, once the intermediate values become the same, the two test data act as one and exhibit the same behaviour with respect to the detection of faults. Suppose, for instance, that one test data kills $f_{t' \ldots i}$ and the other fails to kill it; it is simply not possible in this case for the two intermediate values to become identical before the execution of the last function.

A distinction now needs to be made between those multi-fault alternates whose faults all lie after the two intermediate values become identical and those whose faults do not. In the case of multi-fault alternates belonging to the first class, one can apply the methods of subsection 4.3 to conclude that their survival ratios are $O(n^{-1})$; indeed, it is possible in such cases to compute their exact survival ratios (to leading order in n).

For multi-fault alternates belonging to the second class, however, the following heuristic rule applies. The survival ratio is $O(n^{-2})$ if at least one of the associated single-fault alternates is killed by both test data, otherwise it is $O(n^{-1})$ (the test set being proper, each associated single-fault alternate is killed by at least one test data).

It was shown in the previous subsection that, if the test outputs are distinct, there is a definite advantage in having each test data kill as many single-fault alternates as possible. The situation, if the test outputs are identical, is not as clear-cut; on balance, however, it still seems preferable to have each test data kill many rather than few single-fault alternates. On the other hand, if each single-fault alternate is killed by just one test data, there is no clear advantage in having the two test data kill equal numbers of single-fault alternates, as there would be if the test outputs were distinct.

Two other conclusions must be mentioned, though the detailed explanations are omitted. One is that, for most types of test sets, the coupling effect is clearly stronger if the test outputs are distinct than if they are identical; inefficient test sets prove to be one exception to this rule in that the survival ratios are $O(n^{-1})$, irrespective of whether the test outputs are distinct or identical (the two-function and three-function models reveal that the coupling effect is actually stronger if the outputs are identical, but the difference is marginal). The other conclusion is that, in this case too, double-fault alternates are more likely to survive than triple-fault ones, triple-fault alternates more likely to survive than quadruple-fault ones, and so on.

6 Discussion

One can proceed in the same manner to deal with test sets of order 3, 4 and upwards. In the case of efficient test sets of order r and distinct outputs, for instance, one can write the expected number of survivors as follows :

$$< s(n,q) >_{r(d)} \;=\; \frac{1}{n^r}\sum_{p=1}^{q}(2^{p-1}-1)\,(q-p+1)^r$$

This sum is not too difficult to evaluate if r is small; one thereby finds that the average survival ratio of multi fault alternates is $26/n^3$ if r is 3, $150/n^4$ if r is 4, and so on. In general, the average survival ratio is $O(n^{-r})$ if there are r test data; the coefficient escalates rapidly with r, however. One can use the same arguments as previously to show that the coupling effect is strongest if test sets are efficient or near-efficient; other types of test sets are likely to have much larger average survival ratios, sometimes considerably so.

One notes, for comparison purposes, that the average survival ratio is $1/n^r$ if the original program or composition consists entirely of bijective functions (r is the number of test data). The reason is simple. If the faults manifest themselves after the last fault has been executed, they are guaranteed to produce incorrect outputs; there is then no need to worry about propagation ef fects, as was the case in section 3. This shows clearly the large part played by *function degeneracy* (the deviation of functions from being one-to-one) in the survival of multi-fault alternates, despite the ouputs being distinct.

It requires a bit more effort to find the average survival ratios if some of the outputs are identical. In the case that two of the outputs are identical, for instance, one finds that the average survival ratio is $6/qn^2$ if r is 3, $26/qn^3$ if r is 4, and so on; in general, the average survival ratio is $O(n^{-(r-1)})$ if there are r test data. As expected, the coupling effect is noticeably weaker if two of the outputs are identical; if even more outputs were identical, the coupling effect would be weaker still.

In the case of non-efficient test sets of order r, where r is greater than 2, the conclusions are more or less the same as those reached in section 5. It is advantageous to ensure both that each test data individually kills as many single-fault alternates as possible and that the outputs are all distinct; it is also an advantage that individual test data kill similar numbers of single-fault alternates, but possibly not if the outputs are mostly identical.

There is a case for arguing that the results for test sets of order 1 provide an upper bound for the average survival ratio in other cases. If a test set is proper, each single-fault alternate must be killed by at least one of the test data. The least efficient type of test set (of a specific size) is such that one of the test data succeeds in killing all the single-fault alternates, while the rest fail to kill any. In spite of this, one would expect such test sets to be at least more efficient than proper test sets of order 1; the ineffectual test data should be able to kill at least some of the multiple-fault alternates.

The average survival ratio for proper test sets of order 2 is small enough that one can plausibly claim to have shown the existence of an approximate coupling effect within the model. It is argued elsewhere [4] that, though the model suffers from various shortcomings, they are not such as to vitiate its basic usefulness. The natural presumption is that an approximate coupling effect also operates in the real world; however, one must beware of concluding that the coupling effect is strong enough that one need only worry about killing first-order mutants.

The average survival ratio for test sets of order 1 is $1/n$; assuming that n is equivalent to two bytes, one finds that only one in around 32,000 multi-fault alternates survives. This estimate is not so different from the empirical estimates obtained by Offutt [7, 8], which range from 1 in 10,000 to 7 in 10,000, though it is clearly smaller. The agreement is presumably closer if one restricts attention to double-fault alternates, as Offutt does; the average survival ratio is then $(q+1)/3n$, and thus increases with the size of the program. The other result of Offutt is that higher-order mutants are more likely to be killed than lower-order ones; particular care has been taken to show that this phenomenon does indeed occur in each of the cases considered.

It is important to realise that the above results have been derived within the context of a simple model and involve an average over all possible semantic cases; in consequence, they are not expected to apply to specific programs, except probabilistically. The model itself suffers from a number of defects; it does not properly take account of loops or conditions, it assumes that the domain is the same for all functions, and it is unable to deal with the interactions of faults that occur in the same function, only of those that occur in different functions. Despite all this, the results are clearly of interest; they become more so when it is revealed that the model has two implicit properties as a result of the averaging process.

The first is that fault sizes are large; on average, f_i differs from $f_{i'}$ on $(n-1)$ points, as does f_j and $f_{j'}$, and the rest of them. These are local fault sizes; if fault sizes are judged by the final outputs, they are slightly smaller due to faults being unable to propagate fully. In any case, it is not difficult to show that the coupling effect is strong if fault sizes are small, and weak if they are large (large faults provide more opportunities for faults to interact, disordering outputs in the process).

The second property is that the average *DRR (domain-to-range ratio)* of individual functions is rather small, being only 1.58; the DRR of a function is defined to be the ratio of the number of its inputs to the number of its outputs [9, 10]. DRR's thus range in size from 1 to n; bijective functions, for instance, have a DRR of 1. It is easy to see that the coupling effect is particularly strong if the original functions are all bijective (it does not matter if the faulty ones are not); the reason is that any incorrect intermediate values must propagate to give incorrect outputs.

The outcome in any particular case thus depends on two opposing effects. If faults are small, the coupling effect is stronger than expected; if functions have large DRR's, on the other hand, the coupling effect is weaker than expected. In the programs examined by Offutt, for instance, the input domains are much larger than the output domains, so the coupling effect is presumably weaker than predicted by the model; it is not clear what the fault sizes are, however.

It has been shown that a number of factors are implicated in the coupling effect. Unfortunately, however, it is not yet possible to put these various factors together into a coherent theory that could be used to assess the general adequacy of the testing in individual cases (i.e., not just with respect to first-order mutants). A more realistic model is required that incorporates loops and conditions; such a model should also take account of properties of programs such as fault sizes and function DRR's. One other point needs to be resolved; it is far from clear which is the best measure of the strength of the coupling effect, the expected number of survivors or the average survival ratio.

In the absence of a comprehensive theory, one is left with a few rules of thumb. One should ensure, if possible, that the outputs are all distinct; each test data should also kill as many first-order mutants as possible. There is probably little cause for worry if the program is close to being bijective and faults are small in size; the worry in this case is in finding a test set that kills all the first-order mutants. Finally, if the software to be tested is safety-critical, one should consider requiring that each first-order mutant be killed by two or more test data rather than just one.

7 Conclusion

The coupling effect hypothesis has usually been taken for granted; the prevailing belief is that it is sufficient to focus on killing all first-order mutants since the great majority of higher-order mutants would be killed as well. This approach is probably too complacent; there is no in-built guarantee that the number of surviving higher-order mutants would be small enough to satisfy stringent test-adequacy criteria. It is therefore important, when testing a program, to estimate the number of higher-order mutants likely to survive as this gives a rough idea of the adequacy of the testing.

This paper attempts to do this within a simple model, but does not perhaps altogether succeed. It has shown, however, that the strength of the coupling effect depends on a number of factors. The most important is that the domain be large. For a higher-order mutant to be killed, it is enough that its outputs differ from those of the correct program; this is much more likely if the domain has a large size. A stronger coupling effect also results if the test set is large, the outputs are distinct and each test data kills as many first-order mutants as possible. The nature of the program and the faults it is prone to are also important; it is best that the program be as close to being bijective as possible and that the faults have small sizes.

Even though quantitative agreement between theory and practice is lacking at this stage, it is not too unreasonable to hope that a tool might be developed in the future that would enable one to predict the number of higher-order mutants likely to survive in any particular case. One would then be able to estimate the reliability of the program under test and thereby decide whether the testing has been adequate or not.

Acknowledgments I wish to express my thanks to Robin Whitty and Tracy Hall for their constant encouragement and help during the course of this research. I am also grateful to South Bank University for the award of a fellowship to pursue my research interests.

References

[1] R.A. DeMillo, R.J. Lipton and F.G. Sayward : "Hints on Test Data Selection : Help for the Practicing Programmer," *Computer*, Vol. 11, No. 4 (1978), pp. 34 – 41.

[2] R.A. DeMillo, R.J. Lipton and F.G. Sayward : "Program Mutation : A New Approach to Program Testing," in *Infotech State of the Art Report, Software Testing, Vol 2 : Invited Papers*, Infotech International, 1979, pp. 107 – 126.

[3] K.S. How Tai Wah : "A Theoretical Study of Fault Coupling," *Journal of Software Testing, Verification and Reliability*, Vol. 10, No. 1 (2000), pp. 3 – 45.

[4] K.S. How Tai Wah : "An Analysis of the Coupling Effect : Single Test Data," paper to be submitted for publication, 2000.

[5] K.S. How Tai Wah : "An Analysis of the Coupling Effect : Multiple Test Data," paper to be submitted for publication, 2000.

[6] R.J. Lipton and F.G. Sayward : "The Status of Research on Program Mutation," in *Digest for the Workshop on Software Testing and Test Documentation*, Fort Lauderdale, 1978, pp. 355 – 373.

[7] A.J. Offutt : "The Coupling Effect : Fact or Fiction?" in *Procs of the Third Symposium on Software Testing Analysis and Verification*, Key West, Florida, 1989, pp. 131 – 140.

[8] A.J. Offutt : "Investigations of the Software Testing Coupling Effect," *ACM Trans Soft Eng and Meth*, Vol. 1, No. 1 (1992), pp. 5 – 20.

[9] J. Voas, L. Morell and K. Miller : "Predicting Where Faults Can Hide from Testing," *IEEE Software*, Vol. 8, No. 2 (1991), pp. 41 – 48.

[10] J. Voas, K. Miller and R. Noonan : "Designing Programs that Do Not Hide Data State Errors During Random Black-Box Testing," in *Procs of the Fifth Inter Conf on Putting into Practice Methods and Tools for Information System Design*, Nantes, France, 1992.

Component Customization Testing Technique Using Fault Injection Technique and Mutation Test Criteria

Hoijin Yoon
Department of Computer Science and Engineering
Ewha Womans University
11-1 Daehyun-dong, Seodaemun-Gu, Seoul, Korea
+82-2-3277-3508
hoijin@cs.ewha.ac.kr

Byoungju Choi
Department of Computer Science and Engineering
Ewha Womans University
11-1 Daehyun-dong, Seodaemun-Gu, Seoul, Korea
+82-2-3277-2593
bjchoi@mm.ewha.ac.kr

Abstract

A testing technique to detect failures caused by component customization is necessary. In this paper, we propose a component customization testing technique by using the fault injection technique and the mutation test criteria. We first define the component customization patterns by considering the syntactic and semantic characteristics of customization. Our technique aims to increase the test case effectiveness, which is the ratio of the number of the test cases that can detect error to the number of the selected test cases, by injecting a fault only to a specific part of the component interface. The specific part of the interface is chosen through a component customization pattern defined in this paper and the interaction, which is identified in this paper, between the black-box class and the white-box class of the component. Moreover, we go on to show the applicability of this technique through an example case study, which make it more concrete, using practical component architecture, the EJB.

Keywords

Component, testing, customization, fault injection

1 Introduction

Component-Based Software Development(CBSD) can reduce the cost of development by reusing pre-coded software but there can be some risks involved in using software that is implemented for another purpose [10]. In June of 1996, during the maiden voyage of the Ariane 5 launch vehicle, the launcher veered off course and exploded less than one minute after take-off. The reason for this mishap was that the developers had reused certain Ariane 4 software components in the Ariane 5 system without substantial retesting (having assumed there were no significant differences in these portions of the two systems) [6]. The component-based software that worked without any malfunction on Ariane 4 had erred on Ariane 5. This event lessons that more precise and heavier testing is necessary when components are going to be reused in a system.

This research was partially supported by Korea's BK21 grant.

With the characteristic of components that do not show the source code, there is a limit as to how much the existing testing techniques could be applied to components. Therefore some organized and in depth look at the component based software testing is needed. But there does not seem to be any study that proposes a concrete technique of testing component-based software. The issues that arise in component-based software development can be seen from two perspectives, the component provider and the component user. One factor that distinguishes issues that are pertinent in the two perspectives is the availability of the component source code: the component providers have access to the source code, whereas the component users typically do not [5]. The lack of availability of the source code of the components limits the testing that the component user can perform. Therefore this paper proposes a testing technique that is applicable to a component-based software viewed from the component user, the one who received the service from the component provider. The component user develops component-based software by repeatedly customizing the component provided by component provider to fit into the domain of development. Thus the testing technique that we are proposing in this paper is for the errors that may be caused by component customization.

In Section 2, we define component customization and describe other researches related to the component customization test and fault injection technique. In Section 3, we identify the component customization patterns and develop our component customization testing technique based on these patterns in Section 4. In Section 5, we analyze our technique. Finally in Section 6, we conclude and consider future work.

2 Related Works

This chapter will define what a component customization test is all about and what a software fault injection and mutation testing is.

2.1 Component Customization Test

Component_based software (CBS) is software made through the use of already made components. When developing CBS, a customization occurs to match a component to the requirements of the domain. Paul Allen defined component customization as an important process within CBSD saying "components are made as there are requests, and these requirements need to be expanded through component customization according to the specific requests of the business domain."[1]. Thus the component does not expose its inner workings yet provides an interface whereby the user can change the component's attributes or its methods. This is what is called component customization. Component customization designates every activity to modify the existing component for reuse which includes not only a simple modification of an attribute according to domain specific requirements but also includes adding new domain specific functions as well as assembling with other components to alter a function. In existing component architectures such as the Enterprise Java Beans, these three – modification of attributes, adding domain specific functions, and assembling components – exist [4]. Harrold said that the component provider must therefore effectively test all configurations of the components in a context-independent manner. The component user views the components as context-dependent units because the component user's application provides the context in which the components are used. The user is thus concerned about the configuration [5]. The context that Harrold mentions is the environment that is accomplished through the component customization, and through this component customization various component contexts can be provided. The component context depends on the component user's developing application based on its domain specific requirement.

The testing of CBS tests the resulting errors from component customization that adjusts a component to a new domain for the development of a new CBS. Thus we propose a component customization testing technique in this paper.

2.2 Software Fault Injection and Mutation Testing

Software fault injection is a technique for performing testing by simulating faults at certain locations in the program code and examining how the system behaves. In many systems, the paths taken by a program are quite complex, and the triggering of faults may occur rarely. It becomes difficult to investigate fault-tolerant behavior in such cases. If faults are deliberately injected into the system, this problem can be avoided. In the case of components, because it is hard to identify the execution path due to the private main functionality portion, fault injection technique is appropriate.

An application of adequacy measurement of a test case with the fault injection technique is the mutation test [2]. Mutation test is a technique where a test case is chosen to distinguish between a grammatically correct mutant of the source and the original source. This paper utilizes both the fault injection technique and the mutation test. But we do not simply apply the mutation test to the interface of the component. The fault is injected to the part that has a direct influence on the main functionality of the component. The major contribution of this paper is in where the fault should be injected.

There are two differences between the mutation of the interface that Delamaro uses [3] and the technique that this paper uses. First off, there is a difference between the interface that Delamaro uses and the component interface that we use. Delamaro's interface is a relation between module that has a notion of connection. Delamaro's interface is the relation in the call graphs that is viewed as the call functions between the two modules. Yet our component interface implies a place where the component behavior can be transformed by applying impact on the core functional part of component, apart from Delamaro interface of connection between two modules. Modifying the interface, the component user changes the behavior and the appearance of the components, and its constituents have very diverse qualities with several different techniques of realizing the interface among the various component architectures. Thus it is unreasonable to put Delamaro's testing technique directly to the component-based software. Second, Delamaro's interface mutation mutates call function elements such as function calls, reference to a value returned from a function, and reference to global variables shared by two or more functions as places where faults exist. Yet this paper, rather than mutating every interface element, through the analysis of the interaction between the main functional group and the interface, chooses the fault injection target to provide a efficient component-based software test case. Accordingly, the probability of detecting an error rises with the chosen test case and the problem of computational bottleneck in the mutation test can be minimized.

3 Component Customization Patterns

As described earlier, there is a part of the interface opened to the public and the other part with core functions that is not opened in component. In one of the leading component architectures these days, Enterprise JavaBeans (EJB) provides the core functional parts in JAR files not as the source code, and the interface part is implemented in XML file to enable the modification. To express these characteristics of components, we define the interface as the white-box class, and the core functional part as the black-box class, shown in Figure 1.

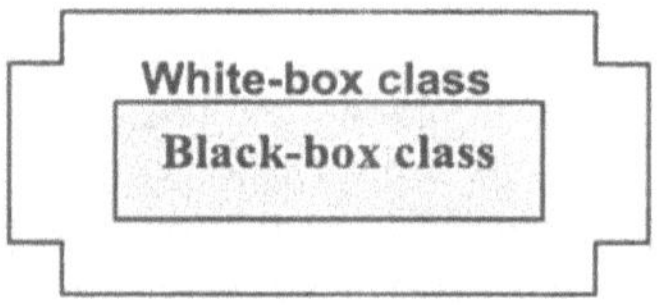

Figure 1 Organization of a component

Definition 1. Black-box class (B)

The black-box class means the core function of the component. And the source code for the black-box class is not disclosed and therefore cannot be modified by component user. This is expressed as B.

Example

The corresponding files to remote interface, home interface, and bean class in Trading Components from Figure 7 are Trading Component's B. These files are in java class file formats, not the java source file, and therefore the code itself is not provided.

Definition 2. White-box class (W)

The white-box class means the interface part of the component, where the source code is opened to the component user and also enabled to modify. Component user can convert the action or characteristic and compose the components by modifying the white-box class. The white-box class is expressed as W. The customized interface, to the requirements of new software developed by reusing the components, is called cW, and the fault-injected cW is called fW.

Example

The Deployment Descriptor in Trading Components from Figure 7 is the Trading Component's W. Trading Component's W consists of XML file where the source core is not disclosed. Through modifying this file by the component user, Trading Component can be customized.

Definition 3. Component (BW)

The component is a combined unit of B and W, which is expressed as BW. BW that has the customized W is called cBW, and fault injected W as fBW.

Example

The Trading Component in Figure 7 consists of B in Example of definition 1 and W in Example of Definition 2, which are organized into BW.

3.2 Component Customization Patterns

We define the component customization patterns from two viewpoints, 'how to customize' and 'why to customize'. The 'how to customize' determines the syntactic patterns whereas the 'why to customize' determines the semantic patterns.

(1) Component Customization Syntactic Patterns

The component customization syntactic patterns show how customization is applied to the component's W syntactically. By referring to the traditional design patterns[11], we define the following three syntactic patterns where 'Customization Code' is the code added or modified by customization and '*New*' stands for the new class created by customization. From hereon, we call the component customization syntactic patterns as *Pattern.syn*.

■ $Pattern.syn_1$

$Pattern.syn_1$ directly inserts the 'Customization Code' to W as shown in Figure 2.

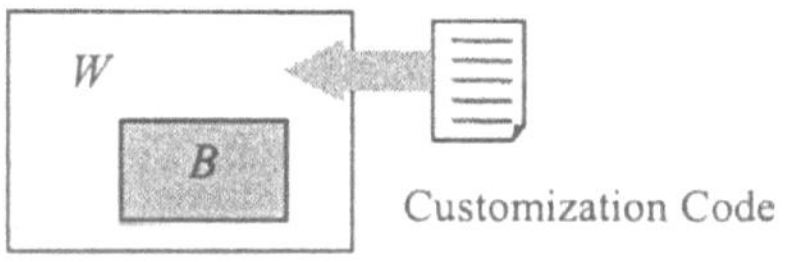

Figure 2 $Pattern.syn_1$

■ $Pattern.syn_2$

$Pattern.syn_2$ creates the class *New* containing the 'Customization Code' then sets an association relation between W and *New* thus making it possible for W refer to as shown in Figure 3.

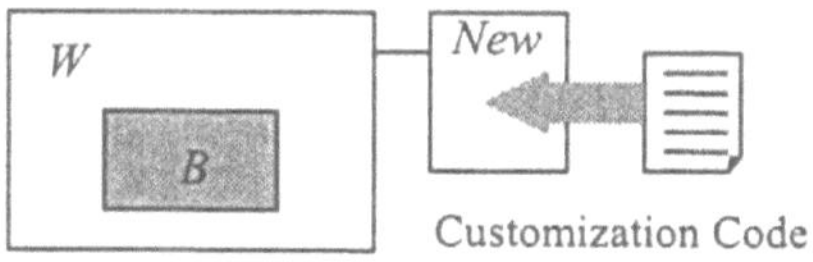

Figure 3 $Pattern.syn_2$

■ $Pattern.syn_3$

$Pattern.syn_3$ creates the class *New* containing the 'Customization Code' then sets an inheritance relation between W and *New* thus making it possible for W refer to as shown in Figure 4.

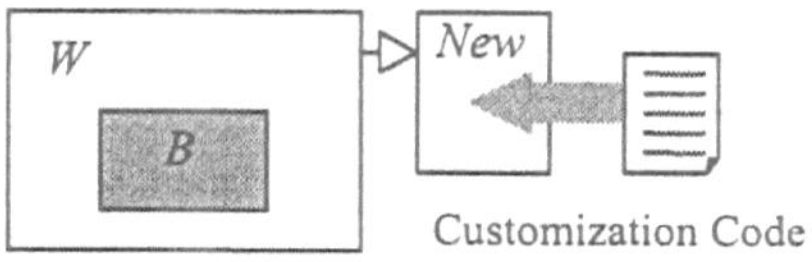

Figure 4 $Pattern.syn_3$

In *Pattern.syn*, we did not consider the relationship between B and W since this relationship cannot be modified by component customization.

(2) Component Customization Semantic Patterns

The component customization semantic patterns define the execution purpose of customization. There are two purposes for customization, setting the component's property and modifying the component's behavior. Therefore there are the following two semantic patterns. From hereon, we call the component customization semantic patterns as *Pattern.sem*.

■ $Pattern.sem_1$

$Pattern.sem_1$ is a customization pattern, which creates cBW by modifying W to set the component properties. For instance, in Trading EJB Component of chapter 4, the customization of TradeLimit to 1000 can be regarded in this pattern.

■ $Pattern.sem_2$

$Pattern.sem_2$ is a customization pattern creating cBW by the composition of new components in order to add or change component's behavior for the domain specific requirements. For instance, in Trading EJB Component of chapter 4, the customization of the component to the requirement by adding the new function that shows the Trading results in different formats can be this pattern. If the new function is implemented in components, the component composition occurs. Meaning, the component composition is one of the component customization patterns.

4 Component Customization Testing Technique

We take the component that the integrator customizes through the appropriate syntactic and semantic patterns and propose a component customization testing technique to test component customization failures on the customized component. Figure 5 shows the component customization process carried out by the integrator using the patterns we defined in the previous section.

Component customization creates *cBW* of Figure 5(b) by adding the dotted area to *W* of *BW* of Figure 5(a) according to the appropriate pattern. Here, the dotted area is the customization code explained in the Section 3.2.(1). The component customization testing technique we propose in this paper tests *cBW* by creating *fBW* by injecting a fault into the *cBW* since this is where the component customization fault exists.

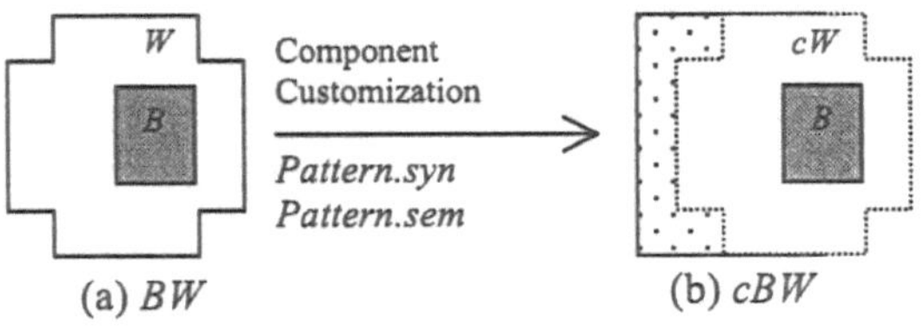

Figure 5 The Component Customization

For Component customization testing, we must especially pay attention to the section where the interaction between *B* and *cW* in *cBW* occur. We define this interaction area as the 'Fault Injection Target' and define the 'Fault Injection Operator' as the operator that injects the fault into this area. Our technique creates Figure 6(b)'s *fBW* by injecting a fault using the Fault Injection Operator not into the whole of *cBW*, but only into Fault Injection Target as shown in Figure 6. Our technique then selects test cases that can differentiate *cBW* and *fBW*.

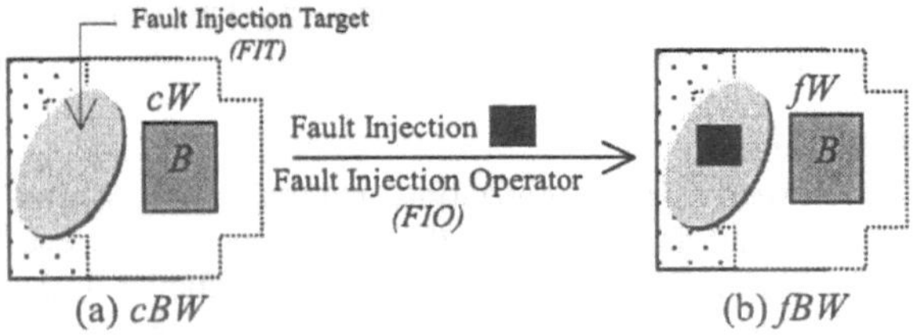

Figure 6 Fault Injection

4.1 Fault Injection Target

Since it is difficult to find the execution path due to the component's black-box, this paper utilizes the software fault injection technique. The point of software fault injection technique lies on where the fault is injected. For selecting more effective test cases, the location where the fault be injected needs to be systematically extracted.

The faults are not simply injected in the entire *cW* or the customization code. Needless to say, the test cases that are selected through injecting the faults in the entire *cW* or the customization code may detect errors caused by the component customization. However, to choose more effective test cases for customization testing, the analysis on the interaction between *cW* and *B* for *cBW*, which are created by CBSD, are undertaken and the effective fault injecting target is selected based on that.

The interaction between *B* and *cW* is mainly depended the specific element (a constituent unit of making *cW*, for instance, a single XML element for EJB). *cBW* operates the behavior appropriate to current domain requirements with referring to the elements in *cW*. This does not mean that *B* directly refers to all elements in *cW*. *B* refers to the specific element out of all *cW* elements, let say *x*, and then indirectly refers to other elements related to *x*. In this paper, *x* is defined as a direct reference element, and the other *cW* elements that are referenced to *B* through *x* are defined as indirect reference elements.

Definition 4. Direct Reference Element (*DRE*)

As an element of organizing *cW*, it means the element that is directly referenced by *B*. This is called *DRE*.

Example

In *cBW*, which is created in EJB component customization pattern 2, *B* is directly referring to <role-link> element of *cW*, and is indirectly affected by elements such as <role-name>, and <method-permission>. In this case, <role-link> is *DRE*.

Definition 5. Indirect Reference Element (*IRE*)

As an element organizing *cW*, Indirect Reference Element reflects the value of itself to *B* through *DRE* indirectly. Namely, *B* uses the value of *IRE* by referring the *DRE* associated with the *IRE*. The set of indirect reference elements related to *DRE*, *d* are expressed as *IRE*(*d*).

Example

In *cBW*, which is created in EJB component customization pattern 2, *B* is directly referring to <role-link> element of *cW*, and is indirectly affected by elements such as <role-name>, and <method-permission>. If <role-link> is *DRE*, namely *d*, the set of elements organized with <role-link> including <role-name>, and <method-permission> is called *IRE*(*d*).

When there are errors in *IRE* modified for the component customization, the error affects B through *DRE*. Therefore, the test cases must detect the errors not only in *DRE* but also in the relevant *IRE*. Based on the interaction between *B* and *cW*, this paper defines where to inject a fault as *DRE* in definition 6. To identify *DRE* as where to inject a fault, the fact that "the test cases selected by injecting a fault to *DRE* not only can detect the errors in *DRE* but also the errors in relevant *IRE*" should be proved.

Definition 6. Fault Injection Target (*FIT*)

This becomes the *cW*'s element that a fault injected to and is called *FIT*. We can get the more effective test cases for component customization testing by injecting a fault to this *FIT*. In this paper, *DRE* of *cW* is selected as *FIT*.

Example

The <role-link> element becomes *DRE* in EJB component customization pattern 2. Therefore the *FIT* for EJB component customization pattern 2 is <role-link> element.

In order to inject faults, the decision on not only the location but also the method of injecting need to be made. The method of injecting a fault to *FIT* depends on how the component architecture implements *W*. In case of EJB,

W is implemented in XML. Therefore, a fault needs to be injected to *FIT* without contradicting DTD of XML. Since the *fBW* needs to be organized without any error in static analysis for component architecture, the fault need to be injected without any mismatch in syntax of each component architecture's *W*. Therefore, the detailed methods vary based on the characteristics of elements organizing *W*. This paper defines the general methods of injecting faults as shown in definition 7, and names this as a fault injection operator. Definition 7 defines the fault injection operator as a principle that must be hold in all component architecture. Based on this definition 7, the concrete operators need to be defined for the testing in a component architecture. In chapter 4 of this paper, the fault injection operators that are for the testing in EJB component architecture are defined concretely and used in the case study.

Definition 7. Fault Injection Operator (*FIO*)

Fault Injection Operator expresses the method of injecting a fault to *FIT*. Fault Injection Operator must inject fault so as to establish *fBW* any syntax error. Namely there should not be any syntax error after the fault injection to *FIT*. We call the fault injection operator as *FIO*. And *FIO* may differ depending on how the component architecture implements *W*.

Example

In EJB, <role-link> element is a *FIT*. As the value of <role-link> element is a type of the name of role, setting a value other than a role name to <role-link> invokes a syntax error in *fBW*. Therefore *FIO* for <role-link> element is the operator that substitutes the value in <role-link> element to a different role name.

As shown in Table 1, Definition 6 and definition 7 can extract *FIT* and *FIO* of EJB in each customization pattern. Since *FIT* in our technique is a *DRE* according to definition 6, the elements specific to *DRE* in each customization pattern out of *cW* elements are extracted to *FIT*.

Table 1. *FIT* and *FIO* in each EJB customization pattern

pattern	*FIT*	*FIO*
1	<env-entry-value>	REV (Replace to another Environment entry Value)
2	<role-link>	RRL (Replace to another Role Link)
3	<ejb-class>	REC (Replace to another Ejb Class)
4	<ejb-link>	REL (Replace to another Ejb Link)

4.2 Component Customization Test Case Selection

Test cases are extracted in the form of a sequence of methods that can differentiate the test target *cBW* from *fBW* created from applying the different *FIO*s only into *FIT*s We define this test case selection technique for component customization test as follows:

Definition 8. Component Customization Test Case Selection Technique

Component customization test case is a sequence of methods that differentiate *fBW* from *cBW*, where *cBW* stands for customized component and *fBW* stands for fault-injected component. *TC* is a set of these test cases.

$TC = \{ x \mid cBW(x) \neq fBW(x)$, where x is a method sequence.$\}$

Definition 8 is similar to the mutation test case selection technique. However, our technique is distinguishable from the mutation testing technique since our technique improves fault-detectability by injecting a fault only into the *FIT* and it also reduces 'computational bottleneck' which was one of the major problems of mutation test case selection technique.

4.3 An Example

This example utilizes EJB component that operates stock trading. This trading component is provided as a single JAR file, and specific to black-box class in JAR file including remote interface, home interface, and bean class are stored as Java class file formats without source files whereas Deployment Descriptor specific to white-box class is stored as a XML source file.

■ Trading Component, *BW*

Figure 7 shows Trading Component, namely *BW*. This is provided in a JAR file as Trader_Session.jar, and there are 4 files for remote interface, home interface, bean class, and Deployment Descriptor. As shown in Figure 7, Trading Component is organized in Trader.class, TraderHome.class, TraderBean.class, ejb-jar.xml.

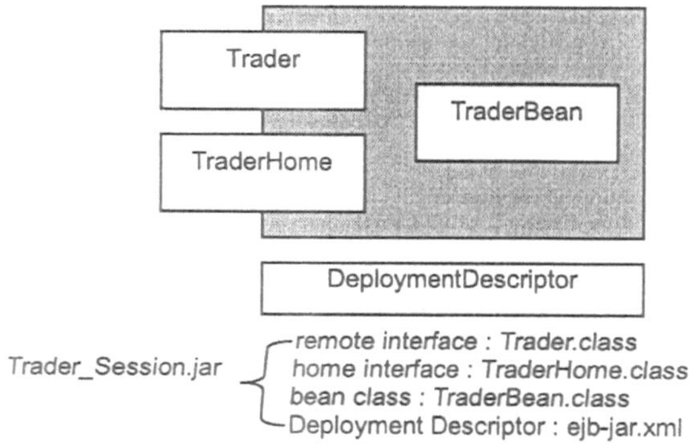

Figure 7. Trading EJB Component

■ *B* in Trading Component

According to definition1, Trading Component's *B* in Figure 7 is associated to remote interface, home interface, and bean class respectively to Trader.class, TraderHome.class, and TraderBean.class. EJB Component contains the contents of implementation in class file formats, and transfers to a black-box similarity.

■ *W* in Trading Component

According to definition 2, Trading Component's *W*

in Figure 7 is associated to deployment descriptor specific to ejb-jar.xml file. Having component's interface in a XML file source code format, EJB Component makes component user modify the contents and transform the component.

■ Customized Trading Component, *cBW*

Our technique applies to *cBW*. In this example, we create *cBW* by customizing Trading Component corresponding to EJB component customization pattern 2. Based on domain specific requirement, the role with limited permission to buy and sell is added to Trading Component's *W*, which creates *cW*.

Figure 8 shows Trading Component's *cW* code customized. Statements in bold fonts indicate the code created or modified by the customization. The *cBW* is organized with Figure 8 and Trading Component's *B*. To visualize the result of test, this case study intentionally puts an error in *cBW*. From the customization of component, instead of offering the permission of buy and sell methods to newly defined role Y, a error is led by only giving buy method permission. This kind of error is put in Figure 8 *cW*. The erroneous *cW* creates *cBW* in EJB Deployer without any problem. Meaning, this error, which can be caused by customization, is a kind that unit test for *cW* cannot detect. This error can cause a critical failure in component-based software implemented to CBSD from an interaction with *B*. So our component customization testing technique proposed in this paper tests this kind of error.

```
...
<security-role>
          <role-name> X </role-name>
  </security-role>
  <security-role>
     <role-name> Y </role-name>
   </security-role>
   <method-permission>
      <role-name> X </role-name>
      <method>
        <ejb-name> statelessSession </ejb-name>
        <method-name> * </method-name>
      </method>
    </method-permission>
   <method-permission>
   <role-name> Y </role-name>
   <method>
        <ejb-name> statelessSession </ejb-name>
        <method-name> buy </method-name>
   </method>
   </method-permission>
  <security-role-ref>
   <role-name> lowQual </role-name>
   <role-link> Y </role-link>
  </security-role-ref>
..
```

Figure 8 Interface of Customized Trading Component

■ Fault Injection Target, *FIT*

According to Table 1, *FIT* of the *cBW* is <role-link> Y </role-link> in <security-role-ref><role-name>lowQual</role-name><role-link> Y </role-link></security-role-ref>.

■ Fault Injection Operator, *FIO*

Based on Table 1, the associated *FIO* is a RRL, which is a substituting operator to a different role link. Applying RRL to the *FIT*, <role-link> Y </role-link>, a different role X is injected as a fault to the *FIT*, <role-link> Y </role-link> to make into <role-link> X </role-link>. The *cBW* injected with the fault becomes *fBW*. Through the fault injection, <role-link> Y </role-link> in cW leads to <role-link> X </role-link> in *fW*.

■ Test Case, *TC*

In order to test *cBW*, many test cases to distinguish *fBW* and *cBW* may be selected based on definition 8. We arbitrarily one test case, lowQual:sell("BEAS",100). The test case, lowQual:sell("BEAS",100), has the *cBW* result of "permission denied", and the *fBW* result of "Selling 100 shares of BEAS", and therefore has selected for a test case according to definition8.

■ Result Analysis

The result which is to apply lowQual:sell("BEAS",100) to *cBW* was "permission denied". However, the expected data of *cBW* for lowQual:sell("BEAS",100) is "Selling 100 shares of BEAS", and the selected test case in our technique shows that *cBW* has an error. The error in *cBW* exists in <method-permission> element as described in section 4.1, and the fault is injected to <role-link>. The places where the error exists and *FIT* totally differ from each other. Our technique allows test cases be tested in all customization relevant to EJB customization pattern 2 as long as they are selected by injecting the fault only to <role-link> that is *FIT* of EJB customization pattern 2, regardless of the whereabouts of the error in the customization code.

5 Analysis

This paper proposed the component customization testing technique by defining the customization patterns, selecting the *FIT*, and then carrying out the customization test by injecting a fault into the *FIT*. In this section, we analyze our technique in view of our customization patterns, *FIT*s, and the scalibility.

5.1 Component Customization Patterns

Our component customization patterns cover the customizations provided by the several popular component architectures, such as JavaBeans, Enterprise JavaBeans, and CORBA. We analyze the customizations of these component architectures in view of our customization patterns as the following.

(1) JavaBeans

In JavaBeans, the customization is made in the following three patterns[7]. First, it customizes by setting the component properties in the property sheet. When using the property sheet, any value within the property variable type can be set. Second, it customizes by setting the component properties in the user property sheet. Utilizing the user property sheet, the component user can set the component's properties under the limitation of what the component developer allows for each property. Third, it customizes by setting Bean properties in the component customizer. The component developer grants the limitation for each property, and the property can be set under the limitation. While User Property sheet involves the same GUI as property sheet format, customizer is designed in various GUI by the component developer.

Three ways of customization mentioned above differ in GUI, but the way of customizing components by setting the component properties are the same in all cases. Therefore, JavaBeans provides customization only for corresponding to our customization patterns of $Pattern.syn_1$ and $Pattern.sem_1$.

(2) Enterprise JavaBeans (EJB)

EJB customizes component using the deployment descriptor in deployment time. There are customization patterns provided as follows[4].

■ EJB Customization Pattern 1

This customization pattern modifies the value of <env-entry-value> in Deployment Descriptor in order to set the property of EJB component to specific requirement for current domain.

Example.

The following is Deployment Descriptor, which set the property to 100.

```
....
<env-entry-name> TradeLimit </env-entry-name>
<env-entry-value> 100 </env-entry-value>
```

■ EJB Customization Pattern 2

This customization pattern adds or modifies the access permission for the component methods. It customizes component by modifying or adding the block of <security-role> in Deployment Descriptor and then setting this security role name to <role-link> for B to refer.

Example.

The following is Deployment Descriptor in which a new role, X is added with having the access permission only to Deposit method, and connected to a role name called client.

```
....
<security-role>
      <role-name> X </role-name>
</security-role>
...
<method-permission>
      <role-name> X </role-name>
      <method>
            <ejb-name> statelessSession </ejb-name>
            <method-name> Deposit </method-name>
      </method>
</method-permission>
...
<security-role-ref>
      <role-name> client </role-name>
      <role-link> X </role-link>
</security-role>
...
```

■ EJB Customization Pattern 3

Among various bean classes that are prepared by EJB component developers and provided with components, the component user chooses according to the domain specific requirement and connects with the corresponding interface. This is possible when the component developer offers several EJB classes per interface.

Example.

The component, RecordResult, used bean class called RecordBean, and then has been customized to use another bean class called RecordBean2 by modifying <ejb-class> in Deployment Descriptor. The following shows the Deployment Descriptor of the RecordResult using RecordBean2. RecordBean2 class was included in the EJB component that was already implemented by component provider.

```
<session>
  <ejb-name>RecordResult</ejb-name>
  <home>example.ejb.basic.statelessSession.RecordHome</home>
  < remote>examples.ejb.basic.statelessSession.Record</remote>
  <ejb-
class>examples.ejb.basic.statelessSession.RecordBean2</ejb-
class>
...
```

■ EJB Customization Pattern 4

This is a customization pattern of EJB component by the composition of other EJB components that has the desired behavior.

Example.

EJB component named Trader using EJB component called RecordResult can be customized to make use another EJB component called RecordResult2. The following is a part of Deployment Descriptor in this customization. RecordResult2 component then can be newly written by component user or be the existing EJB component for the customization. Meaning, the component customization is pursued by composing components such as Trader component and RecordResult2 component.

```
<ejb-ref>
   <ejb-ref-name>ejb/Record</ejb-ref-name>
   <ejb-ref-type>Session</ejb-ref-type>
   <home>examples.ejb.basic.statelessSession.Record2Home</home>
   <remote>examples.ejb.basic.statelessSession.Record2</remote>
   <ejb-link> RecordResult2 </ejb-link>
</ejb-ref>
....
<session>
   <ejb-name>RecordResult2</ejb-name>
   <home>example.ejb.basic.statelessSession.RecordHome</home>
   < remote>examples.ejb.basic.statelessSession.Record</remote>
   <ejb-class>examples.ejb.basic.statelessSession.TraderBean</ejb-class>
...
</session>
```

Since EJB Customization Pattern 1 and 2 are on the levels of the component users to simply select or set the contents provided by the component developers, they correspond to $Pattern.syn_1$ and $Pattern.sem_1$ defined in this paper. EJB Customization Pattern 3 and 4 adds the functions of components or makes changes, and come under $Pattern.syn_2$, $Pattern.syn_3$ and $Pattern.sem_2$.

(3) CORBA 3.0

CORBA3.0 component model precludes customizing a component's behavior by directly altering its implementation or directly deriving specialized sub-types. Component provides a set of optional behaviors and which can be selected and adjusted in each application [9]. Therefore, CORBA 3.0 customization corresponds to $Pattern.syn_1$ and $Pattern.sem_1$.

As mentioned in (1) (2) (3), all the customization patterns provided by the component architecture, which is drawing people's attentions, are included in the component customization patterns defined this paper.

Table 2 Our customization patterns in Component Architectures

Patterns	$Pattern.syn_1$	$Pattern.syn_2$	$Pattern.syn_3$
$Pattern.sem_1$	JavaBeans EJB CORBA		
$Pattern.sem_2$		EJB	EJB

5.2 *FIT*

Our technique used the fault injection technique as we describe in Section 2. Injecting a fault into the whole *cW* is very inefficient for time and cost reasons since it produces too many *fBW*s and test cases. To select an adequate test case for customization test, we must decide where to inject the fault. In this paper, we defined the *FIT*s as where the fault is injected. *FIT*s are a part of *cW*, which affects the interaction between *B* and *cW*. Injecting a fault in our *FIT*s creates a reasonable number of *fBW* and test cases and creates high error detectability for customization testing.

Our *FIT*s are based on the interaction between *B* and *cW*. To analyze this interaction systematically, we developed customization patterns, which stand for 'what to customize' and 'how to customize'. 'What to customize' identifies the *Pattern.sem* and 'How to customize' identifies the *Pattern.syn*. These patterns are based on the traditional design patterns and the features of customization. Also in Section 5.1, we showed that our patterns cover the customizations of the popular component customizations, such as JavaBeans, EJB, and CORBA. Therefore our *FIT*s are valuable for customization test for the application built in the component architectures.

5.3 Scalibility

In section 4.3, a simple error existing in *cBW* was tested by our test case. According to the definition 6, we know the fact that the error existing in *DRE*, *d*, and *IRE*(*d*) can be also detected by our test case. Our test cases can further detect more complex errors in *cBW* based on "coupling effect". "Coupling Effect"[2] is defined as "Test data sets that detect simple types of errors are sensitive enough to detect more complex types of errors". The result of empirical investigation for "Coupling Effect" has been announced as well [8]. Therefore, the test cases selected by our technique can be known for being effective to complex errors due to the component customization.

6 Conclusion and Future Works

Our component customization test technique can be summarized as the following features.

First, our technique tests the component, which provides limited information. Component testing is not solvable by the traditional testing technique, which extracts diverse information from the development artifacts. If the development artifacts of a component are provided at the time of delivery, the cost to manage these artifacts is required. A component is delivered with the minimum number of artifacts and interface, which is the only information our technique requires for testing. Therefore our technique is valuable for component testing.

Second, our technique injects a fault into the *FIT*s. *FIT*s are selected for their high error-detectability of test cases by considering the interaction between *B* and *cW*. Our technique injects a fault not into the whole *cW* or the customization code, but into the *FIT*s. Thus we expect to result in efficient testing time, lower cost, and higher test case effectiveness.

Third, our technique is based on the customization patterns, which can cover the customizations of the component architectures. Thus our technique can be applied to customization testing for the application built in the component architecture, such as JavaBeans, EJB, and CORBA. Therefore our technique can be expanded into each component architecture specific testing technique.

In the future, we will develop component architecture specific testing technique by expanding our technique for the actual CBD domain. We also plan to measure our test case's effectiveness for component customization test through an experiment and justify our *FIT* through a proof. And then we will build the tool that generates *fBW* and the test cases by applying our *FIT*s and *FIO*s automatically.

References

[1] P. Allen, "Practical Strategies for Migration to CBD," *IT Journal Distributed Component Systems*, 1999.

[2] R.A.DeMillo, R.J.Lipton, and F.G.Sayward, "Hints on Test Data Selection : Help for the Practicing Programmer," *IEEE Computer*, 11(4):34-41, Apr 1978

[3] Marcio Eduardo Delamaro and Aditya Mathur, "Integration Testing Using Interface Mutations," SERC-TR-169-P, Apr. 1996

[4] Enterprise JavaBeans Specification 1.1 at URL:http://www.javasoft.com/

[5] Mary Jean Harrold, "Testing : A Roadmap," In Future of Software Engineering, 22nd ICSE, Jun. 2000

[6] J.-M.Jezequel and B.Meyer, "Design by Contract : The Lessons of Ariane," *Computer*, pp. 129-130, Jan. 1997

[7] Micheal Morrison, Randy Weems, Peter Coffee, and Jack Leong, How to Program JavaBeans, Ziff-Davis Press, 1997

[8] A.Jefferson Offutt, "Investigations of the Software Testing Coupling Effect," ACM Trans. On Software Engineering and Methodology, 1(!):5-20, Jan. 1992

[9] OMG, CORBA Component, OMG TC Documentation, Mar, 1998

[10] Weyuker.E.J, "Testing Component-Based Software: A Cautionary Tale," IEEE software, Sep/Oct. 1998

[11] Wolfgang Pree, Design Patterns for Object-Oriented Software Development, Addison-Wesley, 1994

Mutating Network Models to Generate Network Security Test Cases

Ronald W. Ritchey
Booz•Allen & Hamilton
Falls Church, Virginia
ritchey_ronald@bah.com

Abstract

Security testing is normally limited to the scanning of individual hosts with the goal of locating vulnerabilities that can be exploited to gain some improper level of access on the target network. Scanning is a successful approach for discovering security problems, but it suffers from two major problems. First, it ignores security issues that can arise due to interactions of systems on a network. Second, it does not provide any concept of test coverage other than the obvious criteria of attempting all known exploitation techniques on every system on the network.

In this paper, I present a new method for generating security test cases for a network. This method extends my previous work in model checking network security by defining mutant operators to apply to my previously defined network security model. The resulting mutant models are fed into a model checker to produce counterexamples. These counterexamples represent attack scenarios (test cases) that can be run against the network. I also define a new coverage criterion for network security that requires a much smaller set of exploits to be run against the network to verify the network's security.

1. Introduction

Network security installations are frequently implemented using the fortress model. Attackers from the outside need to surmount formidable external obstacles before they can reach the internal protected systems. Most of the security effort is focused on attempting to create this barrier between the outside and the internal resources. Very little effort is focused on internal security. This model has the advantage of allowing the security team to focus on a much smaller set of hosts and configurations when implementing the security policy but it is fundamentally flawed.

Unless the barrier that is set up does not allow any connectivity there is some possibility that an attacker may circumvent the border defenses. This is due to the following issue. For a network to be useful it must offer services. These services are implemented in software and it is difficult to guarantee that any complex piece of software does not contain some flaws [Beizer]. These flaws frequently translate into security vulnerabilities. If exploitable flaws exist in a service, even if the flaws have not been discovered, they still represent a potential for network intrusion. New security bugs are frequently discovered in server software.

Given that it is impossible to state with final authority that there are no possible ways to bypass the border security, it follows that some effort must be expended upon internal systems if the network is truly to be considered secure. This leaves open the problem of how to best protect these internal systems, without overwhelming the security team.

Some sites rely on automated tools to perform vulnerability scanning of each host on the network. Programs such as Computer Oracle and Password System (COPS) [COPS], System Scanner by ISS [ISS], and CyberCop by Network Associates [NAI] are examples of tools that can scan hosts to attempt to discover vulnerabilities in the host's configuration. These tools typically perform a decent job of discovering host vulnerabilities, but they do require significant time and effort to execute and evaluate their results. In addition they do not attempt to identify how combinations of configurations on the same host or between hosts on the same network can contribute to the network's vulnerability.

In my previous work [Ritchey] I demonstrated the value of extending beyond a host-only vulnerability assessment. I created a modeling-based approach to network security that can be used to analyze the overall security of a network based on the interactions of vulnerabilities within a single host and within a network of hosts. This approach relies on model checking technology to analyze the resulting model to determine whether the network's security requirements are met or if there is a method that could be used to invalidate any of the requirements. Security requirements are encoded as assertions in the model checker. If the model checker can invalidate an assertion, it demonstrates this by showing the set of steps it followed to prove the assertion false. This sequence represents a potential path an attacker could use to gain access to the network.

In this paper I apply mutation operators to my network security model to produce new test cases. Mutant models that do not meet the defined security requirements (i.e. the change caused a security requirement to be invalidated) represent single configuration changes to the network that would result in a compromise of the network's security. By identifying which individual configuration changes result in a network compromise, we significantly reduce the total number of system features that must be verified to assure the network's security.

2. An Overview of Model Checking

A model checking specification consists of two parts. One part is the model: a state machine defined in terms of variables, initial values for the variables, and a description of the conditions under which variables may change value. The other part is temporal logic constraints over states and execution paths. Conceptually, a model checker visits all reachable states and verifies that the temporal logic properties are satisfied over each possible path, that is, the model checker determines if the state machine is a model for the temporal logic formula. Model checkers exploit clever ways of avoiding brute force exploration of the state space [Birch]. If a property is not satisfied, the model checker attempts to generate a counterexample in the form of a trace or sequence of states.

The model checking approach to formal methods has received considerable attention in the literature. Tools such as SMV, SPIN, and Murø are capable of handling the state spaces associated with realistic problems [Clark]. I use the [SMV] model checker, which is freely available from Carnegie Mellon University and elsewhere. Although model checking began as a method for verifying hardware designs, there is growing evidence that model checking can be applied with considerable automation to specifications for relatively large software systems, such as TCAS II [Chan]. Model checking has been successfully applied to a wide variety of practical problems. These include hardware design, protocol analysis, operating systems, reactive system analysis, fault tolerance, and security [Holzmann].

The increasing usefulness of model checkers for software systems makes model checkers attractive tools for use in aspects of software development other than pure analysis, which is their primary role today. Model checkers are desirable tools to incorporate because they are explicitly designed to handle large state spaces and they generate counterexamples efficiently. Thus they provide a mechanism to avoid custom building these same capabilities into special purpose tools. For these reasons, I encode the security of a computer network in a finite state description and then write assertions in the temporal logic to the effect that "An attacker can never acquire certain rights on a given host." I then use the model checker to verify that the claim holds in the model or to generate an attack scenario against the network that shows how the attacker penetrates the system.

3. Network Exploitation Methods

This section presents the network intrusion methodology that was used to develop the techniques presented in this paper.

3.1 Vulnerability

Breaking into a computer network requires that vulnerabilities exist in the network and that exploits for the vulnerabilities are known. Any network that an attacker has connectivity with will have some level of vulnerability. The goal of network security is to try to limit this vulnerability to the minimum required to accomplish the purpose of the network.

Network vulnerability is impossible to entirely eliminate. This is due to several factors. For a network to be useful it must offer services. These services are implemented in software and it is difficult to guarantee that any complex piece of software does not contain some flaws [Beizer]. These flaws frequently translate into security vulnerabilities. Sometimes, even when a security flaw is known, the operational need to offer a service with the vulnerability supercedes the need for the network to be totally secure. Network vulnerability may also be created by poor configuration. Given the large number of hosts on some networks, it is not surprising that some of them may not be set up to maximize their defenses. Many hosts are administered by the primary user of the system, who may lack the proper training to configure a secure computer system.

3.2 Exploitation

Before an attacker can attempt to break into a computer system several conditions must be met. An attacker must know a technique (e.g. exploit) that can be used to attempt the attack. However, knowing the exploit is not enough. Before an exploit can be used its preconditions must be met. These preconditions include the set of vulnerabilities that the exploit relies on, sufficient user rights on the target, sufficient user rights on the attacking host, and basic connectivity. The result of a successful exploit is not necessarily a compromised system; most exploits simply cause an increase in the vulnerability of the network. Results of a successful exploit could include discovering valuable information about the network, elevating user rights, defeating filters, and adding trust relationships among other possible effects. Most successful attacks consist of a series of exploits that gradually increase the vulnerability of the network until the prerequisites of the final exploit are met.

Network attackers normally start their work by searching for vulnerabilities on the hosts they can communicate with on the target's network. When a vulnerability is discovered they use it to increase the vulnerability level of the host. Once a host is compromised to the point that the attacker has some remote control of it, the host can then be used to launch attacks further into the network. This will more than likely include hosts that the attacker can not reach directly.

The attacker can use this new point of view to extend the number of hosts that can be searched for vulnerabilities; perhaps discovering new hosts that can eventually be taken over. This process can be continued until the network is fully compromised, the attacker can no longer find additional vulnerabilities to exploit or the attacker's goals are met.

4. Example Network

The purpose of this example is to provide a simple network structure to use for demonstrating the value of this analysis technique. It is composed of a small organization's network that includes a web server that they use to provide information to their customers. Due to budget constraints, public domain software is used throughout the network to reduce costs. The web server they have chosen to use is the widely used Apache web server [Apache]. They have installed the web server using the copy that was included on an old RedHat Linux [RedHat] distribution. Because they are a small company they only maintain one network segment so the web server gets placed on the same segment as their file server. This network structure is shown in figure 1.

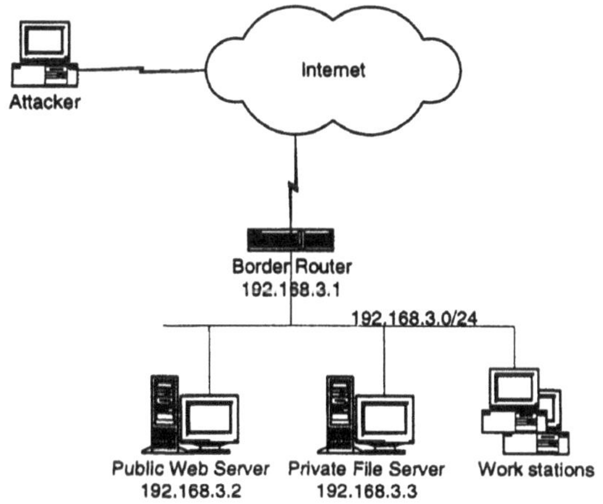

Figure 1

To protect this private server from the Internet they have installed packet filtering rules on their border router. These rules allow hosts on the Internet to connect to the web server, but not with the private server. Table 1 shows the filtering rules that are being enforced at the border router.

Source Address	Destination Address	Action
ANY	192.168.3.2	Allow
192.168.3.0/24	Not 192.168.3.0/24	Allow
Any	Any	Deny

Table 1. Border Filtering Rules

External users use web browsers to communicate with the public web server but they are not supposed to have any other access to the network. Private users rely on the private file server to hold their home directories that often contain company proprietary data. These directories are shared with the users of the network using Network File Service (NFS).

They also occasionally use a custom database application located on the file server that they access by remotely logging in to the server using the rlogin command from their workstations.

5. An Overview of the Network Security Model

This section provides an overview of the network security model that was described in my previous network security analysis paper [Ritchey].

5.1 Composition of the Model

There are five major elements that make up our network security model.

- Hosts on the network including their vulnerabilities
- Connectivity of the hosts
- Current point of view of the attacker
- Exploit techniques that can be used to change the state of the model

- A list of security requirements the model should attempt to validate

Hosts represent potential targets for the attacker and have two major attributes, the attackers current access level on the host and the hosts set of vulnerabilities. A successful attack requires that vulnerabilities exist in the network and that exploits for the vulnerabilities are known. These vulnerabilities are broadly defined. In the model any fact about the host that could conceivably be required as a prerequisite for an exploit is a vulnerability. Taken from the example network, the web server would be described to the model as follows.

Vulnerabilities		Current Access Level
Solaris version 2.5.1 Apache version 1.04 Telnetd Ftpd	Count.cgi Phf.cgi No shadow file Dtappgather	None

Table 2. Sample Host

This list includes vulnerability information such as the version of the operating system and web server, as well as the access level to the server that the attacker will begin with.

It is important that the model be able to represent limited connectivity. Any network that an attacker has connectivity with will have some level of vulnerability. Because of this, a key security technique is network layer filtering. It is important for the model to be able to represent the connectivity between hosts that remains after all filters (firewalls) that exist between the hosts have been examined. To allow a simple example, the model represents connectivity between hosts as a matrix of boolean values. In the example network the router's filtering rules are represented by the following table.

	Attacker	Border Router	Public Web Server	Private File Server
Attacker	N/A	Yes	Yes	No
Border Router	Yes	N/A	Yes	Yes
Public Web Server	Yes	Yes	N/A	Yes
Private File Server	No	Yes	Yes	N/A

Table 3. Connectivity Matrix

Connectivity between different hosts will vary due to the different network filters. If a hacker can gain control of a host, the attacker may be able to launch attacks from the host. It is important to model the point of view of the attacker so that the set of hosts that are reachable by the attacker includes hosts reachable by hosts under the attacker's control. The model maintains a level of access field on each host. Any host that has a level of access higher than none may be used to launch some exploits. When determining which hosts the attacker can reach, the model checker looks for any hosts that are reachable from the union of all hosts with an access level greater than none.

Before an attacker can attempt to break into a computer system the attacker must know an exploit that can be used to attempt the attack. However, knowing the exploit is not enough. Before an exploit can be used its preconditions must be met. These preconditions include the set of vulnerabiiities that the exploit relies on, sufficient user rights on the target, sufficient user rights on the attacking host, and basic connectivity. The model defines exploits by the set of vulnerabilities, source access level, target access level, and connectivity they require, plus the results they have on the state of the model if they are successful. Exploits are used by the model to affect changes to the security of the hosts under analysis. The quality and quantity of exploits encoded in the model have a direct relationship with the quality of the analysis that can be performed with the model. An example exploit included in the demonstration is the PHF.cgi program. This program shipped with several versions of the Apache web server and allowed a remote attacker the ability to execute programs on the host. Table 4 shows how the exploit was represented in the model.

Prerequisites	Source Access Level	Target Access Level	Results
(Apache versions up to 1.0.4 OR NCSA versions up to 1.5a) AND phf program	Any	Any	Access level changed to httpd

Table 4. Sample Exploit

Security requirements are written as invariant statements in the model checker's temporal logic formula language. Each security requirement needs to be formulated as a temporal logic formula. The full expressivity of temporal logic is not normally used. Most assertions take the form of events that should never happen. For example, a typical security requirement might be "An attacker can never access the Private File Server". In SMV this would be formulated as AG (PrivateFileServer.Access = None). If the model checker can reach any state where an invariant statement is false then we know that it is possible for an external attacker to violate one of our security requirements.

5.2 Execution of the Model

After the network has been described to the model checker and initialized, the model checker begins to determine whether the security assertions made about the model are true. The model checker starts by determining the set of hosts the attacker has connectivity with and non-deterministically chooses one. The model checker then tries to locate an exploit that can be used against the host. All prerequisite vulnerabilities for the exploit must exist on the target host. In addition, the prerequisite access levels (source and destination) must be met. If successful, the results of the exploit are used to change the state of the target by adding additional vulnerabilities and/or changing the attacker's access level on the host.

If an exploit is successful it reduces the overall security of the network. This is true because it may be possible to run other exploits against the host if the additional vulnerabilities added match the prerequisite vulnerabilities for another exploit. The attacker may also be able to communicate with new hosts if the attacker's access level on the target host is increased (thereby allowing the attacker to use the target host to launch attacks).

The model checker will continue to locate hosts to attack and will continue to search for valid exploits to use until all possibilities have been explored or all of the security assertions have been proven false. The results are counter examples for each disproved assertion and a validation for any remaining assertions.

6. Mutating the Model

Mutation analysis was originally a code-based analysis technique for automating the development of test cases [Offutt]. Recent applications of this technique have been used to design test cases from specifications. Here mutation analysis is applied to define test cases for network security.

Mutation analysis works by defining mutation operators that are used to create many versions of the original program (in this case model). Mutation operators are defined so that when each is applied it causes some small but significant change to the program. As an example, one mutation operator for code-level analysis changes a less-than comparison to a greater-than comparison.

An individual mutant operator is used to create each mutant version. Each version represents a mutant of the original program that has been intentionally flawed. Test cases are created and run against the mutants with the goal of causing the mutant version to fail. Test cases that cause a mutant to fail are said to *kill* the mutant. The ultimate goal is to design a test set that causes all generated mutant programs to fail. It is important to note that some mutants are impossible to kill. This occurs when the mutant is functionally equivalent to the original program.

6.1 Defining Mutation Operators

For network compromise to be possible, an exploit's prerequisites need to be met. This makes the exploit prerequisites an excellent source for defining our mutant operators. Potential operators include adding vulnerabilities, increasing access levels, and adding connectivity. Each of these changes would have the effect of making the model less secure than the original. There is no point in introducing mutations that remove vulnerabilities, connectivity, or access level as this would have the effect of making the mutant model more secure than the original model.

Each of these potential mutant operators represents a different real-world change that could occur to the network. However, not all changes that are possible in the model are likely in the network. It is important that we recognize what each mutant type represents in the actual network so that we can intelligently filter out inappropriate mutants.

Add connectivity is the simplest of the mutant operators. An add connectivity mutant demonstrates the effect of a change to a firewall's ruleset that allows more traffic past. This type of configuration change is common (though frequently unwise) on production networks. By adding connectivity to the model, we demonstrate what level of access could be gained by an attacker if the firewall configuration was changed. In the example network, there is only one restriction placed upon communication, the attacker cannot talk directly with the private file server. In this case, the add connectivity mutant would allow us to see the ramifications of allowing the attacker direct access to the private file server.

Increase access level is more difficult. Increase access level implies that an attacker is starting with more access than a typical external attacker would have. This could occur if the attacker was an insider or was given information by an insider. One problem in adding access to arbitrary hosts inside the network is the problem of connectivity. The attacker should only be able to use machines during an attack that can be communicated with by the attacker. Any host in the model that has an access level greater than none can be used by the model in the attack. Due to this, it is important that access levels on systems that the attacker cannot gain access to not be modified. As it is unclear at the beginning of the analysis which systems the attacker will eventually be able to communicate with, it is difficult to decide in advance which systems could be correctly mutated by increasing the attacker's access level. An alternative is to introduce a vulnerability that would guarantee the attacker increased access should the attacker gain connectivity to the host. This is easily accomplished by defining a new *super* vulnerability with its matching exploit. With this change, the add vulnerability mutant is sufficient to model the increase access mutant. From the example network, an increase access level mutant would grant the attacker user privileges on the web server, even though the attacker does not normally start with these privileges. This might be valuable if we assume that there is some method (yet unknown) that would allow the attacker to gain this access. This is actually a reasonable assumption as new exploitation methods are discovered daily.

The *add vulnerability* mutant models changes to the configuration of the target system. These could include adding software, changing permissions, modifying settings, etc. There are many changes that are likely to occur during the lifecycle of a system that would result in the addition of vulnerabilities.

In a real-world network, the number of possible changes that could be made would be infinite and would make generating a maximal set of mutants impossible. This is not a problem with the network model though as the model only considers system features that are known prerequisites for an exploit. Since the model has a finite number of encoded exploits, there will only be a finite number vulnerabilities in the model.

An additional issue that must be addressed is the addition of unlikely or infeasible vulnerabilities. A good example would be trying to add Unix specific vulnerabilities to a Windows NT system. These invalid vulnerabilities must be eliminated before the analysis is conducted. In the example network the analysis to weed out invalid add vulnerability mutants was conducted manually. To be able to automate the elimination of unreasonable vulnerabilities requires that more be known about each vulnerability. A structure is required that would allow vulnerabilities to be categorized. One possible structure is shown in figure 2. In this structure, vulnerabilities are separated into four categories, devices, operating systems, software, and basic vulnerabilities. Vulnerabilities can only be applied if their parent vulnerability already exists. For each vulnerability (except devices), a parent vulnerability would need to exist before the vulnerability could be applied. For example, there is an elevation of privilege exploit that relies on a faulty version of a program called dtappgather. The vulnerable version of dtappgather was shipped with several versions of the Solaris operating system. Another way to say this is that the dtappgather vulnerability relies on the host running one of a set of particular versions of Solaris. So we model the dtappgather vulnerability as a software vulnerability that relies on Solaris 2.5, Solaris 2.5.1, or Solaris 2.6. If any host in the model is running any of these operating systems, it would be reasonable to add the dtappgather vulnerability.

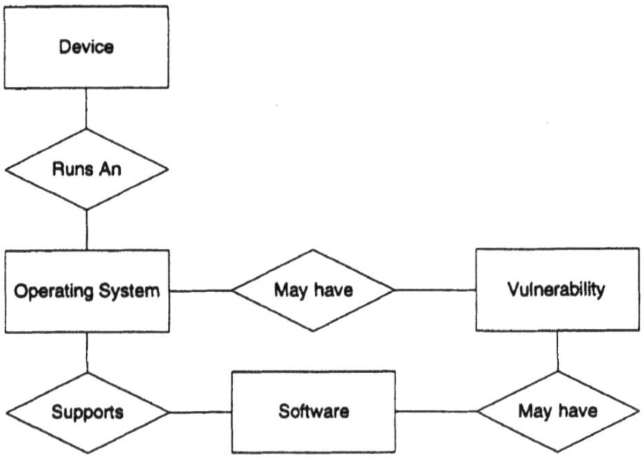

Figure 2

Another consideration is the likelihood of a particular configuration change. It is frequently uninteresting to consider a change in a device type, or an operating system. These types of changes occur very infrequently. In some circumstances, it may also not be interesting to see if adding any possible software package would invalidate the security. These categories of vulnerability should be automatically eliminated from consideration.

6.2 Coverage Criterion for Network Security

A well-designed and configured network should not produce any counter examples when analyzed by this system. However, this analysis is conducted at a particular place in time, and with a particular network configuration. It is unlikely that the network's configuration will remain static. Changes will be made periodically. These changes could introduce additional vulnerabilities that could invalidate the previous analysis. It would be useful to be able to extend beyond a spot check of the network's security and instead address specifically what changes should be avoided in the future to prevent undermining the network's security. This is the advantage of this mutation system.

By introducing a single vulnerability into the model and viewing any resulting counterexamples, the system can identify the individual configuration changes that could lead to network compromise. This would lead to a list of configuration changes that could be phrased as "if we change this parameter, then this security requirement will be invalidated". Extending beyond a single mutation per mutant gives us the ability to look for combinations of configuration changes that would undermine the network. For example, if we allow two mutant operators per mutant model, we could create lists of security issues that could be phrased as "if we change this parameter, and this parameter, then this security requirement will be invalidated".

This definition of network security mutation coverage is based upon the number of mutant operators that can be applied together to produce a counterexample free analysis of the network. If the coverage level is set to one, then the network should be able to have any single configuration value changed without undermining the security of the network. If the level is two, then the network can survive two configuration changes without fear of a compromise. The higher the number, the more difficult it would be for the network to be placed into an insecure state.

6.3 Running the Analysis

To perform the analysis, a network model is created that reflects the current configuration of the network. Security requirements are then encoded into the model in the form of the invariant statements. Next mutants of the model are generated based upon the different mutant operators. Depending upon the coverage level, different numbers of mutant operators may be applied to produce a single mutant model. If any mutants have been generated that are not relevant or reasonable in the context of our network, they are removed in the next step. Finally, the remaining mutant models are run through the model checker. If all mutants verify the security requirements (i.e. none produce counterexamples) the network meets the current coverage level. Otherwise, the network needs to be reconfigured to eliminate the source of the vulnerabilities and the analysis must be run again.

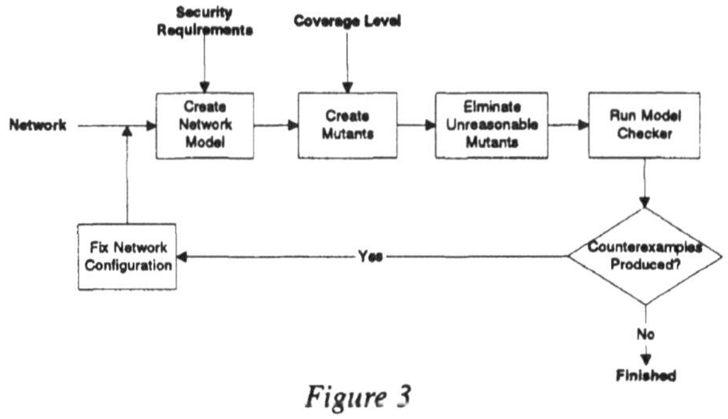

Figure 3

7. Results

A model of the example network was created and a level one analysis was conducted (only one mutation allowed per mutant). The result was a total of 30 different mutant models, one mutant created by an add connectivity mutation, and 29 created by add vulnerability mutations. Of these, 13 were judged to be unreasonable and were removed. This left 17 mutations that were analyzed by the model checker. Six of these models produced counter examples. By evaluating the first couple of steps in the counter examples produced, it is possible for a security analyst to create recommended configuration changes. These counter examples with sample security recommendations are shown in table 5.

Number	Mutant	1st Exploit	Security Recommendation
1	Add Connectivity from Attacker to PrivateFileServer	Add BSD trust from Attacker to PrivateFileServer	Eliminate BSD daemons on PrivateFileServer
2	Add PHF program to PublicWebServer	Use PHF to gain user access to PublicWebServer	Verify PHF not on PublicWebServer
3	Password Hashes known on PublicWebServer	Brute Force Passwords on PublicWebServer	Use strong authentication on PublicWebServer
4	Root password known on PublicWebServer	Telnet to PublicWebServer	Use strong authentication on PublicWebServer
5	BSD trust between Attacker and PublicWebServer	rlogin to PublicWebServer	Eliminate BSD daemons on PublicWebServer
6	User passwords known on PublicWebServer	Telnet to PublicWebServer	Use strong authentication on PublicWebServer

Table 5

8. Conclusions and Future Work

The significant contribution of this work is its ability to provide direct advice to assist security analyst to create highly secure networks. The results of this analysis point out the exact areas of the network that need to have additional protection. This automates the discovery of the factors that could lead to network compromise. In addition, the coverage criterion provides a unique and quantitative way to rate a network's security.

For this technique to be realized as a fully functioning tool several tasks need to be accomplished. First, the basic network modeling analysis this mutation technique relies upon needs to be fleshed out. This requires that the model be populated with a significant set of exploits, that a tool be created that scans for the vulnerabilities these exploits require, and that the connectivity model is extended to provide a more complete representation of TCP/IP functionality. In addition, each vulnerability in the model needs to be categorized, and the system features that the vulnerabilities relied upon needs to be recorded. Finally, the mutation engine needs to be automated so that it accepts as input the network model and the coverage level and either produces a list of mutants that violate the model or verifies that the model meets the coverage criterion.

9. References

[Apache] Apache Web Server information and software on the web at www.apache.com.

[Beizer] B. Beizer, "Software Testing Techniques, 2nd edition," Thomson Computer Press, 1990.

[Birch] J. Birch, E. Clark, K. McMillan, D. Dill, and L.J. Hwang, Symbolic Model Checking: 10^{20} States and Beyond, *Proceedings of the ACM/SIGDA International Workshop in Formal Methods in VLSI Design*, January, 1991.

[Chan] W. Chan, R. Anderson, P. Beame, S. Burns, F. Modugno, and D. Notkin, Model Checking Large Software Specifications, *IEEE Transactions on Software Engineering*, Vol. 24, No. 7, July 1998.

[Clark] E. Clark, O. Grumberg, and D. Long, Verification Tools For Finite-State Concurrent Systems, *A Decade of Concurrency – Reflections and Perspectives*, Springer Verlag, 1994.

[COPS] Computer Oracle and Password System (COPS) information and software on the web at ftp.cert.org/pub/tools/cops.

[Holzmann] G. Holzmann, The Model Checker SPIN, *IEEE Transactions on Software Engineering*, Vol 23, No 5, May 1997.

[ISS] Internet Security Systems, System Scanner information on the web at www.iss.net.

[Mayer] A. Mayer, A. Wool and E. Ziskind, Fang: A Firewall Analysis Engine, *Proceedings of the IEEE Symposium on Security and Privacy*, Oakland, CA, 2000.

[NAI] Network Associates, CyberCop Scanner information on the web at www.nai.com/asp_set/products/tns/ccscanner_intro.asp.

[Offutt] J. Offutt, Practical Mutation Testing, *Twelfth International Conference on Testing Computer Software*, pages 99—109, Washington, DC, June 1995.

[RedHat] RedHat Linux information and software on the web at www.redhat.com.

[Ritchey], R. Ritchey and P. Ammann, Using Model Checking To Analyze Network Security, *2000 IEEE Symposium on Security and Privacy*, May 2000.

[SMV] SMV information and software on the web at www.cs.cmu.edu/~modelcheck.

[Zerkle] D. Zerkle and K. Levitt, NetKuang – A Multi-Host Configuration Vulnerability Checker, In *Proceedings of the Sixth USENIX Unix Security Symposium*, San Jose, CA, 1996.

Keynote

Programs Determined by Mutation-Adequate tests

Dick Hamlet
Department of Computer Science
Portland State University

Abstract

This talk explores the motivation behind mutation as a "data coverage" idea parallel to the usual control-flow-coverage testing. In this view, to kill arithmetic-expression mutants requires a spread of test data, and that data then "covers" the expression. This idea originated about 1970 in partial-recursive function theory, in a study of execution traces that determine the function a program computes. By extension, the mutation-adequate test set determines the only possible program with those traces.

The theoretical ideas led to a mutation system built on a compiler base (1975-1976). Compiled code was executed down to the point of mutation, then mutant expressions were interpretively executed to detect failures of either weak or strong mutation coverage. The system also accepted oracle data to certify test results.

Panel

Future of Mutation Testing and Its Application

Moderator
Jeff Offutt (George Mason University)

Panelists
John Clark (University of York, UK)
Rich DeMillo (Telcordia Technologies)
Dick Lipton (Georgia Institute of Technology)
Martin Woodward (University of Liverpool, UK)

What's in the Future?

- No future for mutation?
- Widely used in unit testing?
- Integrated with compilers?
- Evaluation of other testing techniques?
- Objected-oriented software testing?
- Specification-based testing?
- Design-based testing?
- Web-based software?

Interface Mutation

Interface Mutation

Sudipto Ghosh

Computer Science Department
Colorado State University
Fort Collins, CO 80523
ghosh@cs.colostate.edu

Aditya P. Mathur

Department of Computer Sciences
Purdue University
West Lafayette IN 47907
apm@cs.purdue.edu

Abstract

Applications that utilize the broker-based architecture are often composed of several components that need to be tested both separately and together. An important activity during testing is the assessment of the adequacy of test sets. Testers use one or more adequacy criteria for this activity. Traditional test adequacy criteria have several limitations for commercial use. A test adequacy criterion based on interface mutation has been identified and a testing method that uses this criterion proposed. This method incorporates elements from a component's interface description for per-forming interface mutation.

The interface mutation based test adequacy criterion was evaluated empirically and compared with control flow-based coverage criteria for their relative effectiveness in revealing errors and the cost incurred in developing the test sets. A formal analysis of the fault-detection ability of the testing methods was also carried out.

Proteum/IM 2.0: An Integrated Mutation Testing Environment

Márcio Eduardo Delamaro
Departamento de Informática
Universidade Estadual de Maringá
delamaro@din.uem.br

José Carlos Maldonado
Auri Marcelo Rizzo Vincenzi
Instituto de Ciências Matemáticas e de Computação
Universidade de São Paulo
{jcmaldon, auri}@icmc.sc.usp.br

Abstract

Mutation testing has been used mostly at the unit level. To support its application few tools have been developed and used, mainly in the academic environment. Interface Mutation has been proposed aiming at applying mutation at the integration level. A tool named Proteum/IM was implemented to support such criterion. With the definition of the Interface Mutation criterion the tester has the possibility of applying mutation testing concepts throughout the software development. It seems mandatory to have a single, integrated environment that would support mutation-based unit and integration testing. Such environment, which provides facilities to investigate low-cost and incremental testing strategies, is the focus of this paper.

Keywords: Software Testing, Mutation testing, Interface Mutation, Testing Tool, Proteum/IM 2.0.

1 Introduction

Software testing is an incremental activity that lasts most of the development life cycle. First, each unit developed must be tested on its internal and algorithmical features. Afterwards, these units already tested separately have to be integrated and tested again, in order to check the interacting aspects between them. The former activity is know as **unit testing** and the later, as **integration testing**.

Many testing adequacy criteria have been proposed for the assessment of the test set quality. Most of them are concerned with or directed to unit testing, mainly because their test requirements are limited to the scope of a single unit, failing on exercising interprocedural structures. As a consequence, only functional testing has been used at the integration level testing most of the time.

A few exceptions can be identified, of non functional testing criteria for integration testing, for example [11, 12, 14, 17]. Even so, it is not clear what are the consequences of combining a criterion C_U in the unit testing with a criterion C_I in the integration level. An interesting point to address is: "What could one avoid in a C_I-based integration testing if the tester knows that C_U criterion had been applied at the unit level?" or in similar way, "what could one avoid in a C_U based unit testing if the tester knows that criterion C_I would be used at the integration testing?"

Mutation testing has traditionally been used at the unit testing. In a recent work, its use was extended to deal with interprocedural aspects, allowing its use for integration testing. A criterion, named Interface Mutation was proposed [7, 9, 10]. This paper describes a tool named Proteum/IM 2.0 which supports the application of mutation concepts throughout the software development: traditional mutation testing at the unit level and the Interface Mutation criterion at the integration level. Proteum/IM 2.0 is an evolution of *Proteum* [8], for unit testing, and Proteum/IM [10], for integration testing.

Thus, Proteum/IM 2.0 allowsthe application of a single concept (mutation) for the unit and the integration testing phases. It favors the conduction of studies that help to understand and improve mutation based testing strategies.

In the next section we briefly describe Interface Mutation. In Section 3 we show the main functionalities of Proteum/IM 2.0 presenting its graphical interface and its execution through shell scripts. In Section 4 we discuss some issues of its implementation. We comment about the approaches used to the two most important tasks required in such a tool: the generation and storage of mutants and their execution. In Section 5 we show a simple application of the tool where we try to expose some advantages of using a single environment that supports mutation testing and Interface Mutation testing. In Section 6 we make our final remarks and present ongoing and future work.

2 Interface Mutation

Mutation testing has been used mostly at the unit level, mainly because the kind of error the mutant operators aim at is restricted to unit errors. Interface Mutation [7] extends mutation testing to the integration level. When applying Interface Mutation the tester is concerned with integration errors, i.e., those errors related to a connection between two units and the interactions along that connection. In general, a connection is defined by a subprogram call and interactions defined by parameters and global variables.

Given a connection between units f and g (f calls g), there are two groups of mutations: operators in the first group apply changes to the body of function g, for instance, incrementing a reference to a formal parameter. Operators in the second group apply mutations to the places unit f calls g, for example, incrementing an argument.

Before presenting the Interface Mutation operators we need to define:

$P(g)$: The set of formal parameters of g. This set also includes references to pointer and array parameters. For example, when a parameter v is defined `int *v` or `int **v`, v and *v belong to this set.

$G(g)$: The set of global variables accessed by g.

$L(g)$: The set of variables declared in g (local variables).

$E(g)$: The set of global variables not accessed in g.

$C(g)$: The set of constants used in g.

Also the set R is defined; it does not depend on the tested connection under test. This is the set of "required constants". It contains some special values, relevant for each data type and associated operators. Table 1 summarizes these constants.

Table 1. Required constant sets.

Variable Type	*Required Constants*
signed integer signed char signed long	-1, 1, 0, MAXINT, MININT
unsigned integer unsigned char unsigned long enum	-1, 1, 0, MAXUNSIGNED
float double	-1.0, 1.0, 0.0, -0.0

Constants MAXINT, MININT and MAXUNSIGNED correspond respectively to the largest positive integer, smallest negative integer and largest unsigned integer. These values are machine and data type dependent.

Each operator has a name that identifies it uniquely amongst all the Interface Mutation operators. Table 2 list the name and meaning of the Interface Mutation operators.

It is important to note that the application of Interface Mutation is related to one connection between two units.

Table 2. Interface Mutation Operators.

Group-I	
Operator	*Description*
CovAllEdg	Coverage of all edges
CovAllNod	Coverage of all nodes
DirVarAriNeg	Inserts arithmetic negation at interface variable
DirVarBitNeg	Inserts bit negation at interface variable
DirVarIncDec	Inserts/removes ++ and – at interface variable
DirVarLogNeg	Inserts logical negation at interface variable
DirVarRepCon	Replaces interface variable by set C
DirVarRepExt	Replaces interface variable by set E
DirVarRepGlo	Replaces interface variable by set G
DirVarRepLoc	Replaces interface variable by set L
DirVarRepPar	Replaces interface variable by set P
DirVarRepReq	Replaces interface variable by set R
IndVarAriNeg	Inserts arithmetic negation at non interface variable
IndVarBitNeg	Inserts bit negation at non interface variable
IndVarIncDec	Inserts/removes ++ and – at non interface variable
IndVarLogNeg	Inserts logical negation at non interface variable
IndVarRepCon	Replaces non interface variable by set C
IndVarRepExt	Replaces non interface variable by set E
IndVarRepGlo	Replaces non interface variable by set G
IndVarRepLoc	Replaces non interface variable by set L
IndVarRepPar	Replaces non interface variable by set P
IndVarRepReq	Replaces non interface variable by set R
RetStaDel	Deletes return statement
RetStaRep	Replaces return statement
Group-II	
Operator	*Description*
ArgAriNeg	Inserts arithmetic negation at arguments
ArgBitNeg	Inserts bit negation at arguments
ArgDel	Remove argument
ArgIncDec	Argument Increment and Decrement
ArgLogNeg	Inserts logical negation at arguments
ArgRepReq	Replaces arguments by set R
ArgStcAli	Switches arguments of compatible type
ArgStcDif	Switches arguments of compatible type
FunCalDel	Removes function call

As a consequence, a mutant is associated to a call and not to a unit. Figure 1 shows what happens, for example, when a unit f calls unit g twice. In this case, the mutants associated to the first call should be killed only if that call is been exercised. For the Group II mutants this is trivial because the mutation is done exactly where f calls g. But for the Group I operators the same is not true. Since the mutation is applied inside g, it is necessary to know which call was used. If it was not the desired one, them the mutant should not be killed. In Proteum/IM 2.0 this feature is implemented by enabling the mutation at the right call in f and checking inside g whether or not the mutation is enabled. More details about such mechanism is given in Section 4.

3 Functionality of Proteum/IM 2.0

Proteum/IM 2.0 provides mechanisms for the assessment of test case set adequacy for testing units and for testing the interactions among the units of a given program P. Based

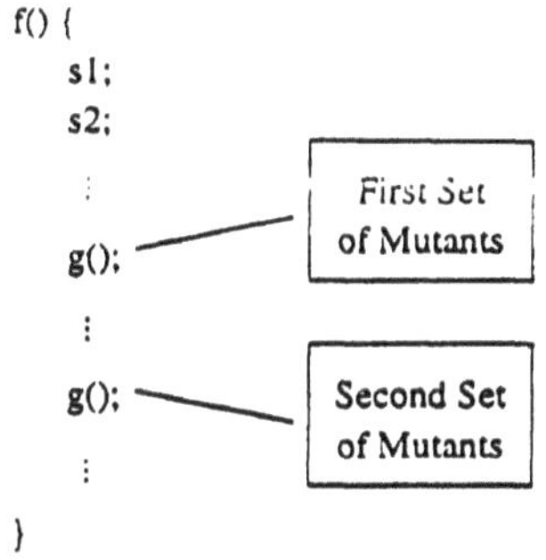

Figure 1. Interface Mutation: Sets of mutants generated for the two connections f–g.

on the adequacy evaluation, the test case set may be enhanced to obtain an adequate test set. If the program under test running against this adequate test set behaves according to the specification the confidence in the program's reliability increases [13].

There is a minimal set of operations that must be provided by any mutation based testing tool:

- Test case handling: execution, inclusion/exclusion and disabling/enabling;
- Mutant handling: creation, selection, execution, and analysis; and
- Adequacy analysis: mutation score and reports.

Proteum/IM 2.0 supports the execution of such tasks, some of them in a completely automatic way and some with the intervention of the tester. There are two ways to conduct a test session in Proteum/IM 2.0: either by a graphical interface or by scripts. The graphical interface allows the beginner to explore and learn the concepts of mutation testing and to use Proteum/IM 2.0 in a controlled manner. Advanced users, on the other hand, would probably prefer to use scripts, for reasons of productivity and evaluation of alternative testing strategies.

3.1 Graphical Interface

The interface allows the beginner to explore and learn the concepts of Proteum/IM 2.0 and mutation testing. It also provides better ways to visualize test cases and mutants and in this way facilitates the task of identifying the equivalent mutants. A general view of the possible operations available through the interface is shown in Figure 2.

Testing Sessions

In Proteum/IM 2.0 the testing activity is guided by testing sessions. A testing session is characterized by a database created and managed by Proteum/IM 2.0 to store the necessary information about the program being tested, its mutants and the test cases provided by the tester. Thus, the first step required when using Proteum/IM 2.0 is the creation of a test session. To this creation operation the tester has to provide some basic information, as shown in Figure 3. A test session can be created, interrupted and resumed later using the operation *Program Test/Load*. In this case, Proteum/IM 2.0 asks for the directory and the name of the test session and resumes it.

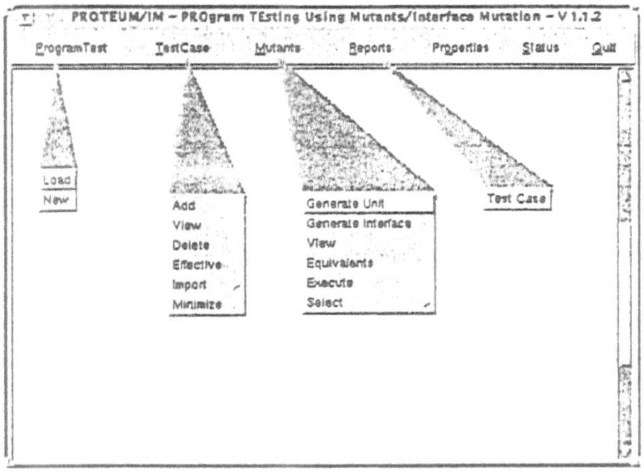

Figure 2. Operations available in the interface

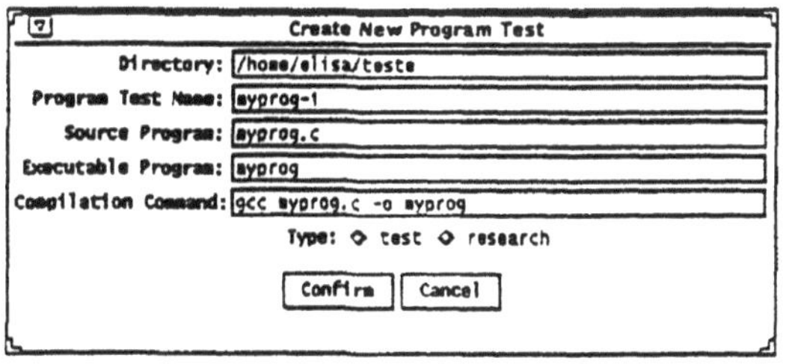

Figure 3. Creating a test session

Test Set Handling

Once a test session is created, a couple of operations can be performed to build up a test case set database. The first is the interactive insertion of test cases by the tester. With this functionality the tester provides 'command line' parameters and then interacts with the program being tested. Proteum/IM 2.0 grabs and stores the inputs and outputs that will constitute the test case.

Another way to insert test cases in the data base is importing from files that describe the test cases. There are three types of files currently imported from Proteum/IM

2.0: 1) another Proteum/IM 2.0 test case database; 2) *Poke-Tool* [5]– a dataflow-based testing tool – test case files and; 3) plain ASCII files. Proteum/IM 2.0 executes the original program using the data in any of these files as input, grabs the output and stores the test case in its own format.

Test cases can also be removed from the data base. Proteum/IM 2.0 also provides a way to logically remove a test case by disabling it. In this case, the test case is not physically removed from the database but is not considered in the future operations like mutant execution. Later, the test case can be re-enabled and is back to the logical database. This allows the tester to try different combinations of the test cases in the database. Proteum/IM 2.0 offers a way to examine the test case database by the operation *Test Case/View.*

Mutant Handling

The central task of Interface Mutation concerns the manipulation of mutants. First, it is necessary to choose what kind of mutants will be used in the test. Proteum/IM 2.0 provides a set of 33 Interface Mutation operators divided in two groups, 24 operators in Group I and 9 in Group II, as shown in Table 2. For the unit testing, a set of 75 operators exists. They are further classified in Constant, Operator, Statement, and Variable operators. The unit operators are based on the Agrawal *et al.* work and the initial nomenclature has been kept [2].

For each operator it is possible to select a percentage of generation and the maximum number of mutants per mutation point. In Figure 4 some of the Group I operators are shown. A generation percentage and maximum number per mutation point can be determined to the whole group or individually for each operator. The generation process is not necessarily done at once. It can be repeated several times. Those facilities ease the investigation of Randomly Selected Mutation [1], Constrained Mutation [19] and Selective Mutation [3, 21–23].

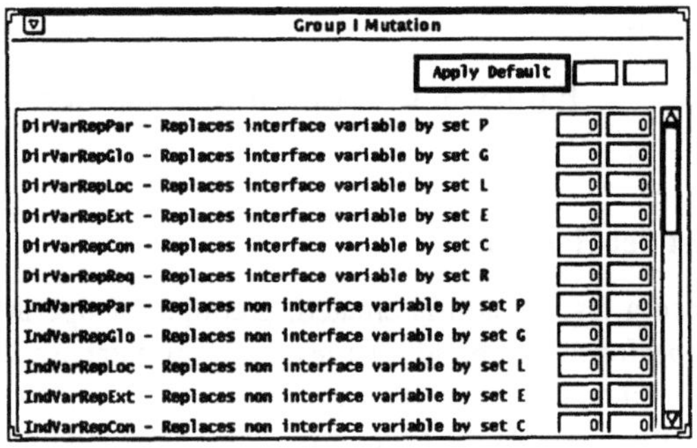

Figure 4. Mutant generation

At this point, once a test case set is provided and mutants are created, it is necessary to start the execution of the mutants. Proteum/IM 2.0 then executes each mutant with the test cases and compares their behavior against the behavior presented by the original program. There are two possible ways to execute the mutants. The first is the ordinary way of executing a mutant only until it is killed by a test case (or up to the end of the test case set if no test case kills it). Another way is to execute each mutant with all the test cases, regardless the mutant is killed or not. This approach enables some extra data collection, useful in several experiments. Which way to apply is determined at the test session creation. If 'Test' is chosen as the type of the test session, then the first approach is used. If it is 'Research', the second approach is used.

As a result of mutant execution, Proteum/IM 2.0 marks mutants as 'dead' or 'alive'. After the execution, the tester can analyze the live mutants and decide, whether they are equivalent or not. Proteum/IM 2.0 presents each mutant, allowing the tester to browse the set of mutants, as shown in Figure 5. The type of mutants (alive, dead, or equivalent) to be analyzed can be chosen using the buttons in the right corner of that panel. If the tester decides a mutant is equivalent, it can be marked by checking the box labeled 'Equivalent'.

In the same way a test case can be disabled or enabled, sets of mutants can also be activated or desactivated. Proteum/IM 2.0 provides this feature so different sets of mutants can be tried in a same test session. This feature, already existent in the previous versions of the Proteum family, has been proved very useful for experiments that want to measure the usefulness or efficiency of determined subsets of mutant operators [26]. The selection of mutants is also based in a percentage of mutants per mutant operator, as it happens in the mutant generation step. The difference in this case is that in the selection step, the percentage is applied over the already generated mutants. Desactivated mutants are not considered in the adequacy computations.

Reports

The current state of a session can be obtained by reports provided by Proteum/IM 2.0. There is a summary report, which pops up pressing the button *Status* in the main menu, where only the main information is given. There is also a report with information about the test case set and the mutants they killed.

Next section describes how a test session is run via shell scripts. Running a test session using Proteum/IM 2.0's graphical interface is probably easier but less flexible than by a shell script. The interface depends on the constant tester's intervention, at least to go from one operation to the next. The advantages of using Proteum/IM 2.0 in this way are: 1) there is no additional effort to create scripts to run the session, what in general is not a trivial task; and

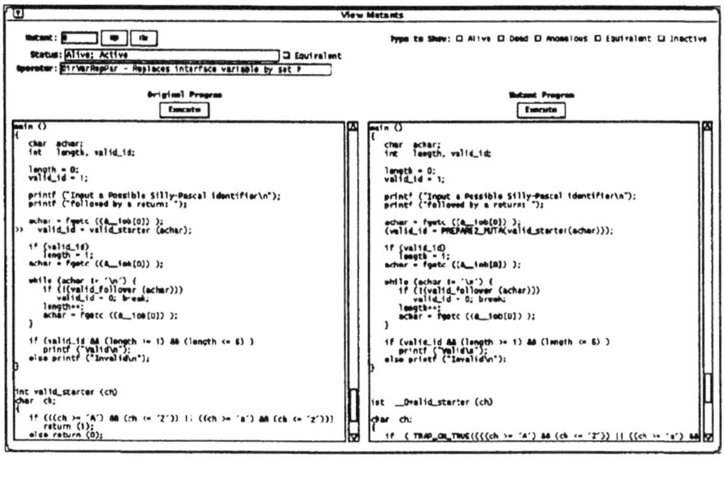

Figure 5. Analyzing a mutant

2) operations that require visualization and interaction are privileged.

3.2 Testing Scripts

The same operations performed through the graphical interface can also be performed by directly calling the programs that compound Proteum/IM 2.0 in a shell command line or in a shell script. This allows a 'programmed' way to run a test session. Actually, the graphical interface is just a "shell" that takes parameters from the tester and feed them to the same programs described herein.

Proteum/IM 2.0 is formed by two sets of programs, the 'basis' programs and the 'utility' programs. The first are lower level programs that act directly on the files that characterize a test session. The later uses the first to perform some specific operations on a test session. For instance, there is a basis program to create an empty test case database, another basis program to create an empty mutant database and there is an utility program that call both to create an empty test session that is compound by the test case and mutant databases. This section shows how to run a test session using some of the utility programs.

Testing Sessions

There is a program named `test-new` to create a test session. The same information provided via graphical interface can also be supplied to this program as parameters. For example, here is how to create in the current directory a test session named `myprg-1`, with a source file `myprg.c`, an executable file `myprg`, and a compilation command as '`gcc myprg.c -o myprg`'.

```
test-new -D . -E myprg -S myprg -C "gcc myprg.c -
o myprg" myprg-1
```

To avoid command lines as long as that one, Proteum/IM 2.0 assumes some default parameters. For example, the command line "`test-new myprg`" creates a test session similar to that above, named `myprg`. The result of a well succeed `test-new` execution is a test case and mutant databases and a few auxiliary files.

Test Set Handling

Program `tcase-add` is used to interactively insert a test case. As it happens in the graphical interface, the execution of the program being tested is started and `tcase-add` grabs the input and output and measure the execution time as well. Command line parameters for the test case can be provided by parameters to `tcase-add`. There is also the program `tcase` used to manipulate the test case database. With it the tester can import, enable or disable a test case, delete a sub-set of test cases and look at the database.

Mutant Handling

A specific program is designed to generate mutants. Program `muta-gen` creates mutant descriptors and inserts them in the mutant database. The parameters are the name of the mutant operators to be applied and the corresponding generation percentage. For script use we have added a prefix to the names of the operators, identifying the class of each operator. For Group I operators we added prefix 'I-', for Group II we added 'II-' and for unit operators we added 'u-'. Since Proteum/IM 2.0 allows the use of incomplete names for identifying operator, these prefix are useful. They allow, for example, the following statement to generate mutants to all the unit Constant operators:

```
muta-gen -u-c 100 0 myprg
```

All operators beginning with 'u-c', it means, *u-cccr*, *u-ccsr* and *u-crcr* will be used.

Program `exemuta` is mainly used to execute the mutants. It can also be used to activate and deactivate mutants. The same parameters used to `muta-gen` to determine the operators and percentages are used. The last function of this program is to create the source and executable files for a specific mutant or set of mutants so the tester can use them, for example, to visualize the mutant and compare it against the original program.

There is also a very simple program to visualize the mutants, called `muta-view`. This is a "curses"-based program and just displays the statement in the original program that was changed to create the mutant and the correspondent mutated statement. Using program `muta` the tester can change the status of the mutants providing their numbers and new status as parameters. For example, the statement below sets mutants 1, 19 and 34 as equivalent (if they are alive) in test session `myprg`.

```
muta -equiv -x "1 19 34" myprg
```

Reports

At last, the program `report` generates the report of test cases. The selection of which information to be presented in the report is done through a parameter to the program. The report produced is exactly the same cited before but is stored in a file, instead of displayed as in the graphical interface.

Figure 6 shows an example of test script using Proteum/IM 2.0. This script evaluates 10 different test case sets in relation to a program 'search' and a set of mutants composed by 10% of each Group I Interface Mutation operator and 20% of each Statement unit operator. The test cases are imported from ASCII files stored in sub-directories named I, II, ..., X. The results of the evaluation are stored in the same subdirectories.

4 Implementation Aspects

In this section we discuss the most critical aspect in a mutation tool: mutant management. The tool must analyze the original program, apply the mutant operators chosen by the tester and somehow create and execute a bunch of similar programs. Since the main drawback imposed to mutation testing is about cost, the tool must find an efficient way to perform mutation management. This section describes the approach used in Proteum/IM 2.0.

Most mutation tools described in the literature, Mothra [16] for instance, use the interpretative approach to do mutations. In this approach the original program is translated to an intermediate form where the mutations are applied, then the original and mutated programs are interpreted and their results compared. The main problems with this approach are: 1) the interpreted mutants can not execute at the same speed as a compiled program and; 2) the interpreter may fail to reproduce the actual environment where the program (and mutants) should run.

Another possible approach, used by Proteum/IM 2.0, is to apply the mutations on the original source code and compile the mutated source code to create an executable mutant. This mutant is then executed against the test case set and its result compared with the results of the original program. In this way the environment where the mutants are executed is the actual environment, not depending on an interpreter. On the other hand, this requires an extra time spent to create the source and to compile the mutants. The approach taken by Proteum/IM 2.0 tries to reduce this time in order to keep low the global speed of mutant execution. The next two sections show the main points to achieve that: 1) the generation and storage; and 2) the execution of mutants.

```
#!/bin/csh ######################################
# This script uses Proteum/IM 2.0 to evaluate 10
# test case sets to test program "search.c".
# The test case sets are
# in  ASCII files in subdirectories I, ..., X.
# At the end of each evaluation, the report
# file is placed in the same subdirectory
# from where test set was imported
################################################

# create a test session
test-new -C "gcc search.c -o search -w" search

foreach tset (I II III IV V VI VII VIII IX X)

#### generate 10% of the mutants for Group I
#### and 20% for statement operators
#### for all connections/units
    muta-gen -I- 10 0 -u-S 20 0 search

#### import test cases from ASCII
#### files in1, in2, ...,in100
    tcase -ascii -D $tset -I input \
               -f 1 -t 100 search

#### execute mutants
    exemuta -exec search

#### produce report and copy it to the
#### same subdirectory
    report -tcase search
    mv search.lst $tset

#### reset test case and mutant set for
#### next interaction
    tcase -create search
    muta -create search
end
```

Figure 6. A Test Script using Proteum/IM 2.0

4.1 Generation and Storage of Mutants

The application of Interface Mutation operators is done in two steps. The first is performed when the test session is created. At that time, an intermediate representation of the source program – called LI [4] – is created. In the second step the LI program is analyzed and the structures of the program suitable to the application of Interface Mutation operators are identified and mutant descriptors are generated and incorporated to the mutant database. Figure 7 represents this process.

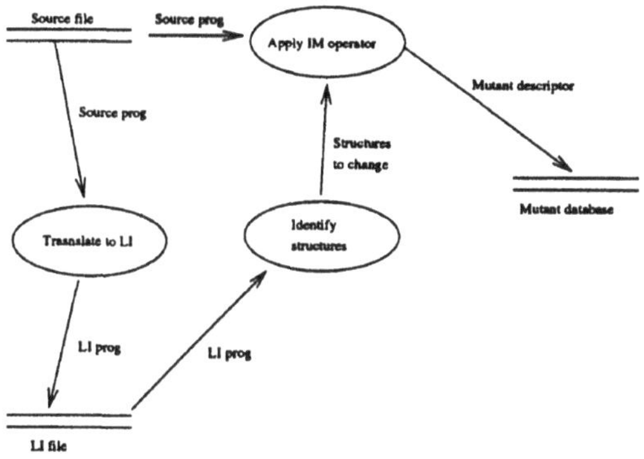

Figure 7. Application of the Interface Mutation operators

The first step is the translation from source code to LI. Each "statement" in the LI program identifies a structure in the source program. The example in Figure 8 shows a C program and its corresponding LI representation

The first column in the LI program identifies the type of the structure that appeared in the source code. For example, `$DCL` for declarations, `$IF` for an `if` statement and `$Sn` for the nth simple statement. The second column gives the number of the node in the program graph (also generated with the LI program). The third column gives the offset of the structure in the source program, the fourth gives the size in characters of the structure in the source program and the last column gives its line in the source program

The second step corresponds to the analysis of the LI program and generation of the mutants. The manipulation of mutants in Proteum/IM 2.0 is designed in a way to privilege mutant execution. It means that when it is time to execute mutants the delay to build up the source codes and to compile them must be as short as possible. At the generation time Proteum/IM 2.0 analyzes the original program, applies the mutant operators and creates, for each mutant, a description that is stored in the mutant database. These descriptors basically contain information of where the mutation is done and a sequence of string substitution to be applied. Note that these string substitutions are not related with the program structure or the programming language. The descriptor basically says: "From offset X in the original file, take off N characters and replace them by string S".

```
int a;

main()
{
    a = g();
}

int g()
{
int i, x[10];

    for (i = 0; i < 10; i++)
    {
        scanf("%d", &a);
        if (a < 0)
          x[i] = 0;
        else
          x[i] = a;
    }
    return 0;
}
$DCL        1    1   6   1
@main       1    9   4   3
$DCL        1    9   6   3
{           1   16   1   4
$S01        1   21   8   5
}           1   30   1   6
@g          1   37   1   8
$DCL        1   33   7   8
{           1   41   1   9
$DCL        1   43  13  10
$FOR        1   61   3  12
$S0         1   66   6  12
$C(01)01    2   73   7  12
$S03        6   81   3  12
{           3   89   1  13
$S04        3   92  16  14
$IF         3  110   2  15
$C(01)02    3  113   7  15
{           4    0   0   0
$S05        4  125   9  16
}           4    0   0   0
$ELSE       5  136   4  17
{           5    0   0   0
$S06        5  145   9  18
}           5    0   0   0
}           6  158   1  19
$RETURN     7  163   9  20
}           8  173   1  21
```

Figure 8. A C program translated to LI

For example, the application of operator *I-RetStaDel* (deletes a `return` statement) in the program of Figure 8 would produce the mutant descriptor of Table 3.

This kind of mutant description favors the execution process because the creation of mutant source becomes easy and fast. It requires only a few strings substitution, with-

Table 3. A mutant descriptor

Field	*Value*	*Meaning*
Calling	main	name of the calling function
Called	g	name of the called function
Node	main:1	node of the program graph where "`a = g();`" is
Change at	21	offset from the beginning of the file of "`a = g();`"
Size	8	size of "`a = g();`"
Include	a = PREPARE_MUTA(g());	string that replaces the original statement "`a = g();`"
Node	g:7	node of the program graph where "`return 0;`" is
Change at	163	offset from the beginning of the file of "`return 0;`"
Size	9	size of "`return 0;`"
Include	IF_MUTA(;, return 0;);	string that replaces the original statement "`return 0;`"

out any concern about language structures or syntax. In addition, it is independent of the language. Once the descriptors are create, the process of physically generating the mutants does not depend on the target language. In this way it becomes easier to configure the tool to deal with different languages.

Another important point about Group I Interface Mutation operators application refers to those applied in the body of the called function. Lets take a function *h* that is called from *f* and from *g*. If we want to test connection *f–h* then we generate mutants that have *h* changed somehow. If such mutants are generated simply by changing *h*, they can be distinguished by a test case that executes connection *g–h*, leaving the aimed connection untested. Thus, we need a mechanism that ensures that a mutant is killed only if the desired connection is been exercised. In Proteum/IM 2.0 a mutant generated for connection *f–h* has, besides the mutation inside *h*, a "guard" in the point where *f* calls *h*. This guard would enable the mutation. If *h* is called from *g*, the absence of such guard would not enable the mutation and *h* should behave exactly as in the original program.

For example, lets take Interface Mutation operator *I-DirVarIncDec* that generates a mutant with a pre-increment operator inserted. Suppose it is applied to connection *f–g* to the program in the top of Figure 9. The mutant generate would be as shown on the bottom-part program in the same figure.

The macro `PREPARE_MUTA` sets a global variable that is tested in the other macro `IF_MUTA`. If this variable is not set then original code `a+1` is executed, otherwise mutated code `++a + 1` is executed. The mutant may be distinguished only if the mutated code is executed, i.e, only if function `g` was called by `f`.

4.2 Execution of Mutants

The execution of mutants is one of the bottlenecks for mutation testing. To speed up this process Proteum/IM 2.0 uses two approaches: 1) creation of executable mutants instead of their interpretation; and 2) reduce the time to create the mutant sources. The process is show in Figure 10.

```
int g(int a)
{
    return a + 1;
}

int f()
{
int i;
    i = g(0);
}
```

```
int g(int a)
{
     return IF_MUTA(++a + 1, a + 1);
}

int f()
{
int i;
     i = PREPARE_MUTA(g(0));
}
```

Figure 9. Example of how Proteum/IM 2.0 creates mutants to assure a given connection is exercised

The compilative approach contributes to speed up the execution of mutants but on the other hand introduces a delay in building mutant sources and executables. To reduce this delay, Proteum/IM 2.0 builds source files that hold several mutants at once, not only one mutant. This aspect has been addressed by many authors [6, 15, 20, 24]. The process construction/compilation is not realized for each mutant. Instead, it is done once for a "large" number of mutants (currently at most 100). Lets take as an example the program of Figure 8 and the application of operator *I-IndVarRepReq* (in this case, replaces a constant by another constant). Two mutants would be created: `return 0;` is replaced by `return 1;` and `return -1`. Figure 11 shows the code that joins these two mutants.

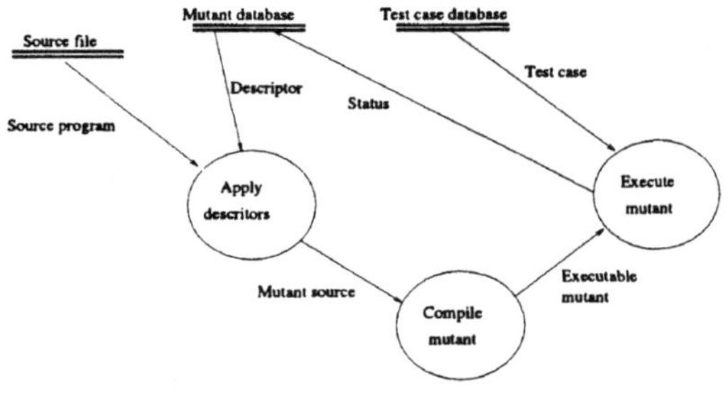

Figure 10. Process of mutant execution

The called function g() is replaced by two functions named __1g() and __2g(). At the execution time the new g() function takes care of calling one of them, according to the environment variable MUTANTTOEXEC, set by Proteum/IM 2.0 to indicate which mutant is being run (in this case, mutant 1 or 2). Even though the growing of the source file, caused by the replication of g(), the time consumed to build up and compile this single file is considerably shorter than it would be if each mutant had to be constructed and compiled separately.

The code in Figure 11 also shows the mechanism, already mentioned, used by Proteum/IM 2.0 to decide at the execution time whether the mutation is applied or not, depending on if the desired connection is executed or not. This is done using the variables __flg_muta__ and __LOCAL_COUNTER__ to enable and disable the mutated code.

Proteum/IM 2.0 also uses control flow information to speed up mutant execution. When a test case *t* is included in the test set, the tool stores information about the nodes of the program graph that were reached by its execution. Before trying to kill a mutant M, using the test case *t*, Proteum/IM 2.0 checks if *t* really can kill M, i.e., checks whether the node(s) where the mutation was done in the original program is reached by *t*. If not, there is no use of executing M against *t* because the mutant would certainly stay alive. This feature may be used or not, according to the tester's wish. In general a large number of executions is avoided and the execution process is speeds up significantly.

5 A Simple Example

In this section we show a simple example of using Proteum/IM 2.0 to compare unit and integration mutant operators. We use the *Cal* Unix calendar program to show the effectiveness of test sets generated by different sets of mutant operators. The objective here is not to deeply analyze the data presented, but just show the kind of data we can derive using an integrated testing environment.

For program *Cal*, 4 adequate test sets were generate, each one for a different set of mutant operators, according to the selective approaches proposed in the literature [1, 3, 18, 19, 21–23]. Then these test sets were used against the mutants generated by the other sets and the mutation scores were assessed. This approach has been used in several other studies to evaluate and compare testing criteria. Table 4 shows the mutation scores obtained. The label *Unit* refers to all the unit operators implemented in Proteum/IM 2.0; *Interface* refers to all the Interface Mutation operators; *Suff-MA* refers to a set of 6 sufficient unit operators determined in a previous experiment [3]; and *Suff-IM* refers to a set of 8 interface operators obtained in a first attempt to determine the set of sufficient interface mutant operators [25].

```
int __flg_muta__ = 0;
int a;

main() {
   a = (__flg_muta__ = 1) ? g(): g();
}

int __1g() {
  int i, x[10];

  for (i = 0; i < 10; i++) {
      scanf("%d", &a);
      if (a < 0)
          x[i] = 0;
      else
          x[i] = a;
  }
  return (__flg_muta__) ? 1 :0;
}

int __2g() {
  int i, x[10];

  for (i = 0; i < 10; i++) {
      scanf("%d", &a);
      if (a < 0)
          x[i] = 0;
      else
          x[i] = a;
  }
  return(__flg_muta__) ? -1 :0;
}

int g() {
  int __LOCAL_VAR__;
  static int __LOCAL_COUNTER__ = 0;

  if ( __flg_muta__ )
        __LOCAL_COUNTER__++;
  switch ( atoi(getenv("MUTANTTOEXEC")) ) {
     case 1:
        __LOCAL_VAR__ = __1g();
        break;
     case 2:
        __LOCAL_VAR__ =  __2g();
        break;
  }
  if ( __flg_muta__ )
        __LOCAL_COUNTER__ --;

  if ( __LOCAL_COUNTER__ == 0)
        __flg_muta__ = 0;
  return __LOCAL_VAR__;
}
```

Figure 11. Example of the mutant construction

Briefly analyzing these data we observe that the test set adequate for the unit operators (MA-adequate) determines a mutation score of 0.870 with respect to (w.r.t.) the Interface Mutation criterion. In the other way, the IM-adequate test set determines a mutation score of 0.944 w.r.t. mutation testing. These data show that these criteria are incomparable since neither mutation testing subsumes Interface Mutation nor Interface Mutation subsumes mutation testing. Thus, it is worth investigating their complementary aspects.

Table 4. Example of using Proteum/IM 2.0 on *Cal*

	Unit	*Interface*	*Suff-MA*	*Suff-IM*
Unit	1.000	0.870	1.000	0.851
Interface	0.945	1.000	0.963	1.000
Suff-MA	0.999	0.869	1.000	0.851
Suff-IM	0.941	0.997	0.952	1.000

In another work, using a suite of five UNIX programs we investigated the combinations of mutant operators and the testing strategies, according to different parameters as cost, effectiveness and mutation score [25]. With this kind of experiments we try to reduce the cost of mutation testing and provide guidelines for the establishment of a low-cost, effective testing strategy.

Analyzing the sufficient sets we observe that a Suff-MA-adequate test set determines a mutation score of 0.999, 0.868 and 0.8512 w.r.t. the mutation testing, Interface Mutation and Suff-IM criteria, respectively. The Suff-IM-adequate test set determines a mutation score of 0.940, 0.996 and 0.952 w.r.t. the mutation testing, Interface Mutation and Suff-MA criteria, respectively. These data show that even the sufficient sets are incomparable since one does not subsume the other. It should be highlighted that in this case using only the sufficient set it was possible to obtain a high mutation score w.r.t. the full set of operators at each level.

6 Conclusion

This paper presented the main functional characteristics of Proteum/IM 2.0, a testing tool that supports mutation based unit and integration testing for C programs. The two modes of operation, via a graphical interface and via shell scripts, were described. Also some important aspects about its implementation were discussed. In special, the process of generation/execution of mutants was highlighted, since these are the central tasks in a mutation tool. The approach used by Proteum/IM 2.0 differs from previous approaches taken to implemant other tools. The use of compiled mutants, in contrast with interpreted mutants, requires special care to keep the time for mutant execution in accepted limits. The solutions adopted by Proteum/IM 2.0 in these matters were presented. An example of its use on comparing unit and Interface Mutation operators was shown.

The Proteum family has being used mainly for teaching and research. As a teaching instrument Proteum/IM 2.0 has being used at Universidade de São Paulo – Campus of São Carlos, at Universidade Estadual de Maringá, and at Universidade Estadual de Campinas, Brazil in courses of Computer Aided Software Engineering to undergraduate and graduate classes. Other research institutes, universities and industries in Brazil and abroad have also used the tools.

Currently, the experience on developing Proteum/IM 2.0 is been used to extend mutation testing to object oriented languages. The problems related to OO development are being studied, aiming at the development of a OO fault model. Based on this fault model, mutant operators will be designed and a tool to support mutation testing for OO programs will be planned.

The development of Proteum/IM 2.0 has been mainly carried out by Masters and Ph.D. students. At the end, the students have a too short time to really improve it. This has been among the obstacles to bring Proteum/IM 2.0 to an industrial level. In the scope of our activities we are interested in identifying partners to conduct empirical studies in industry and in establishing a collaboration to turn Proteum/IM 2.0 into the state of the practice.

Acknowledgments

The authors would like to thank the Brazilian Funding Agencies – CNPq, FAPESP and CAPES – and the Telcordia Technologies (USA) for their partial support to this research. The authors would also like to thank the anonymous referees for their valuable comments.

References

[1] A. T. Acree, T. A. Budd, R. A. DeMillo, R. J. Lipton, and F. G. Sayward. Mutation analysis. Technical Report GIT-ICS-79/08, Georgia Institute of Technology, Atlanta, GA, Sept. 1979.

[2] H. Agrawal, R. A. DeMillo, R. Hataway, W. Hsu, W. Hsu, E. Krauser, R. J. Martin, A. P. Mathur, and E. H. Spafford. Design of Mutant Operators for C Programming Language. Tech Report SERC-TR41-P, Software Engineering Research Center, Purdue University, March 1989.

[3] E. F. Barbosa, J. C. Maldonado, and A. M. R. Vincenzi. Towards the determination of sufficient mutant operators for C. In *First International Workshop on Automated Program Analysis, Testing and Verification*, Limerick, Ireland, June 2000. (Accepted for publication in a special issue of the Software Testing Verification and Reliability Journal).

[4] M. Carnassale. GFC – a multilanguage tool for program graph generation. Master's thesis, DCA/FEE/UNICAMP, Campinas, SP, Feb. 1991. (in Portuguese).

[5] M. L. Chaim. Poke-tool - a tool to suport data flow based structural test of programs. Master's thesis, DCA/FEEC/UNICAMP, Campinas, SP, Apr. 1991. (in Portuguese).

[6] S.-S. Chen. Design of a mutation testing tool for C. Department of Computer Sciences, Purdue University, Apr. 1992.

[7] M. E. Delamaro. *Interface Mutation: An Interprocedural Adequace Criterion for Integration Testing*. PhD thesis, Instituto de Física de São Carlos - Universidade de São Paulo, São Carlos, SP, June 1997. (in Portuguese).

[8] M. E. Delamaro and J. C. Maldonado. Proteum - a tool for the assesment of test adequacy for C programs. In *Conference on Performability in Computing Systems (PCS'96)*, pages 79–95, Brunswick, NJ, July 1996.

[9] M. E. Delamaro, J. C. Maldonado, and A. P. Mathur. Integration testing using interface mutation. In *VII International Symposium of Software Reliability Engineering (ISSRE'96)*, pages 112–121, White Plains, NY, Nov. 1996.

[10] M. E. Delamaro, J. C. Maldonado, and A. P. Mathur. Interface mutation: An approach for integration testing. IEEE Transactions on Software Engineering, (accepted for publication), 2000.

[11] A. Haley and S. Zweben. Development and Application of a White Box Approach to Integration Testing. *The Journal of Systems and Software*, 4:309–315, 1984.

[12] M. J. Harrold and M. L. Soffa. Selecting and Using Data for Integration Test. *IEEE Software*, 8(2):58–65, March 1991.

[13] J. R. Horgan and P. Mathur. Assessing Testing Tools in Research and Education. *IEEE Software*, 9(3):61–69, May 1992.

[14] Z. Jin and A. J. Offut. Integration Testing Based on Software Couplings. In *Proceedings of the X Annual Conference on Computer Assurance (COMPASS 95)*, pages 13–23, Gaithersburg, Maryland, January 1995.

[15] M. Kim. Design of a mutation testing tool for C. Department of Computer Sciences, Purdue University, Apr. 1992.

[16] K. N. King and A. J. Offutt. A Fortran language system for mutation based software testing. *Software-Practice and Experience*, 21(7):685–718, July 1991.

[17] U. Linnenkugel and M. Müllerburg. Test Data Selection Criteria for (Software) Integration Testing. In *Proceedings of the First International Conference on Systems Integration*, pages 709–717, Mornstown, NJ, April 1990.

[18] J. C. Maldonado, E. F. Barbosa, A. M. R. Vincenzi, and M. E. Delamaro. Evaluation N-selective mutation for C programs: Unit and integration testing. In *Mutation 2000 Symposium*, pages 32–44, San Jose, CA, Oct. 2000.

[19] A. P. Mathur. Performance, effectiveness and reliability issues in software testing. In *15th Annual International Computer Software and Applications Conference*, pages 604–605, Tokio, Japan, Sept. 1991.

[20] A. P. Mathur. Cs 406 software engineering. Course Handout, Purdue University, Fall 1992.

[21] E. Mresa and L. Bottaci. Efficiency of mutation operators and selective mutation strategies: an empirical study. *The Journal of Software Testing, Verification and Reliability*, 9(4):205–232, Dec. 1999.

[22] A. J. Offutt, A. Lee, G. Rothermel, R. H. Untch, and C. Zapf. An experimental determination of sufficient mutant operators. *ACM Transactions on Software Engineering Methodology*, 5(2):99–118, 1996.

[23] A. J. Offutt, G. Rothermel, and C. Zapf. An experimental evaluation of selective mutation. In *15th International Conference on Software Engineering*, pages 100–107, Baltimore, MD, May 1993.

[24] R. Untch, M. J. Harrold, and J. Offutt. Mutation analysis using mutant schemata. In *International Symposium on Software Testing and Analysis*, pages 139–148, Cambridge, Massachusetts, June 1993.

[25] A. M. R. Vincenzi, J. C. Maldonado, E. F. Barbosa, and M. E. Delamaro. Unit and integration testing strategies for C programs using mutation-based criteria. In *Symposium on Mutation Testing*, pages 56–67, San Jose, CA, Oct. 2000.

[26] W. E. Wong, J. C. Maldonado, M. E. Delamaro, and A. P. Mathur. Constrained Mutation in C Programs. In *Proceedings of the 8th Brazilian Symposium on Software Engineering*, pages 439–452, Curitiba, PR, Brazil, October 1994.

Tool Session

TDS: A Tool for Testing Distributed Component-Based Applications

Sudipto Ghosh*
Computer Science Department
Colorado State University
Fort Collins, CO 80523
ghosh@cs.colostate.edu

Priya Govindarajan†
Intel Corporation
Hillsboro OR 97124
priya.govindarajan@intel.com

Aditya P. Mathur‡
Department of Computer Sciences
Purdue University
West Lafayette IN 47907
apm@cs.purdue.edu

Abstract

Applications that utilize the broker-based architecture are often composed of several components that need to be tested both separately and together. An important activity during testing is the assessment of the adequacy of test sets. The interface mutation based test adequacy criterion for components can be used for test adequacy assessment. TDS is a tool that assists a tester in performing Interface Mutation testing. The architecture of the tool and the features are described here.
Index terms: *CORBA, coverage measurement, distributed applications, fault injection, interface mutation, monitoring, test adequacy.*

1. Introduction

Software testing is an integral part of the software development process. Testing an application involves the creation of test cases, the execution of the application against these test cases and the observation of application behavior to determine its correctness. Correctness may be determined with the help of an oracle that compares the observed output with the expected or the correct output. When an application behaves incorrectly it needs to be debugged to determine the cause. Debugging often leads to the identification and removal of faults.

This research is concerned with the testing of component-based distributed applications. Various definitions of components are provided by researchers and software professionals [1]. We adopt the following definition of a component given by Szyperski.

> *A software component is a unit of composition with contractually specified interfaces and explicit context dependencies only. A software component can be deployed independently and is subject to third-party composition.*

Let $\mathcal{A}$ be an application comprised of a set $\mathcal{C}$ of distinctly identifiable components where $\mathcal{C}=\{C_1, C_2, \ldots, C_n\}$, $n \geq 1$. A component in $\mathcal{C}$ could be a client, a server, or both. Each server exposes an interface. The interface usually consists of one or more method signatures and is specified in an Interface Description Language commonly known as IDL. These methods can be invoked on the corresponding server by clients. A method signature specifies its name, parameters passed between the server and its clients when the method is invoked, a return type, and zero or more exceptions that could be raised during its execution.

Each component is written in one or more programming languages. Components are assumed to be distributed over a network of machines that may not all have the same run-time environment. Using the CORBA standard [4] it is possible to develop applications of the kind described above.

*Sudipto Ghosh's work was supported in part by NSF award CCR-9102331 and a grant from Telcordia Technologies and the Purdue Research Foundation. This work was done when he was a graduate student at Purdue University.

†Priya Govindarajan's work was supported by a grant from the Software Engineering Research Center. This work was done when she was a graduate student at Purdue University.

‡Aditya P. Mathur's research was supported in part by NSF award CCR-9102331 and a grant from Telcordia Technologies and the Software Engineering Research Center.

1.1. Test Adequacy Assessment

Test sets are created to test an application for conformance with functionality-related requirements. *Code coverage* of some sort is a measure of "how much" of the application code has been tested by the test sets. The term *coverage domain* denotes a set of program related entities that are checked and counted for measuring coverage. Within an application these entities include functions, statements, decisions, and definition-use pairs. For example, the set of all functions in a C program forms a coverage domain.

During testing, at any time, the tester has a test set $\mathcal{T}$ containing one or more test cases. The "goodness" of $\mathcal{T}$ is an important indicator of how well the program has been tested. Assessment of test adequacy is done using one or more test adequacy criteria. One concern is what criteria to select. Cost considerations often favor one criterion over another.

The following problems have been identified in the context of testing distributed component-based applications.

1. *Component testing*: Given a test set $\mathcal{T}$ to test component C_i of $\mathcal{S}$, how does one assess the adequacy of $\mathcal{T}$?
2. *Application testing*: Given a test set $\mathcal{T}$ to test an application $\mathcal{A}$, how does one assess the adequacy of $\mathcal{T}$?

1.2. Other Testing-Related Activities

In the context of testing and debugging distributed applications, testers need to monitor and control system execution. The activities are listed below:

- Monitoring system behavior:
  - Visualization of system state transition in the presence of a given input sequence.
  - Visualization of system state transition in the presence of injected faults.
- Evaluation of system performance:
  - Measurement of instantaneous and average load distribution in both hardware and software.
  - Measurement of instantaneous and average response time.
- Controlling system behavior:
  - Temporary or permanent shutdown of selected services.
  - Injection of a arbitrary stream of requests directed at selected servers.

1.3. Heterogeneity of Language, Platforms and Architectures

The components of an application may by written in different programming languages and for use on different hardware and software platforms. With middleware conforming to standards like CORBA and DCOM, components can interact with each other independent of the language and the platforms. When an application composed of such components is tested, it is useful to require the test method and the tool to be independent of the language and the platforms or support a variety of these. The tool implementation is built on the CORBA architecture and meets this requirement.

1.4. Monitoring and Control Mechanism in Distributed Software Testing

Components in a distributed application may be distributed over multiple computers on a network. This renders the test monitoring and control mechanism more complex than that used to control a centralized software application. Mechanisms for centralized or distributed monitoring and control need to be devised. Distributed data collection and storage mechanisms need to be designed taking care of possible data buffer overflows. Usually the amount of data collected for monitoring and control is large because of the number of components and their long life-times. Care must be taken to ensure that the monitor and controller do not become bottlenecks during the monitoring and control process. The tool implementation addresses this issue with the help of a hierarchical set of *observers* and data collectors called *listeners*.

1.5. Testing for System Scalability and Performance

To improve performance, components may be implemented using threads. The same single-threaded system that has been tested perfectly may not work when re-implemented using multiple threads. Concurrency issues, race conditions and deadlocks could occur.

Various threading models are used in server implementations and object adaptors in CORBA, each having different consequences. Testing for the thread-safe property is a major concern.

Stress testing or load testing has to be done to ensure that the system performs well under high load factors. The same server components may perform well under small loads, but may cause poor performance or even crash under a heavy load of requests. This feature is implemented in an advanced version of TDS, called Wabash [1].

1.6. Testing for Fault-Tolerance

Computer systems are often used in environments critical to life and property. These situations call for high reliability and availability. Often, such environments also add the requirement of fault-tolerance to software systems. Hence,

[1] http://www.cs.purdue.edu/homes/ghosh/html/project.html

software systems need to tolerate failures that occur due to faults in its components or changes in the environment in which the components execute. Examples of such environments include those found in nuclear plants, space missions, medical applications and defense establishments.

Fault injection testing [3] is used to test for fault-tolerance by injecting faults into a system under test and observing its behavior.

The site where a fault is injected is called a *fault-site*. Code is inserted into the site so that a fault is *triggered* if control reaches the fault-site.

A set of faults is required for the purpose of injection. Having a generic set of faults for a class of system helps in automating the process of fault injection. The faults can be provided in a fault-injection tool and can be selected by the tester for injection. Fault injection has mostly been performed only on selected systems because of a lack of tools that can perform fault-injection testing.

2. Proposed Testing Methodology

To address the above issues, we propose a methodology called *TDS*, for *Testing Distributed Systems*. In Ghosh [2], a criterion based on interface mutation has been proposed for assessing test adequacy. Interface fault injection testing has been proposed for testing for fault tolerance.

We propose that components be tested first. We follow the following steps:

1. Identify the interfaces of the components.
2. Identify the methods and exceptions that are present in the interface and have to be covered.
3. Identify the parameters in the methods and create mutants of the programs using the mutant operators.
4. Create a test set based on the requirements of the component and execute the component against the test cases in this set.
5. Remove any error revealed in the process of testing.
6. Improve the test sets to increase all interface-based coverage measures (method coverage, exception coverage, interface mutation score) to 100%.

For testing applications we identify two cases, 1) the server components have themselves been tested and the test set for each server has satisfied the interface-based adequacy criteria, and 2) the server components have not been tested. Server components are those that present their services through an interface. If the server components have not been tested, we propose that they be tested individually using our proposed test adequacy criteria. Once all the server components have been tested, the application should be tested with the clients and the server components together.

The following steps are proposed when testing a distributed application for fault tolerance.

1. Select the faults.
2. Inject the faults into the application.
3. Generate test sets based on the requirements for fault tolerance.
4. Execute the application against the test sets.
5. Observe if the fault has been triggered.
6. Trace the execution after the fault has been triggered.
7. Observe application behavior for fault tolerance.
8. If the behavior does not conform to the requirements for fault tolerance, make appropriate changes to the fault-recovery code.

A prototype that implements the interface-based testing methodology has been developed. The current version of the tool is 1.1.

3. Features of TDS

TDS meets the needs of the tester by providing the following features.

1. It gives a scalable measure of test adequacy for a distributed system running on heterogeneous platforms and architectures. Method coverage, exception coverage and fault coverage can be measured for each interface.
2. It assists in system monitoring and debugging. The execution counts of methods and the times spent in selected servers can be measured.
3. It allows the evaluation of system performance. It measures CPU usage, memory usage and available file handlers on Windows NT.
4. It provides a facility for fault injection to assess the tolerance of the system to failures in the components.
5. It provides a facility for performing interface mutation testing.

4. Architecture of TDS

TDS helps the tester focus on testing the interfaces between components defined using CORBA IDL. TDS has been developed in Java. Currently it supports the Orbix implementation of CORBA and handles C++ and Java programs. The following terms are used in the context of tool design.

- A **project** is used to denote the configuration of the system under test. It consists of the location of files on the machines, the machines on which the application is executing and the files themselves. When either the file set is modified, or modifications are made to any file, the project is considered to be a new one. A project could have several sessions with the same project settings.

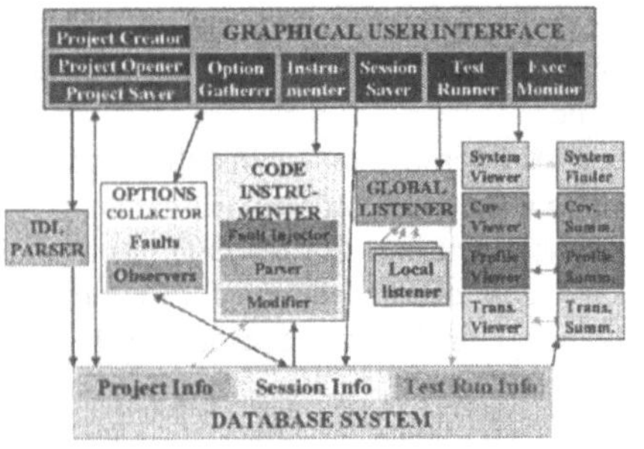

Figure 1. Architecture of TDS.

- An **observer** monitors the execution based on the selection made by the tester in order to view coverage, performance or events.
- A **session** is used to denote test runs with a set of selected observers and injected faults. Within a session, one can use different test suites but with the same set of observers and faults.

The tool, as shown in Figure 1, consists of several interacting components. At a high level, the tool consists of a GUI, a parser for IDL files, a parser and instrumenter each for Java and C++, local listeners that are CORBA servers running on each machine for monitoring the execution and gathering data, a global listener that communicates with the local listener and gathers the raw data, a database system that is used to store the data, a data processor that performs analysis of the raw data, and different viewers that present different views of the data.

The features of the tool can best be described by looking at three distinct phases — pre-test, testing and post-test.

4.1. Pre-test phase

This refers to the phase when the tester sets up the system under test and selects observers and faults to be injected.

4.1.1. Creation of Projects

The following steps are related to the creation of projects:

1. **Create a new project** — The tester specifies details about the project like the project name, component names, names of files containing the IDL descriptions. A project could contain several components and each component could consist of several IDL files. After the tester provides the names of components and IDL files, the IDL parser goes through each file and gathers the details of each interface and module in terms of exceptions and methods defined and the names and types of parameters, return values and exceptions raised by the methods.
2. **Save a project** — The project configuration can be saved in a file.
3. **Open a project** — A saved project configuration file can be opened later. This saves the effort of re-entering the project details.

4.1.2. Selection of Interface Related Observers

The tester can place observers in the system in order to assess test adequacy. For observer selection, the information gathered by the IDL parser is presented in a hierarchical form and the tester can select the methods and exceptions to be observed. This information can be saved and retrieved later. For each interface described in an IDL file, the tester can select methods or exceptions to be monitored. This is done to find out coverage information (whether or not a method is ever executed or an exception ever thrown), profile information (how frequently a method is invoked and executed, at what instant of time, and which objects are involved — server and client), what parameters are sent and received and what exceptions are raised.

4.1.3. Selection of Mutant Operators

The tester can mutate the parameters of a method defined in the interface. This is done by swapping parameters, changing return value, or changing parameter values.

4.1.4. Selection of Faults to be Injected

Fault selection is similar to observer selection. The tester is presented with a list of faults and locations for injection. The tester can introduce faults into the system and observe the fault handling capability of the system. The faults are introduced at the interface. We assume that the components of the system have already been tested. We are only concerned with faults at the interface. The kinds of faults available for injection are:

1. **Insert delays** — By inserting delays, the return of a request to a client can be delayed.
2. **Force exceptions to be thrown** — To check the fault handling capability of the system, the tester can force a component to throw exceptions. The current implementation enables exceptions to be thrown irrespective of the actions taken by the execution of server code.

Using the information of selected observers and faults, code instrumentation is performed. The appropriate parser and instrumenter for the language is invoked by the tool on the stubs and skeletons created by the IDL compiler for the interfaces. Here the tool is limited to C++ and Java, but it

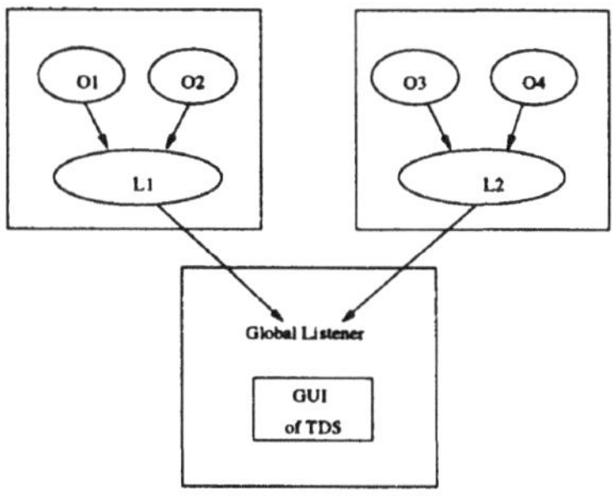

Figure 2. Observer-Listener Architecture

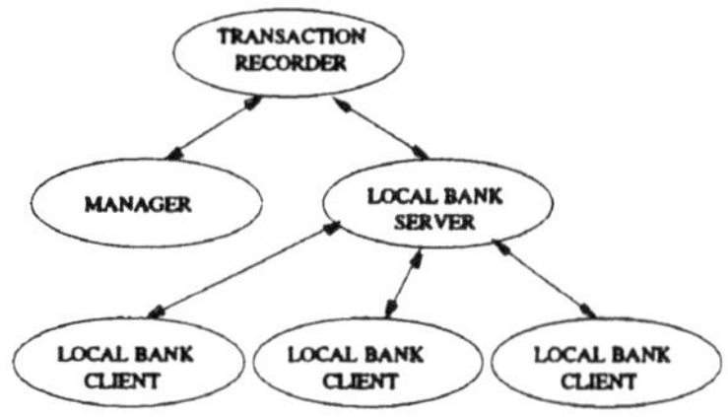

Figure 3. Bank System Architecture

can be easily extended for other languages if we add parsers and instrumenter modules for them.

4.2. Testing Phase

In the testing phase, the tester is allowed to view coverage details and various system characteristics during execution. The test is initiated by starting local listeners on all the machines. These listeners are CORBA servers. Observers that were instrumented into the program code send data to these listeners. The global listener pulls the data from the local listeners on demand or at fixed intervals. Local listeners are used instead of a single global listener in order to minimize the network traffic that would have occurred between the CORBA objects with a single global listener. Now, the extra network traffic is limited to that between the local listeners and the global listener. Figure 2 shows the observer-listener architecture.

Whenever a selected method is invoked or a selected exception thrown, a message is sent to the local listener. Whenever a fault is triggered, the local listeners are notified. When the tester wants to obtain execution information, a number of options are available for viewing the data in the form of tables, graphs or charts. The data summarizer, the database system and view presenters interact with the global listener and produce the appropriate views.

4.2.1. Viewing System Performance

For each machine in the network, the tester can view all the active servers. Machine characteristics such as memory and CPU usage can be viewed.

4.2.2. Coverage Related Views

Data regarding method and exception coverage is displayed through tables and graphs. A bar chart displays the coverage in a hierarchical manner starting from all methods in the system, followed by methods component-wise, and finally methods defined in an interface. A comparison can be made among the methods defined in an interface, the methods selected by the tester and the methods covered during testing. In order to facilitate easy test set enhancement, a list of the methods that have been covered and also a list of the methods that need to be covered is also provided. Pie charts show similar hierarchical views of profiling information in terms of time spent in a module or the number of times methods were executed or exceptions were raised.

4.3. Post-test phase

The post-test phase deals with the analysis of all the data gathered and saved in a database. Coverage analysis can be performed with the help of data regarding methods, exceptions and faults. In the next version, debugging information can be obtained regarding sequences of method calls and how exceptions were raised. Analysis regarding the data collected in the database can be done by the tester with the help of SQL queries that can be written independently of the tool. Figure 2 shows the architecture of TDS.

5. Using TDS

TDS requires the availability of Orbix_2.3c or OrbixWeb3.0 and JDK 1.1.5 or higher with Swing 1.0.3.

The use of TDS will be explained through the use of a bank example as shown in Figure 3. The bank system has four components:

1. The Local Bank Client acts as a client which sends requests to the local bank server to create or delete accounts, deposit or withdraw money or transfer money between accounts.
2. The Local Bank Server acts as both server and client. It services the requests of the local bank client, and records the transactions with the Transaction Recorder.
3. The Transaction Recorder acts as a server which records the transaction as requested by the local bank server and also reports the transactions to the manager.
4. The Manager acts as Client which requests the reports on transactions made by the Local Bank Client.

Interface I_1 is provided by the Transaction Recorder and

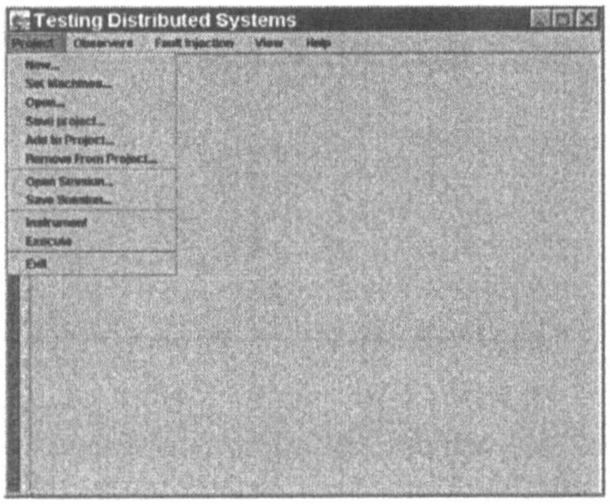

Figure 4. Project menu.

used by the Manager and Local Bank Server. The following methods are defined in the interface:

1. newTransactionEntry(transactionEntry)
2. getTotalNumTransactions()
3. getNumTransaction(memberName)
4. getNumDeposits(memberName)
5. getNumWithdrawls(memberName)

Interface I_2 is provided by the Local Bank Server and used by the Local Bank Client. The following methods are defined in the interface *Bank*:

1. createAccount()
2. deleteAccount()
3. transfer(from, to, amt)

The following methods are defined in the interface *Bank*:

1. balance()
2. makeDeposit()
3. makeWithdrawl()

The steps are outlined in the following paragraphs. Illustrations in the form of screen dumps accompany each step.

5.1. Pre-test Phase

On starting up TDS, one can select the project menu as shown in Figure 4.

5.1.1. Create a new project

Provide details of components and IDL files with the following steps. This is a required step as shown in Figure 5.

1. Click on "Project" followed by "New."
2. Type server component name.

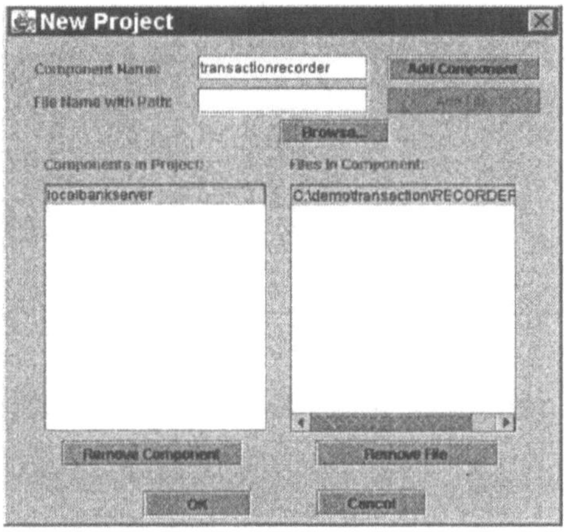

Figure 5. Creation of a New Project.

3. Type IDL file name or browse for file. If all the IDL files that are in a directory need to be included, then it is enought to select the directory itself. All the IDL files will be automatically included for the component.
4. Click on Add component.
5. Double clicking on a component in the left list box will list all the files included for it and changes(addition or removal of files) can be made as necessary.
6. Remove files or component, if necessary.
7. Repeat above for other server components.

5.1.2. Set Machine Names

Set the names of the machines on which the application to be tested is going to run. This step is required in order for the global listener to know the machines on which to start the locallistener. (Figure 6).

1. Click on "Project" followed by "Set Machine Names..."
2. Type Machine Name
3. Hit "Enter" or Click "Add."
4. Repeat above steps to add new machine names.
5. Click "Ok."

5.1.3. Saving a Project

For future use in different sessions, one may wish to save these settings in a file.

5.1.4. Opening an Existing Project

One may wish to open an existing project by not having to type in all the settings.

5.1.5. Viewing System

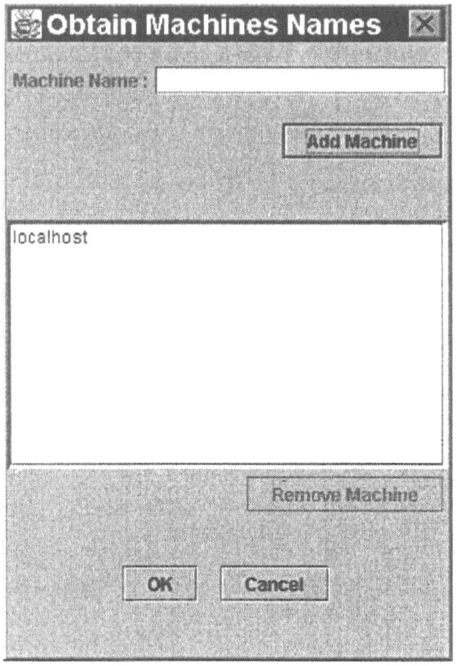

Figure 6. Set Machine Names.

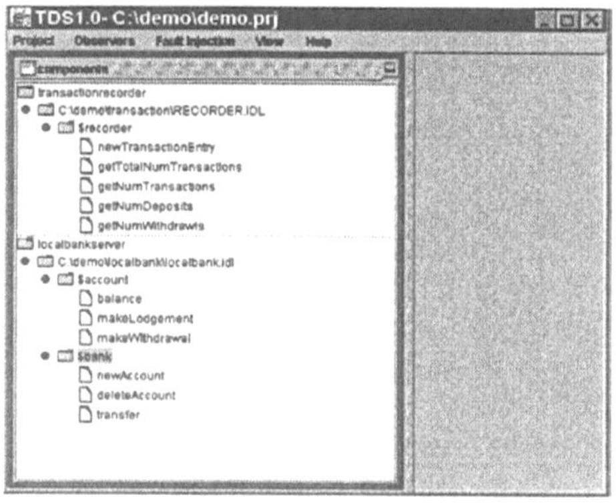

Figure 7. System View.

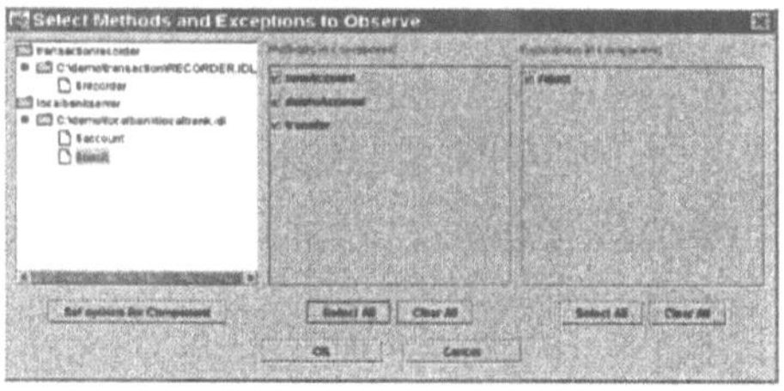

Figure 8. Observer Selection.

After the project is created, one can view the system in a hierarchical manner - system components, followed by the IDL files in each component and the modules (if present) and interfaces defined in each IDL file with all the defined methods. Figure 7 shows the view.

- Double-click on the line in the empty panel and observe the names of components.
- Double-click on the component to see the IDL files.
- Double-click on the IDL file to see the modules and interfaces.
- Double-click on the interface to see the methods.

Similar hierarchical views are used throughout the tool.

5.1.6. Select Observers for Methods in Interfaces

The tester can make the selection of coverage observers by clicking on Coverage in the Observer menu. The window is shown in Figure 8.

1. Double-click the component.
2. Double-click the IDL file.
3. Double-click the Interface Name.
4. Select Observers by clicking in the check box of the methods and exceptions.
5. Click "Set Options in Component."
6. Repeat for other interfaces.
7. Click "Ok."

5.1.7. Select Faults

The fault injection interface is shown in Figure 9.

1. Click on the Fault Injection Menu.
2. Select "Mutation Faults."
3. Click on the Component.
4. Click on the IDL File.
5. Click on the Interface Name.
6. Click on the Method Name.
7. Click on "Show Faults."
8. Select different types of faults.

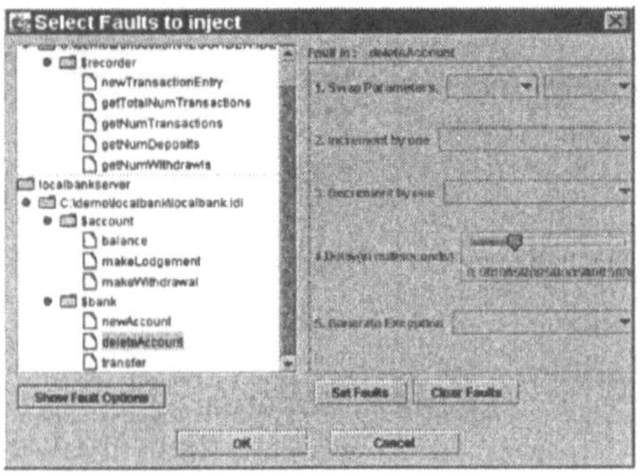

Figure 9. Fault Selection Interface.

(a) Increment Paramenters – Select parameter to be incremented from drop-down list.
(b) Decrement Parameters – Select parameter to be decremented from drop-down list.
(c) Swap Parameters — Select parameter to be swapped in the left drop-down list and choose the other parameter in the next drop-down list. The other list will only display those parameters that can be swapped. The first window shows all parameters.
(d) Insert Delay[2]

9. Click on "Set Faults." Only one fault can be selected per method.
10. Repeat for other methods.
11. Click "Ok."

5.1.8. Saving a Session

The selection of observers and faults can be saved in a file.

5.1.9. Opening an Earlier Session Settings

A previously saved sessions file can be reopened later. This saves the tester the time required for selection of observers.

5.1.10. Instrumentation and Re-compilation

After the tester has selected the kinds of observations that he wishes to perform, the code needs to be instrumented and the instrumented code has to be recompiled. The following steps are required:

1. Click on "Project" followed by "Instrument."
2. Click on "Ok" in the "Completed Instrumentation" Box.
3. Recompile the instrumented stub and skeleton code.

[2]Though this is not a mutation fault, this was listed here because a new interface was not made at that time.

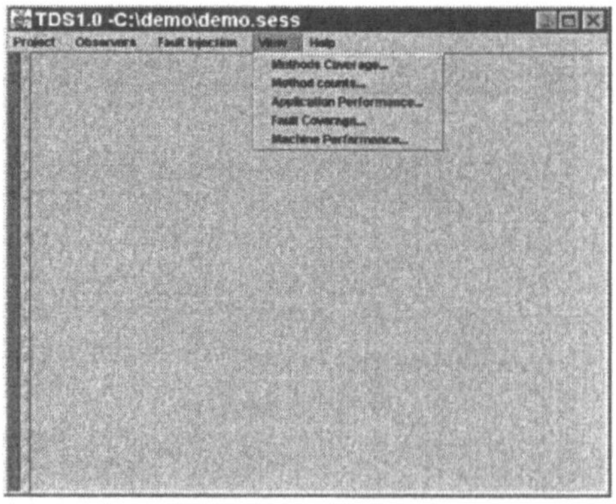

Figure 10. View Menu.

5.1.11. Starting the global Listener

Once the code has been instrumented, before running the test cases, the global listener has to be started. This will cause the global listener to connect to all the local listeners. The following step is required:

1. Click on "Project" followed by "Start Global Listener"

5.2. Testing Phase

The system can now be executed and observation can be done during the system execution. Orbix daemons should be running on all the machines and the Oracle database should be started up. The Oracle driver will start it up if needed. The View menu can be used for dynamic monitoring of system execution (Figure 10). All the method related views are given in a hierarchical fashion. All method coverage is from the server side.

5.2.1. Observe Method Coverage

1. Select "Method and Exceptions Coverage" from "View Menu."
2. Click on component.
3. Click on IDLfile.
4. Click on interface.
5. Click on interface for summary (Figure 11), and details of methods not covered (Figure 12).

5.2.2. Observe Method Execution Count

1. Select "Method Execution Count" in "View Menu."
2. Click on components for component level counts, i.e. number of times calls have been made to each component in the system.

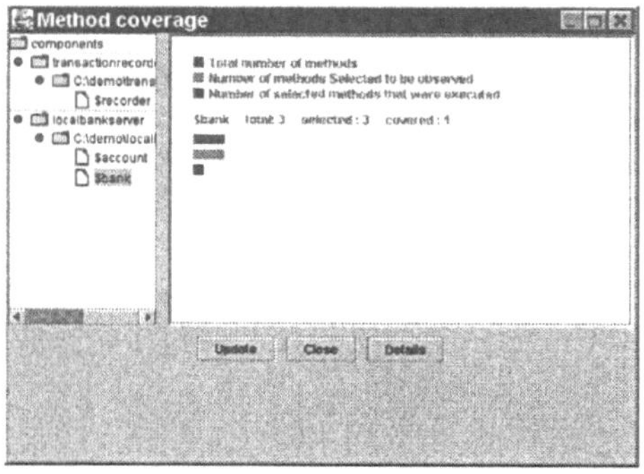

Figure 11. Method Coverage at Interface (Summary).

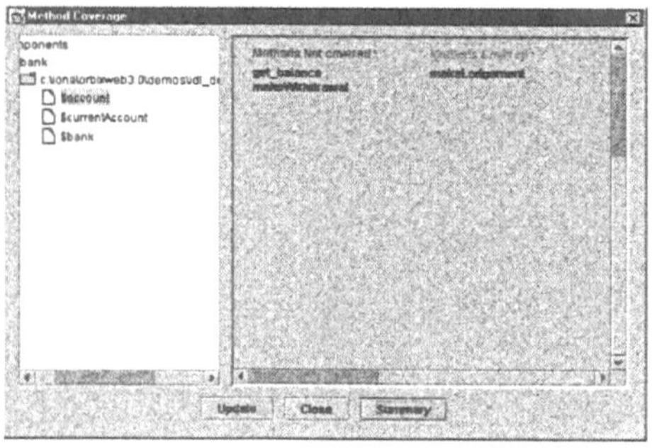

Figure 12. Method Coverage at Interface (Details).

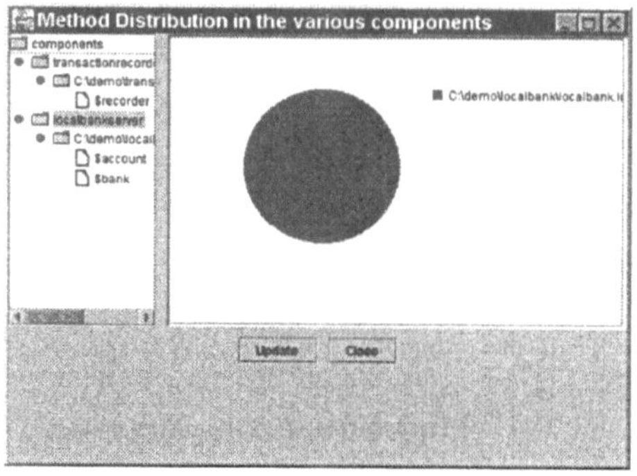

Figure 13. Method Execution Counts at IDL-File Level.

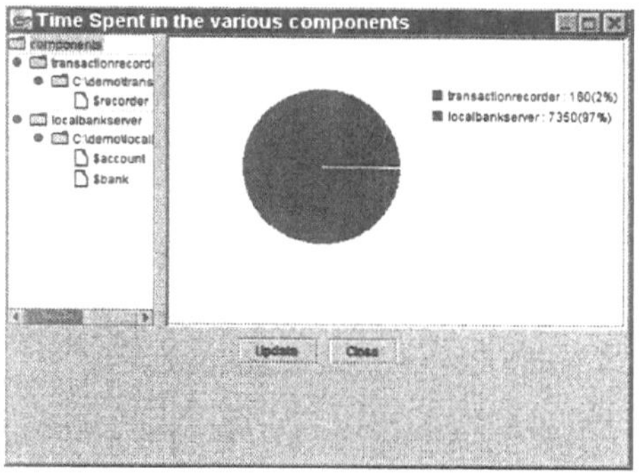

Figure 14. Method Time Spent in Servers at Component Level.

3. Click on a particular component for counts at the IDL file level, i.e. number of times calls have been made to each IDL file in the selected component (Figure 13).
4. Click on particular IDL file for counts at interface level, i.e. number of times calls have been made to each interface in the selected IDL file.

5.2.3. Observe Method Execution Times in Server

1. Select "Method Execution Time" in "View Menu."
2. Click on components for the time at component level, i.e. time spent at each component in the system (Figure 14).
3. Click on a component in the system for execution time at IDLFile level, i.e time spent at each IDL file in the selected component.
4. Click on an IDL file of the component for execution times at interface level, i.e. time spent at each interface of the IDL file.

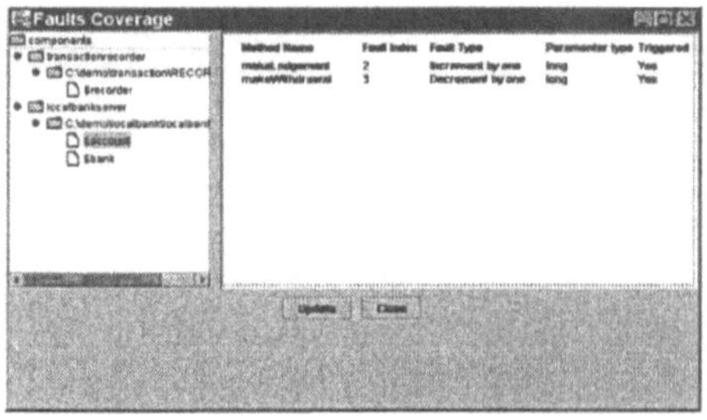

Figure 15. Faults Covered.

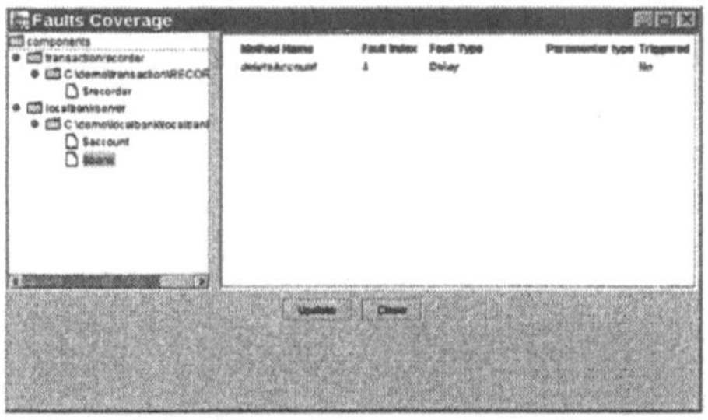

Figure 16. Faults Not Covered.

5.2.4. Fault Coverage at Interface Level

1. Select "Faults Coverage" in "View Menu."
2. Click on component.
3. Click on IDL file name.
4. Click on interface name.

If a injected fault is triggered, it shows up in blue (Figure 15), otherwise, in red (Figure 16). The fault type and the method in which it was injected are also shown. The fault injection is done at the stub side.

Figure 17 shows a picture of TDS with many views at the same time. During execution one may click on the "Update" button and refresh the views that may have changed during execution.

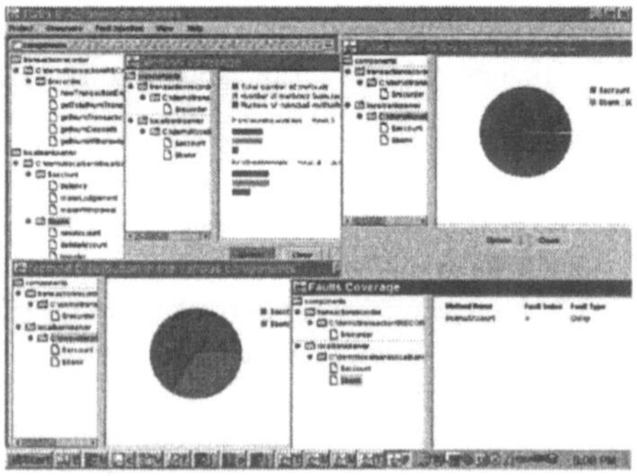

Figure 17. TDS with Many Views.

6. Evolution of TDS into Wabash

TDS has evolved into Wabash 2.0. Wabash implements interface mutation and fault injection using interceptors provided in CORBA. Thus, instrumentation of stubs and skeletons is not required. Recompilation is also unnecessary. Wabash also provides fine-grained monitoring and control capabilities. One can specify control actions based on specified events. These control actions can be applied to components, objects, interfaces and individual methods in the interfaces. Load testing can be performed with the creation of dynamic clients.

Work is going on to enhance the architecture of Wabash so that it can support Jini and JMX in addition to CORBA-IDL.

References

[1] Alan W. Brown and Kurt C. Wallnau. The Current State of CBSE. *IEEE Software*, pages 37–46, September/October 1998.

[2] S. Ghosh. Testing Component-based Distributed Applications - a Thesis. Technical Report SERC-TR-180-P, Software Engineering Research Center, Purdue University, West Lafayatte, IN, USA, August 2000.

[3] M. C. Hsueh, T. K. Tsai, and R. K. Iyer. Fault Injection Techniques and Tools. *IEEE Computer*, pages 75–82, April 1997.

[4] OMG — The Object Management Group. *The Common Object Request Broker: Architecture and Specification, Revision 2.0.* OMG, 1995.

Proteum: A Family of Tools to Support Specification and Program Testing Based on Mutation

José Carlos Maldonado[1]
Márcio Eduardo Delamaro[2]
Sandra C. P. F. Fabbri[3]
Adenilso da Silva Simão[1]
Tatiana Sugeta[1]
Auri Marcelo Rizzo Vincenzi[1]
Paulo Cesar Masiero[1]

[1]*Instituto de Ciências Matemáticas e de Computação*
Universidade de São Paulo
{jcmaldon, adenilso, tatiana, auri, masiero}@icmc.sc.usp.br

[2]*Departamento de Informática*
Universidade Estadual de Maringá
delamaro@din.uem.br

[3]*Departamento de Computação*
Universidade Federal de São Carlos
sfabbri@dc.ufscar.br

Abstract

The quality of the VV&T – Verification, Validation and Testing – activity is extremely relevant to the software development process. The establishment of a low-cost, effective testing and validation strategy and the development of supporting tools have been pursued by many researchers. This presentation discusses the main architectural and operational aspects of a family of tools that support specification and program testing based on mutation. The testing of C programs is supported by Proteum/IM 2.0, at the unit and at the integration level as well. Proteum *is an acronym for PROgram Testing Using Mutants. At the specification level the application of mutation testing for validating Reactive Systems (RS) specifications based on Finite State Machines (FSM), Statecharts and Petri Nets is support by* Proteum/RS.

Keywords: Testing Tools, Mutation Testing, Specification Testing, Program Testing.

1 Introduction

Due to communications and transformations that are unavoidable during software development, the resultant products are subject to be delivered with errors. The earlier these errors are detected in the life cycle the less onerous is the process to remove them. Moreover, if errors are not discovered, this does not necessarily mean that the software or an intermediate product does not have one or more; it could be the case that the test case set used is simply not adequate enough to reveal them.

The quality of the testing activity is by itself an issue in the software development process. Software testing adequacy assessment constitutes a key factor for producing high quality software. One way to evaluate the quality of a test case set is to use coverage measures derived from the required elements of a given testing criterion.

Considering Reactive Systems – systems whose main feature is to interact with the environment reacting to stimuli, usually under time constraints –, the quality of the testing activity is even more relevant as faults in these systems can provoke economical or human losses, making the specification and testing activities much more critical.

The software development activities should be supported by tools. In this paper the focus is on mutation testing tools. In the next section, an overview of the mutation-based tools developed in the scope of the cooperation between the ICMC-USP (Instituto de Ciências Matemáticas e de Computação - Universidade de São Paulo, the DC-UFSCar (Departamento de Computação - Universidade Federal de São Carlos) and the DIN-UEM (Departamento de Informática - Universidade Estadual de Maringá) is provided.

2 An Overview of the Proteum Family Tools

Mutation testing, proposed by DeMillo *et al.* [10], is an adequacy criterion used to assess test set quality, originally at the unit level. It requires the development of a test set T that reveals the presence of a well-specified set of faults. The faults are modeled by a set of mutant operators which, when applied to a program (or product) P under test, generate syntactically correct programs(or products) called mutants. The quality of T is measured by its ability to distinguish the behavior of the mutants from the behavior of P.

It must be pointed out that applying the testing criteria without the support of a tool is an error prone, unproductive activity. The availability of a testing tool increases the quality and the productivity of the testing activity and may ease the technology transfer to the industry, contributing to the continuous evolution of such environment, indispensable for the production of high quality software products. Testing tools have also proved invaluable to research end education, helping software engineering students acquire the basic concepts and experience on comparison, selection and establishment of testing strategies [17].

Proteum is the first tool to support the testing of C programs based on mutation testing at the unit level [5]. With the proposition of the criterion Interface Mutation [8], that uses a set of mutant operators developed to model integration errors, the Proteum/IM has been developed [4]. At the integration level, Delamaro *et al.* provided evidences that Interface Mutation is also effective in detecting faults [8]. Recently, *Proteum* and Proteum/IM have been integrated in a testing environment, named Proteum/IM 2.0 [9]. In this way, the tester can use the same concept during the unit and the integration testing phases.

The authors have also been investigating the adequacy of mutation testing to validate Finite State Machines (FSM) [11, 13], Statecharts [12, 15] and Petri Nets [14, 24]. Supporting tools have also been developed and referred to as *Proteum/RS*: *Proteum/FSM* [11], *Proteum/ST* [15] and *Proteum/PN* [14, 24, 25].

We are interested in exploring the adequacy, the cost and the complementary aspects of the testing techniques to validate system behavioral specification. The aim is to provide coverage criteria in the context of Reactive Systems. The relevance of this kind of information in the context of communication protocol has been discussed by Petrenko and Bochmann [23].

The *Proteum* family is composed of the following tools:

- *Proteum* [5, 7]: supports the unit testing of C programs. It has 71 operators, categorized into four mutation classes [2]: Statement (15), Operator (46), Variable (7) and Constant (3). These operators are taken from the Agrawal *et al.* work [1].

- Proteum/IM [4]: supports the integration testing of C programs based on the Interface Mutation criterion. It has 33 operators divided into two groups [4]: 24 of Group I, and 9 of Group II. Given a connection between units A and B (A calls B), operators in the first group apply changes to the body of function B. Operators in the second group apply mutations to the places unit A calls B. Proteum/IM provides mechanisms for the assessment of test case adequacy for testing the interactions among the units of a given program.

- Proteum/IM 2.0 [9]: is an evolution of *Proteum* and Proteum/IM. It is a single, integrated environment that provides facilities to investigate low-cost and incremental testing strategies based on mutation.

- *Proteum/FSM* [11]: supports the application of mutation testing to validate Finite State Machine based specifications. It has 9 mutant operators. These operators are based on the error classes defined by Chow [3] and on heuristics about typical errors made by designers during the creation of Finite State Machines.

- *Proteum/ST* [15]: supports the application of mutation testing to validate statecharts based specifications. Statecharts [16] are an extension to Finite State Machines. The approach taken to implement *Proteum/FSM* makes it easier to extend the ideas, concepts and tools to Statecharts considering hierarchy, concurrency, history and others statecharts features. *Proteum/ST* operator set is divided into three categories: 9 Finite State Machine operators; 11 Extended FSM (EFSM) operators; and 17 Statecharts-feature-based operators. Three abstraction strategies to abstract all the FSM and EFSM components of a statecharts at the different hierarchical levels are available. In this way, incremental strategies are supported.

- *Proteum/PN* [14, 24, 25]: supports the application of mutation testing to validate Petri Net based specifications. Two kinds of errors have been considered to define the Petri Net mutant operators [14]: alteration in the net arcs (8 operators) and in the net initial marking

(3 operators). It includes facilities for test case generation and equivalent mutant determination [24].

All the *Proteum* family tools support the minimal set of operations that must be provided by any mutation based testing tool:

- Test case handling: execution, inclusion/exclusion and disabling/enabling;
- Mutant handling: creation, selection, execution, and analysis; and
- Adequacy analysis: mutation score and reports.

The *Proteum* family supports the execution of some of these tasks in a completely automatic way and some with the intervention of the tester. It has been developed as a set of Unix-like modules. There are two ways to conduct a test session: either by a graphical interface or by scripts. The graphical interface allows the beginner to explore and learn the concepts of mutation testing and to use the *Proteum* family in a controlled manner. Advanced users, on the other hand, would probably prefer to use scripts, for reasons of productivity and evaluation of alternative testing strategies.

In addition to the minimal set of operations, the *Proteum* family tools have some features and facilities that support the evaluation of alternative criteria that have been proposed for mutation testing application [2, 19–22, 29, 31], such as selective and randomly mutation. Some of the facilities make feasible to adequate the testing rigorousness according to the criticality of the product under test and the budget restrictions. For instance, to select a subset of mutant operators, to generate just a percentage of the mutants, test set miminization, and so forth. These alternatives are in the direction of making mutation testing useful in industry; in other words, establishing low-cost, practical ways to apply mutation testing, aiming at reducing the number of mutants and keeping a high mutation score. Many empirical studies have been conducted using these tools [2, 6, 8, 12–15, 18, 19, 27–30].

3 Conclusion and Future Work

We have presented the *Proteum* family tools that support specification and program testing based on mutation. The testing of C programs is supported at the unit and at the integration level as well. At the specification level it is supported the application of mutation testing for validating Reactive Systems (RS) specifications based on Finite State Machines (FSM), Statecharts and Petri Nets. The *Proteum* family tools have being mainly used for teaching and research in Brazil and abroad.

The short term goals of our work on this subject are directed to three lines of research: improvement and refinement of the mutation operators, establishment of selective mutation criteria by conducting empirical studies aiming at evaluating the cost and the effectiveness of the operators, and evolution of *Proteum* family to an integrated environment to support the testing process from the specification to the implementation phase.

The experience on developing the *Proteum* family is also been used to extend mutation testing to object oriented languages. Other specification language, such as Estelle and SDL, are also in the scope of our research. For instance, the mutation testing has been applied for validating Estelle specification, addressing the communication between the modules and the structure of the specification, as well as other aspects [26].

The development of the *Proteum* family has been carried out by Master and Ph.D. students. In the scope of our activities we are interested in identifying partners to conduct empirical studies in industry and in establishing a collaboration to turn the *Proteum* family tools into the state of the practice.

Acknowledgments

The authors would like to thank the Brazilian Funding Agencies – CNPq, FAPESP and CAPES – and the Telcordia Technologies (USA) for their partial support to this research. The authors would also like to thank Eric Wong for his encouragement along these years.

References

[1] H. Agrawal, R. A. DeMillo, R. Hathaway, W. Hsu, W. Hsu, E. W. Krauser, R. J. Martin, A. P. Mathur, and E. H. Spafford. Design of mutant operators for the C programming language. Technical Report SERC-TR41-P, Software Engineering Research Center, Purdue University, West Lafayette, IN, Mar. 1989.

[2] E. F. Barbosa, J. C. Maldonado, and A. M. R. Vincenzi. Towards the determination of sufficient mutant operators for C. In *First International Workshop on Automated Program Analysis, Testing and Verification*, Limerick, Ireland, June 2000. (Accepted for publication in a special issue of the Software Testing Verification and Reliability Journal).

[3] T. S. Chow. Testing software design modeled by finite-state machines. *IEEE Transactions on Software Engineering*, 4(3):178–187, 1978.

[4] M. Delamaro and J. Maldonado. Interface mutation: Assessing testing quality at interprocedural level. In *19th International Conference of the Chilean Computer Science Society (SCCC'99)*, pages 78–86, Talca – Chile, Nov. 1999.

[5] M. E. Delamaro and J. C. Maldonado. Proteum - a tool for the assesment of test adequacy for C programs. In *Con-*

ference on Performability in Computing Systems (PCS'96), pages 79–95, Brunswick, NJ, July 1996.

[6] M. E. Delamaro, J. C. Maldonado, and A. P. Mathur. Integration testing using interface mutation. In *VII International Symposium of Software Reliability Engineering (ISSRE'96)*, pages 112–121, White Plains, NY, Nov. 1996.

[7] M. E. Delamaro, J. C. Maldonado, and A. P. Mathur. Proteum - a tool for the assesment of test adequacy for C programs - user's guide. Technical Report SERC-TR168-P, Software Engineering Research Center, Purdue University, Apr. 1996.

[8] M. E. Delamaro, J. C. Maldonado, and A. P. Mathur. Interface mutation: An approach for integration testing. IEEE Transactions on Software Engineering, (accepted for publication), 2000.

[9] M. E. Delamaro, J. C. Maldonado, and A. M. R. Vincenzi. Proteum/IM 2.0: An integrated mutation testing environment. In *Mutation 2000 Symposium*, pages 124–134, San Jose, CA, Oct. 2000.

[10] R. A. DeMillo, R. J. Lipton, and F. G. Sayward. Hints on test data selection: Help for the practicing programmer. *IEEE Computer*, 11(4):34–43, Apr. 1978.

[11] S. C. P. F. Fabbri, J. C. Maldonado, M. E. Delamaro, and P. C. Masiero. Proteum/FSM: A tool to support finite state machine validation based on mutation testing. In *XIX SCCC - International Conference of the Chilean Computer Science Society*, pages 96–104, Talca, Chile, 1999.

[12] S. C. P. F. Fabbri, J. C. Maldonado, and P. C. Masiero. Mutation analysis in the context of reactive system specification and validation. In *5th Annual International Conference on Software Quality Management*, pages 247–258, Bath, UK, Mar. 1997.

[13] S. C. P. F. Fabbri, J. C. Maldonado, P. C. Masiero, and M. E. Delamaro. Mutation analysis testing for finite state machines. In *5th International Symposium on Software Reliability Engineering (ISSRE'94)*, pages 220–229, Monterey - CA, Nov. 1994.

[14] S. C. P. F. Fabbri, J. C. Maldonado, P. C. Masiero, and M. E. Delamaro. Mutation analisys applied to validate specifications based on petri nets. In *FORTE'95 – 8th IFIP Conference on Formal Descriptions Techniques for Distribute Systems and Communication Protocols*, pages 329–337, Montreal, Canadá, Oct. 1995.

[15] S. C. P. F. Fabbri, J. C. Maldonado, T. Sugeta, and P. C. Masiero. Mutation testing applied to validate specifications based on statecharts. In *ISSRE – International Symposium on Software Reliability Systems*, pages 210–219, Nov. 1999.

[16] D. Harel. Statecharts: A visual formalism for complex systems. *Science of Computer Programming*, 8:231–274, 1987.

[17] J. R. Horgan and P. Mathur. Assessing testing tools in research and education. *IEEE Software*, 9(3):61–69, May 1992.

[18] J. C. Maldonado, E. F. Barbosa, A. M. R. Vincenzi, and M. E. Delamaro. Evaluation N-selective mutation for C programs: Unit and integration testing. In *Mutation 2000 Symposium*, pages 32–44, San Jose, CA, Oct. 2000.

[19] A. P. Mathur and W. E. Wong. Evaluation of the cost of alternative mutation strategies. In *VII Simpósio Brasileiro de Engenharia de Software*, pages 320–335, Rio de Janeiro, RJ, Brazil, Oct. 1993.

[20] A. P. Mathur and W. E. Wong. An empirical comparison of data flow and mutation based test adequacy criteria. *The Journal of Software Testing, Verification, and Relability*, 4(1):9–31, Mar. 1994.

[21] E. Mresa and L. Bottaci. Efficiency of mutation operators and selective mutation strategies: an empirical study. *The Journal of Software Testing, Verification and Reliability*, 9(4):205–232, Dec. 1999.

[22] A. J. Offutt, G. Rothermel, and C. Zapf. An experimental evaluation of selective mutation. In *15th International Conference on Software Engineering*, pages 100–107, Baltimore, MD, May 1993.

[23] A. Petrenko and G. V. Bochmann. On fault coverage of tests for finite state specifications. Technical report, Département d'Informatique et recherche opérationnelle – Université de Montréal, 1996. http://www.iro.umontreal.ca/pub/teleinfo/TRs/Petr96b.ps.gz.

[24] A. S. Simão and J. C. Maldonado. Mutation based test sequence generation for Petri nets. In *III Workshop of Formal Methods*, João Pessoa, Oct. 2000.

[25] A. S. Simão, J. C. Maldonado, and S. C. P. F. Fabbri. Proteum-RS/PN: A tool to support edition, simulation and validation of Petri nets based on mutation testing. In *Brazilian Symposium on Software Engineering – SBES'2000*, João Pessoa, Oct. 2000.

[26] S. R. S. Souza, J. C. Maldonado, S. C. P. F. Fabbri, and W. Lopes de Souza. Mutation testing applied to estelle specifications. In *33rd Hawaii Internacional Conference on System Sciences, Mini-Tracks: Distributed Systems Testing*, Maui, Havaí, Jan. 2000. (Accepted for publication in a special issue on Distributed Systems Testing of the Software Quality Journal).

[27] A. M. R. Vincenzi, J. C. Maldonado, E. F. Barbosa, and M. E. Delamaro. Unit and integration testing strategies for C programs using mutation-based criteria. In *Symposium on Mutation Testing*, pages 56–67, San Jose, CA, Oct. 2000.

[28] E. W. Wong, J. C. Maldonado, and M. E. Delamaro. Reducing the Cost of Regression Testing by Using Selective Mutation. In *VIII International Conference of Software Technology (CITS)*, pages 93–109, Curitiba - PR - Brazil, June 1997.

[29] W. Wong, J. Maldonado, M. Delamaro, and S. Souza. A comparison of selective mutation in C and fortran. In *Workshop do Projeto Validação e Teste de Sistemas de Operação*, pages 71–80, Águas de Lindóia, SP, Jan. 1997.

[30] W. E. Wong, J. C. Maldonado, M. E. Delamaro, and A. P. Mathur. Constrained mutation in C programs. In *8th Brazilian Symposium on Software Engineering*, pages 439–452, Curitiba, PR, Brazil, Oct. 1994.

[31] W. E. Wong and A. P. Mathur. Reducing the cost of mutation testing: An empirical study. *The Journal of Systems and Software*, 31(3):185–196, Dec. 1995.

Index of Authors

MIX
Papier aus verantwortungsvollen Quellen
Paper from responsible sources
FSC® C105338

If you have any concerns about our products,
you can contact us on
ProductSafety@springernature.com

In case Publisher is established outside the EU,
the EU authorized representative is:
Springer Nature Customer Service Center GmbH
Europaplatz 3, 69115 Heidelberg, Germany

Printed by Libri Plureos GmbH
in Hamburg, Germany